A HISTORY OF THE CHURCH IN WALES

A HISTORY

OF THE

CHURCH IN WALES

EDITED BY

DAVID WALKER

Canon of Brecon
Senior Lecturer in History,
University College of Swansea

FOREWORD BY

THE ARCHBISHOP OF WALES

PUBLISHED FOR
THE HISTORICAL SOCIETY OF THE CHURCH IN WALES
BY
CHURCH IN WALES PUBLICATIONS
EDUCATION AND COMMUNICATIONS CENTRE
WOODLAND PLACE, PENARTH, S. GLAM

ISBN 0 85326 0 10 9 Hardback

0 85326 0 11 7 Paperback

Printed in Wales by
D. BROWN AND SONS LIMITED
COWBRIDGE AND BRIDGEND, GLAMORGAN

CONTENTS

v

34961

ILLUSTRATIONS

FOREWORD

It is a joy to greet the appearance of this badly needed history of the Church in Wales and to commend it to a wide readership. Adherents of that Church in particular need accurate knowledge and understanding of the past if they are to appreciate properly its situation today and its relationship with other Christian traditions in this land. As we see how previous generations assessed their responsibility, how they discerned or failed to discern the will of God in their day, the outward and inner obstacles they encountered and the extent to which they enhanced or impoverished the inheritance they had received, we shall hopefully become that much wiser and more determined as we labour at our contemporary task.

The authors write with the inherent authority of people who know their subject through-and-through. It is very fitting that since there is no such thing in the strictest sense as "denominational" Church history the chapter on Relations between Anglicans and Dissenters should have been contributed by Dr R. Tudur Jones, the learned historian of Congregationalism and Welsh Independency. Having been privileged to read the proofs in full, I know that every chapter has corrected my ignorance and given me invaluable food for thought. On behalf of all those who will read the work with deep appreciation, I thank the authors for doing us this fine service and the Historical Society of the Church in Wales for its initiative in the undertaking.

JULY 1976

+ ffricjer Cambrensis

ix

CONTRIBUTORS

E. T. DAVIES, MA, formerly Editor of the Historical Society of the Church in Wales and Canon of Monmouth.

R. W. D. FENN, BD, MA, FRHISTS, FSA (Scot), Head of Department of Classics, Lady Hawkin's School, Kington; Vicar of Staunton-on-Wye, Hereford.

OWAIN W. JONES, MA, FRHISTS, Vicar of Builth Wells; Canon and Treasurer of Brecon.

R. TUDUR JONES, DD, DPHIL, Principal, Coleg Bala-Bangor, Bangor.

DAVID WALKER, DPHIL, FSA, FRHISTS, Senior Lecturer in History, University College of Swansea. Hon. Editor of the Historical Society of the Church in Wales; Canon of Brecon.

ABBREVIATIONS

Arch. Camb.	Archaeologia Cambrensis
B.B.C.S.	Bulletin of the Board of Celtic Studies
Ep.Acts	Episcopal Acts and Cognate Documents relating to Welsh Dioceses, 1066-1272 edited by J. Conway Davies
J.H.S.C.W.	Journal of the Historical Society of the Church in Wales
James, Church History	J. W. James, A Church History of Wales
N.L.W.J.	National Library of Wales Journal
S.P.C.K.	Society for the Promotion of Christian Knowledge
Trans. Cymm.	Transactions of the Honourable Society of Cymmrodorion
Trans. R.Hist.S.	Transactions of the Royal Historical Society
W.H.R.	Welsh History Review
Glanmor Williams, Welsh Church	Glanmor Williams, The Welsh Church from Conquest to Reformation

ACKNOWLEDGEMENTS

The publication of this volume has been made possible by grants from

   The Catherine and Lady Grace James Foundation
   The Archdeacon Bevan Memorial Fund
   The Welsh Church Act Fund of
      West Glamorgan
      Clwyd
      Gwynedd
      Powys

We are grateful for this generous support.

My first debt is to the contributors for their prompt and ready support in producing this volume. The original intention was that each chapter would be written by a historian long familiar with the problems and sources of a particular period. I had hoped that the story of the Welsh Church in the sixteenth and seventeenth centuries might have been written by one of the small group of specialists working on Tudor and Stuart Wales. When pressure of work made that impossible, I had to undertake that chapter myself. My colleague of long standing, Professor Glanmor Williams was kind enough to read the draft of this chapter. My last debt is to my wife; in discussion, and in the practical business of seeing the volume through the press, her help has been invaluable.

David Walker

INTRODUCTION

A SURVEY of the history of the Church in Wales must cover a wide range of topics which are not always bound together by an obvious or common theme. Those who, like Chancellor J. W. James, can assert that 'the Church in Wales, in the Celtic period, in the late Medieval period, and since the Reformation, has been identically the same' avoid many problems. That there has been a basic conformity of belief embracing fundamental tenets of the Christian faith as they are expressed in the creeds and in the work of the early councils is incontestable. But there has been a wide variety of accretion and emphasis, and there have been changes of organisation and outlook which, in their day, have been of the first importance. The isolation of the Celtic churches in the Age of the Saints obscured, though it did not destroy, the links which existed between the Church in these islands and the papacy. The centralisation of power in Rome and the emergence of the power-structure described as caesaro-papalism in the eleventh and twelfth centuries gave a new appearance to the medieval Church. By comparison, the Church in Wales then seemed old-fashioned, not to say anachronistic, and the process of modernisation was by no means a painless one.

In the medieval Church changing emphasis in teaching and devotion led to changes in perspective which caused widespread criticism. In particular, a concentration on purgatory and hell, on punishment and on the means of escaping from the dark and terrifying consequences of sin played a major and unhealthy part in popular religion. Critics of the Church in the fourteenth and fifteenth centuries were much concerned with abuses which sprang too easily from such a concept of religion. Medieval historians may, if judgment is allowed, regret that the European Church failed to find from within the means of purification and reform. When changes came in the sixteenth century, they came through revolt and through the widespread rejection of a system which had countenanced distortion and abuse.

How great was the break? How strong the sense of continuity? These questions have exercised theologian and historian alike. The Church of England, as an ecclesiastical entity separated from the Church of Rome, is a product of the sixteenth century. Its origins lie in the reign of Henry VIII;

its growth towards maturity owes much to Elizabeth I, and there
are those who would argue that the English Church cannot be seen in its
fully-developed form until as late as the restoration of Charles II in 1660.
In structure it was as the medieval Church had been, though it now
lacked the monasteries which, at their best, had been a source of new life
during the high Middle Ages: in allegiance to the crown it was new; in
doctrine it sought to return to the position of the early Church. It eschewed
the cult of the Virgin, so popular in the Middle Ages, which became a
mark of a minority within anglicanism. It concentrated on the two basic
sacraments of baptism and holy communion, abandoning as unscriptural
the concept of purgatory and all the methods of seeking amelioration so
characteristic of the recent past. It professed a view of the holy communion which was entirely at variance with the teachings of the medieval
Church. The contrast between the doctrine and teaching of the new
Church of England and those of the medieval European Church was very
great. Contemporary apologists concentrated on the assonance of
anglican teaching with the teaching of the primitive Church, or sometimes
with that of the Church of their Saxon forbears. In Wales there was a
parallel appeal to the glories of the Celtic past. There was no wish to
seek continuity with all that had been characteristic of the late Middle
Ages. Only in the seventeenth century would the Laudian Church seek
to rediscover its affinities with the Roman Church, or in the nineteenth
century would the tractarians seek to reshape anglicanism in a catholic
mould.

Yet it is often claimed with some measure of accuracy that the
anglican Church was the heir of the medieval Church, and that there was
a continuous history of the Christian faith in these islands in which any
breach which occurred was legal rather than doctrinal, local rather than
fundamental. On that basis the anglican Church has claimed to represent
the catholic Church in Great Britain. Roman Catholics had to wait
until the nineteenth century before a Roman Catholic hierarchy and a
formal church-structure were reintroduced into England and Wales.
During the last hundred years there has been a tendency to assume, as
for example, Cardinal Heenan assumed throughout his active ministry,
that this restored Roman Church is the true representative of the catholic
tradition in Britain. From the sixteenth century to the twentieth century
the dissenting traditions have maintained a firm opposition to the claims
of the Church by law established, and have defended their own theology
and their own form of church order. In some studies of the history of
anglicanism the Dissenters have been treated with scant consideration.

We have tried to deal with the relations between Anglicans and Dissenters in terms which do not discredit either side.

Throughout this long period Wales was part of the English Church and faced the Reformation and its consequences as part of the province of Canterbury. That remained the case until 1920 when, under the terms of an Act of 1914, Wales was set up as an independent province in its own right. As we look back behind that short spell of independent existence, we have to ask how much of the past we may properly claim as our own heritage.

These considerations set the terms of reference of this *History*. We are concerned with the ancestry and affiliations of the Church in Wales. While we are aware of controversy, we do not seek to establish any particular case in the debate. From the Age of the Saints is drawn much of the setting and ethos of the Welsh Church, for the imprint of Dewi, Teilo, Dyfrig, Deiniol, and other leading missionary figures of the Dark Ages lies deep upon the land and the Church. In the Middle Ages the Church was made over in a new, continental image. The sixteenth century, with its ferment of ideas, its challenging theological debate, and its turbulent politics, introduced many far-reaching changes in Wales as elsewhere in Britain. The old dissent has an honourable, though not perhaps a major role in the story of Christianity in Wales. The new dissent, associated with the name of John Wesley, and among his Welsh associates with that of Howel Harris, radically altered the pattern of Welsh religious life. The coming of the industrial age resulted in a sweeping transformation of the valleys of south Wales and created new and grave problems for Church and Chapel alike. The Church was handicapped at first by the legacy of its past, but as the nineteenth century advanced the churchmen of south Wales built up a new network of parishes and found the men to tackle the problems of an industrialised society. In the nineteenth century, too, conflicting movements of thought and devotion—the evangelicals and the tractarians—made a great impact on the Welsh dioceses. There was a recurrent threat that the Church would be disestablished, a threat which became a political reality in the first decades of the twentieth century. By 1914 all was ready and the necessary legislation had been passed, but the realisation of Parliament's scheme was delayed until after the first world war. Since 1920 the Church in Wales has faced up to the responsibilities of independence and has been seeking to discover and implement her rôle, not only in Wales, but in a wider sphere. That, too, is now part of the unfolding story which must be told.

CHAPTER 1

THE AGE OF THE SAINTS
by
R. W. D. Fenn

BY[1] the middle of the fifth century A D, Britain was being governed by her native princes and four centuries of Roman occupation were over. Christianity was one of the legacies of this period of occupation. However, this Romano-British Christianity was predominantly urban so that at the time of the Roman withdrawal rural Britain was still largely pagan whereas every town of any size had its bishop at the head of the local Christian community. In this kind of urban environment Christianity worked its way up the social scale to make considerable progress even with the wealthiest classes. Two hundred years earlier Tertullian claimed that those parts of Britain inaccessible to the Romans had been conquered by Christ, and a little later Origen supported this claim. Both men, however, were lawyers, members of a profession somewhat given to exaggeration, and even at the beginning of the fifth century Wales, the south-western peninsula, and the north were still outside the orbit of organised Christianity in Britain. Celtic heathenism flourished throughout the Roman period and Irish traditions point to the continued existence of wizards and druids in fifth-century Britain. Even in urban centres Christianity was not unchallenged.

On the other hand, Bede's picture of Christianity as an extinct religion, at least in southern England when St. Augustine landed in Kent in 597 to begin his mission to the English, is overdrawn. It is true that the British Church had become so disorganised that there were no bishops in south-east England to take part in the early negotiations with Augustine, and Pope Gregory I seems to have had no knowledge of where the sees of Roman Britain were located. Indeed, by 597 the bishoprics of York, London and Colchester, whose occupants had represented the British Church at the council of Arles in 314, had ceased to exist, whereas in Kent the pagan temples of Saxon idols were numerous and in good repair. The Romano-British Church, deriving its strength from the towns and villas was weakened by the decline in urban life and the villa system which followed the Roman withdrawal, and there was by then still little organised Christianity in Wales and the west. There were, no doubt, individual Christians or small Christian communities in Roman settlements like Chester, Cirencester, Gloucester, Wroxeter, and Caernarfon. Julian and Aaron were martyred at Caerleon as Christians. The graves unearthed at Llantwit Major on the site of a Roman villa were probably of fourth-century Christians, and the Christian chapel found at Caerwent also belongs to the sub-Roman period. Cunedda and his sons were settled in north Wales in the middle of the fifth century to strengthen those parts against enemy attack, and they, too, were Christians, representing the descendants of St. Ninian's converts in southern Scotland. Rough pillar-stones, found in various parts of Wales, also commemorate fifth-and early sixth-century Christians. But all this is evidence for the existence of isolated Christians and small Christian communities in Wales rather than for any widespread organised Church.

Such scattered Christian congregations as did exist suffered in the Irish expansion along the shores of the Severn Sea and the Welsh coast from the Gower to the Llŷn. This pagan, Irish expansion, already extensive in the Roman period, reached a pressure in the fifth century second only to that of the Anglo-Saxons in south-east England. But the Christian will to survive, despite these pressures, is illustrated by the life of St. Patrick. The most probable site of his birth-place is near the Severn estuary whence he was carried off in his youth by Irish pirates. He escaped after six years to find his family villa and its Romano-British Christianity carrying on just as they were before he left them.

The Saxon settlement gradually strangled communications between the British Church and continental Christianity, but in the Celtic west this growing isolation was relieved by a renewal of trade with the Mediter-ranean in the middle of the fifth century. Pottery, decorated with Christian emblems, found at Dinas Emrys and Tintagel illustrates how the fifth-century reorientation of the Celtic west towards the Mediterranean also opened routes along which spiritual ideas could travel as freely as com-mercial traffic. Missionaries as well as traders made their way to Wales where the main centre of their activities seems to have been in Erging. Erging, or Archenfield, is that part of Herefordshire embraced by the Wye, the Monnow, and the Black Mountains. Both the English and the Welsh names of the district are derived from the Latin name *Ariconium*, the local capital and a Roman mining town, some two miles east of Ross-on-Wye. This was the most Romanised area in Wales and at the centre of a network of Roman roads leading to all parts of England and Wales. Gloucester, where Christians were to be expected, was not far away, and some latent Christianity, inherited from the Roman occupation, was not unlikely in Erging itself. An environment such as this offered missionaries good ground for their evangelistic seed and it is not coincidental that a generation after the renewal of trade and communication between Wales and the Mediterranean the historical figure of St. Dyfrig should appear in Erging.

St. Dyfrig's life and work divide into two parts: first as a missionary and teacher, and then as a bishop. Though Christianity had but slender roots in Erging when St. Dyfrig was young, the pattern of his dedications shows its strength at his death. The centre of this missionary activity was Hentland whose fame should equal that of St. Paulinus's *Ty Gwyn* and St. Illtud's *Llanilltud Fawr* in the chronicles of the Welsh Church. From Hentland St. Dyfrig could use the roads converging on nearby *Ariconium* not only to facilitate the conversion of Erging and Gwent but also for access to places further afield. The question of communications led to his move to Mocrhos, near the Chester-Caerleon road and the main route to west Wales. St. Dyfrig now changed his emphasis, and there were several other monastic schools growing in south Wales: Mocrhos slipped into obscurity. Laying aside the spurious Germanus traditions about his consecration, it has to be remembered that, unlike other Celts, Dyfrig was not a tireless traveller. He has no continental dedications and few beyond Wales. Thus, it seems he was consecrated by some other bishops before him in south-east Wales. Such bishops certainly existed and the *Life* of St. Samson, generally considered reliable, tells how St. Dyfrig was joined by some of them for St. Samson's consecration. St. Dyfrig stands out against this background of anonymous episcopal predecessors and contemporaries as a far less shadowy and insubstantial figure.

St. Dyfrig's early efforts in south-east Wales were augmented by a succession of Irish saints who followed the earlier influx of Irish raiders and settlers. Men like Brynach, Brychan, and Tathan settled on the western peninsulas, along the shores of the Severn estuary, and as far inland as Brycheiniog. But St. Dyfrig's greatest fellow-worker was St. Illtud, of whom it has been said that 'he turned Wales into a monastery'. Monastic Christianity appealed to Celtic society. It was far better suited to its social pattern than the urbanised Christianity it superseded. Following the example of the great Gallic house of Lerins, St. Illtud saw monasticism primarily as a withdrawal from the world and not as a means of its conversion. The original Llanilltud Fawr was probably established on an island off the Pembrokeshire coast, and Celtic monasteries were often built on rocky headlands like Tintagel in Cornwall, in isolated valleys like Glascwm, or on storm-beaten islands like Ynys Seiriol off the coast of north Wales. The Celtic saint often expressed his desire for withdrawal by going into voluntary exile from his native land and at times this quest for the land of promise inadvertently resulted in the expansion of the Celtic Church. The early seventh-century *Life* of St. Samson gives an authentic picture of a sixth-century saint, and it tells how St. Samson, after his consecration as bishop of Llanilltud in 521, was bidden in a vision to become an ecclesiastical wanderer, and so became an apostle to Cornwall and Brittany.

The settlement of Brittany is another illustration of the extension of Celtic Christianity without any deliberate missionary strategy. Dedications to Welsh saints like David, Teilo, and Padarn have Breton counterparts, implying a connection between the two countries. By the sixth century a British-speaking population of considerable size had become established in Armorica, forming the nucleus of modern Brittany. Why so many of the Welsh saints sought out new homes for themselves and their kinsmen in Brittany remains a mystery, but the most likely explanation is that they were escaping the periodic ravages of the yellow plague. There was no deliberate missionary strategy involved, no particular quest for spiritual isolation, no political motives behind it, nor was it an escape from the pressures generated by Saxon and Irish invaders. All the same, it was the means whereby the Celtic Church became established in Brittany.

The Welsh Church made little impact upon Saxon paganism as it extended westwards. This religious inactivity becomes all the more remarkable when it is remembered, for example, that in the sixth century Powys was far more extensive than would later be the case and that its eastern limits were only drastically reduced by the rise of Mercia in the mid-seventh century. A considerable part of what was later Mercia had been influenced by Celtic saints. Moreover, Romano-British cities like Gloucester, Cirencester, and Bath seem to have partly survived the Saxon settlement and so did numerous Celtic-speaking communities which passed under Saxon leadership. It is not unreasonable to suppose that these communities retained some measure of the Celtic Christianity imparted to them by St. Dyfrig and his contemporaries, and yet they handed little of it on to the new settlers. The *Hwicce* and the *Magonsaete*, Powys's new neighbours, probably owed their faith to the Celtic Christianity of the Northumbrian rulers set over them by the pagan, Penda, their Mercian overlord.

Augustine landed in Kent in 597 and it was six years before he made his first formal contacts with the Celtic Church in Britain. Unfortunately, Bede's *Ecclesiastical History of the English People* is our only source of information about what happened at this meeting and Bede compiled his *History* when the controversy in Britain between the Celtic and the Roman Churches was at its height. He says that Augustine met the bishops and learned men of the nearest British province at a place called Augustine's Oak which he says is on the border dividing the *Hwicce* and the West Saxons. These bishops and doctors were Celtic Christians from Wales and the south-west, but the whereabouts of Augustine's Oak is uncertain. The Oak at Down Ampney, near Cricklade, and at Aust on the Severn, are both possible sites. So too, are Cressage in Shropshire and Bistre now in Clwyd, though the strongest candidate is probably the Oak in Abberley in Worcestershire. According to Bede, Augustine's first encounter with the British clergy was followed by a second and fuller conference, but the place where this met is not mentioned. This was attended by many very learned men from an apparently nearby monastery usually identified as Bangor-is-coed or Bangor-on-Dee, twelve miles or so south of Chester. It is now thought, however, that Bede's account of these two meetings between Augustine and the British is an expansion of a single incident at Augustine's Oak.

Augustine's first concern was to end the enmity which had grown up between himself and the British clergy. Gregory the Great had seen the potential value of Celtic missionary zeal and religious devotion for the Church as a whole and hoped, by the Romanisation of the Celtic Churches, to obviate the risk of schism at some later stage. If the conversion of Anglo-Saxon England had been Augustine's first intention, then he was particularly slow, taking six years to approach the British bishops and clergy, his natural allies for the work. The origin of this delay lies in Augustine's invitation to the British to enter into catholic unity with him. This unity did not yet exist, so that the encounter at Augustine's Oak was not so much a tardy approach to the Britons as the successful fruition of the attempts of six years to arrange a meeting between the leaders of the two Churches. This had been impossible hitherto on account of the not unfounded British suspicions as to Augustine's real motives in seeking brotherly relations with them. The second demand at Augustine's Oak was that the British should abandon those customs which were contrary to the unity of the Church. These were liturgical matters; a reference to the keeping of Easter which precedes this in the text was a later gloss, for in 603 the Easter controversy was not yet acute in western Europe. There is no mention of Augustine making any metropolitical claims over the Britons.

The demands which Bede recorded at Augustine's second encounter (at Chester) were quite different. The Britons are now asked first to keep Easter at the correct time, then to administer baptism according to the rites of the Roman Church. The invitation to join in preaching to the English is placed third. The British refused to do all these things and replied that they would not have him as their archbishop. However, Augustine's metropolitical authority over the British Church was a purely personal concession granted to him by Pope Gregory. It was not until the time of Archbishop Theodore (668-690) that English archbishops were able to assert fully their authority over their fellow-bishops. Thus, like the Easter controversy, this was not an issue of the early seventh century.

The encounter at Augustine's Oak was more eirenic than that at Chester which, in Bede's *History*, leads into an account of the subsequent British disaster at the battle of Chester. This again suggests that it is the earlier composition, framed before Anglo-Welsh theological attitudes had hardened. The moral underlying the Chester narrative is that the British refusal to accept Augustine's demands was a rejection of eternal salvation. The atmosphere at Augustine's Oak was quite different. The Britons admitted there that Augustine's teaching was the true path of righteousness, and this recognition that there was some point to Augustine's arguments places the composition of this account in a period before the controversy between British and Roman Christianity had become inflamed by the eighth-century bitterness which underlies Bede's own thought. Augustine was at a disadvantage in dealing with the British through his lack of experience. He had no knowledge of any Church beyond that of his native Rome and he arrived in Kent prejudiced against Celtic Christianity for in 596 Pope Gregory had complained that though 'the English nation eagerly desires to be converted to the Christian faith, the priests in the neighbourhood reject it and refrain from kindling the desires of the English.' This combination of ignorance and lack of sympathy foredoomed any confrontation between Augustine and the British to failure from the start.

In 601 Gregory committed all the bishops of the Britons to Augustine's jurisdiction, but it is difficult to believe that the pope really commissioned him to use this authority 'that the ignorant may be taught, the weak strengthened by his persuasion, and the perverted corrected.' The Age of the Saints was not yet over at the beginning of the seventh century and in Wales alone leaders of the calibre of St. Beuno and St. Tysilio were still active. Pope Gregory anticipated no difficulty in placing the British under Augustine's authority. But Augustine's approach lacked tact: for the British bishops it was a summons not an invitation to confer with him at Augustine's Oak. There is an underlying refusal in his dealings to accept them on terms of equality. The British suspected his intentions, detecting political implications in placing themselves under the direct control of Rome through a bishop established at Canterbury under a Saxon king. The concept of metropolitical authority, everything to Augustine, was new and strange to them. There had never been an ecclesiastical province of Britain with its own archbishop and primate. However, the British repudiation of Augustine's claims was not a rejection of papal authority and the later traditions about the confrontation incorporated into the Chester narrative record that the British rejection of Augustine was personal. He was not rejected as the pope's representative. The Mercians who recounted this tradition in the eighth century, like the Welsh about whom it was told, knew perfectly well that Augustine's refusal to stand up from his chair to greet the British churchmen was based upon something far more subtle than a lack of humility.

Augustine's parochialism affected his policy. He was amazed when he encountered liturgical variations during the journey to Britain. The papacy made no attempt to insist upon uniformity and it was only Augustine's lack of experience which made him demand of the British that they should abandon their liturgical customs where these were at variance with those of Rome. The whole episode becomes even more difficult to understand if it is compared with what happened thirty years later when St. Birinus began to work amongst the West Saxons. Oswald was then *bretwalda* of the English and confirmed the grant of Dorchester as Birinus's see-city. He was a devout Celtic Christian, but Birinus accepted him without any apparent hesitation as the baptismal sponsor of Cynegil, king of the West Saxons. Oswald's Celtic background did not prevent him from becoming the patron of a Roman missionary bishop. Moreover, Birinus worked without let or hindrance amongst the *Gewisse* of Wessex whose background was strongly Celtic. This points to the possibility that in the hands of a more adept negotiator Augustine's encounter with the British would have produced an abundant harvest. But, as it was, apart from a single entry in the *Annales Cambriae*, this first meeting with Roman Christianity made no impact upon Welsh tradition. Augustine himself does not seem to have been unduly disturbed by the conference's failure. No record of his writing to Gregory for further advice has survived, nor did he make any other formal overtures to the Britons before he died in the May of the following year, 604.

The prominence given in its day to the Easter controversy and the bitterness it inflamed emphasised the divergences between the Celtic and English Churches. When the controversy was settled, the racial self-consciousness of the Welsh and the need to resist growing Mercian territorial claims retarded the integration of their Church into the evolving pattern of western Christendom.

This Welsh self-consciousness and ecclesiastical sensitivity hid a basic lack of confidence. It is almost as if Wilfrid's jibe at the synod of Whitby that the special characteristics of Celtic Christianity were no more than the religious idiosyncracies of an off-shore island had hit home. St. Aldhelm's account of the fate of those English who went to live amongst the Welsh suggests that the Celts had developed a pathological dread of the Anglo-Saxons. This was the work of churchmen who saw theological contact with the Saxons as dangerous and disastrous as contact with a leper. In an early chapter of his *History*, Bede tells how, in 156 A D, Lucius, a British king, wrote to Pope Eleutherius asking to be made a Christian. His request, it is said, was quickly granted. The chronology of the story is confused and some think Lucius was a Mesopotamian ruler rather than a Briton. However, some three quarters of a century after Bede, Nennius incorporated a slightly different version of the story into his *History*, and later, in the Norman period, various amplified versions were in circulation. In the *Book of Llandaff* Lucius sent Elvan and Medwy as his ambassadors to Eleutherius. The former was consecrated bishop, the latter became a doctor of the Church, and through 'their eloquence and knowledge of holy writ, Lucius and all the nobles of Britain were baptised.' It is likely that Bede acquired the Lucius legend by way of Wales, where the theological and political events of the day gave the legend new importance. It guaranteed the ancestry of the Welsh Church by showing it had as direct a contact with Rome as the Church established by the Augustinian mission, a useful antidote to the growing failure of nerve of Celtic Christianity. Both Bede and Nennius derive their versions of the legend from the *Liber Pontificalis*, a collection of early papal biographies, though they obtained them independently. The *Book of Llandaff* shows that the church at Llandaff possessed a copy of the *Liber Pontificalis* though, of course, the date of its acquisition is uncertain. The Norman versions of the Lucius legend were also probably derived from earlier Welsh traditions. It is significant that in the various amplifications of the legend names appear which have been identified with dedications in the vicinity of Llandaff.

By the end of the seventh century the lower Wye, from Hereford to the Severn, represented the Anglo-Welsh border and there had been considerable Mercian encroachment and hostility, eventually halted by King Ithel ap Morgan. It was against this background in which Welsh churches as well as lands were lost to the Mercians that the Lucius story was propagated by the bishops of Llandaff. The intention was, no doubt, to minimise, by a claim to antiquity, the dilution of the ecclesiastical Celticism of an area claimed by the bishops of Llandaff and won by Mercian conquest for the Romanised bishops of Hereford. The conquest continued into the Norman period when imaginative hagiographers strengthened the historicity of their tale by identifying its heroes with patrons drawn from Llandavian church dedications of Irish origin.

The Lucius legend appealed to the Welsh Church because it established it on terms of equality with the Roman party in England which saw Celtic Christianity as a second-class version of the real thing. This is also reflected in the emergence of the journey to Rome as a hagiographical common-place in the seventh and eighth centuries. The Celtic saints were losing some of their lustre and had to be reinstated. This was done by associating them with those whose orthodoxy was unimpeachable and by crediting them with a journey to Rome where they were made welcome. Gildas, Cadoc, Brynach, and Winifred are all portrayed in their *Lives* as welcome visitors to Rome. Another example of this process occurs in the hagiographers' desire to connect Welsh saints with St. Germanus, the light of Cornwall and the pillar of western orthodoxy. St. Dyfrig, St. Illtud, and St. Paulinus were all associated with St. Germanus by their hagiographers, improbable though this may be in historical terms.

There was no need for the Welsh to have felt so defensive in the face of English Christianity which still had a Celtic content. The use of the Roman liturgy was still only partial in England where rogation days, a Celtic introduction, were now observed. The crown as episcopal head-gear was another Celtic custom absorbed by the Anglo-Saxon Church, and Celtic monastic ideals were still observed in England after the intro-duction of the Benedictine Rule at Wearmouth in 674. Another con-spicuous example of the survival of Celtic religious ideals amongst the English is the *clericatus;* it was common practice amongst Celtic princes to abdicate and enter the religious life. Maelgwn Gwynedd did this, though he later abandoned the cloister. So also did Petran, father of St. Padarn, St. Carautoc, St. Tysilio, and Ynyr Gwent. The development of English Christian art is a further example of the survival of Celtic

Christianity: English manuscripts and memorials reflected Celtic skills and Celtic literary influence affected the themes and style of Saxon poetry.

Economic and emotional factors contributed to the belief that the Welsh and English Churches were essentially different in the pre-Norman period. This belief undermined the self-confidence of the Welsh in the seventh and eighth centuries and they justified themselves by developing legends tracing their connections with the Holy See. But despite these feelings of Celtic inferiority the organisation of both churches was virtually identical. The kingdom-bishopric was the normal unit of episcopal organisation for Celt and Saxon alike. The Welsh kingdom-bishoprics evolved slowly. This was largely due to the pre-eminence of the abbot in the Celtic Church. Though St. Kentigern, St. David, St. Padarn, and St. Dyfrig were bishops who ruled monastic houses, other Welsh monasteries, far from having a bishop as their superior, appear not even to have had a bishop in the community. St. Dyfrig travelled specially to Llanilltud to ordain men for Illtud and there is no mention of a bishop as part of the community at Llancarfan.

The Celtic monastery represented the religious activity of the tribe. Its close tribal connections meant that, if necessary, a layman could be its abbot rather than allow the monastery to be ruled by an alien monk. This emphasis on the tribal connections of the monastery was maintained at the expense of the prestige of the episcopate, so that the bishop came to be deprived of the power of discipline, normally regarded in the Church as one of his essential prerogatives. The discrepancy between the status of the Celtic and Roman episcopates is illustrated in the legal codes. In Anglo-Saxon law a bishop had the status of an ealdorman, the king's principal administrator in the shire, whereas in Welsh law his status was no more than that of a free tribesman. But despite their superior legal status Anglo-Saxon bishops could be deposed by their king. In Wales there is no corresponding record of this, and bishops, at least in Morgannwg, seem virtually to have deposed their kings by excommunicating them and exiling them for grave offences. The otherwise inferior status of Welsh bishops is reflected in their numerical predominance. Gildas refers to a large number of bishops in his day and he is supported by Rhigyfarch's *Life of St. David* which says that one hundred and eighteen bishops attended the synod of Brefi. Gildas also implies that some bishops in the Celtic Church served particular *parochiae:* perhaps they were abbots as well. As in Gaul, at the beginning of the seventh century communities living together in the Celtic Church under an abbot had a *parochia* attached to them. In Wales the *parochia* consisted of the smaller monasteries subject to the mother house, the population of the tribe for which they were responsible, and the churches established by the founder or his disciples. The *parochia* of Llancarfan, for example, consisted of the cantref of Penychen in which it had been founded, the two Llanellis, and various churches with Cadoc dedications scattered throughout south Wales, Dumnonia, and Brittany.

In Ireland the custom of attaching sees to monasteries became common in the sixth century when the ecclesiastical government of the country was shared almost equally by abbots who were bishops and by abbots who were priests. The extent of the monastic *parochiae* was not as strictly defined as that of the continental dioceses of the period. Instead they probably waxed and waned with the fortunes of the monastery which was regarded as their religious centre. In the eighth century the offices of abbot and bishop were separated and there existed by this time provision for every tribe to have its own bishop to supervise its spiritual affairs. Wales was slower than Ireland to accept the idea that there should be one bishop for one kingdom and its eventual development was encouraged by the complete absence of bishops in some Welsh monasteries. In these instances the abbot usually exercised at least some episcopal functions, for example, that of excommunication.

The legendary life of St. Teilo in the *Book of Llandaff* may contain a reference to the evolution of the Welsh kingdom-bishoprics in its account of how Teilo consecrated 'Ishmael to Menevia and many others he likewise raised to the episcopate, sending them throughout the land and dividing *parochiae* to them for the convenience of clergy and people.' As it stands the account is unhistorical, but it may well reflect the process of development which took place in Wales. The *Annales Cambriae* for 809 record the death of Elbodugus 'archbishop in the region of Gwynedd' which suggests that he had episcopal colleagues there. In all probability this was also the case in sixth-century Gwynedd where inscriptions on two early Christian monuments suggest the existence of other bishops thereabouts besides those connected with the Bangor Fawr of St. Deiniol. Bangor, however, is the only church in Gwynedd traditionally associated with a bishop's chair. The episcopal traditions of important *clas* churches like Clynnog Fawr and Caergybi (now Holyhead), where, no doubt, there were originally bishops on the monastic establishment, had disappeared long before 809. It is reasonable to suggest that this was brought about by the steady flow of travellers to and fro over the Irish Sea keeping the church in Gwynedd well informed about developments in Ireland. The title of archbishop given to Elbodugus in the *Annales Cambriae* was purely honorific and was derived from the fact that the see of York became an archbishopric in 734, a fact known to Nennius, editor of the *Annales*. To the Celts, however, the new title reflected added honour rather than an increase in authority, which in the case of Elbodugus was justly deserved, at least in the eyes of Nennius, for his work to further the acceptance of the Roman Easter in Wales.

In his *Life* of Alfred, written at the end of the ninth century, Asser refers to the *parochia* of St. David's as being by then well known 'on the left and western bank of the Severn.' This has been interpreted as meaning the area over which the monastic *clas* of St. David's had authority, rather than the diocese of St. David's ruled over by a bishop. This seems unlikely, however, in view of the reference in the Laws of Hywel Dda, *c.* 942, to the bishop's seven houses in Dyfed. Indeed, by the end of the ninth century the *clas* was a declining institution. This had been brought about largely by the Danish invasions which reached their peak in 878. The *clas* system allowed clergy to marry and it became increasingly common for laymen to be head of the *familia*. Such lay abbots would not, though, be called as in the past to assist the bishop in excommunications or to advise him in synod. Instead the bishop was able, at least in Morgannwg, to exercise his authority alone and the influence of the principal abbots declined correspondingly. The mention of the bishop's seven houses in Dyfed and the decline in the authority of the *clas* show that by the tenth century the bishops had for some time been the dominant ecclesiastical figures. Any mention of a *parochia* was a reference to their sphere of authority and not to that of the abbot or the *clas*.

The origin of the Welsh kingdom-bishopric seems to lie in the work of St. Dyfrig in south-east Wales. His ecclesiastical career began as an abbot and teacher and he belongs to the period of the great monastic schoolmasters in Wales. St. Paulinus at Whitland, St. Illtud at Llanilltud Fawr, and St. Tathan at Caerwent all were his contemporaries, while he himself is remembered as a bishop rather than as an abbot-teacher. He was active in Erging where the kingdom-bishopric was paralleled by another in adjoining Gwent. When in the late sixth century Meurig ap Tewdrig united Glywyssing, Gwent, and Erging into Morgannwg, the whole kingdom seems to have been served by one bishop whose principal seat was at Llandaff which provided Morgannwg with its bishops for the next three centuries.[2]

The evolution of the kingdom-bishopric in south-east Wales was accompanied by a change in the character of the Celtic monastery. The day of the smaller monastery seems to have been over by the end of the sixth century and the ecclesiastical scene is then dominated by the abbots of the great houses of the Vale of Glamorgan, Llancarfan, Llantwit Major, and Llandough. At the same time, it is probably significant that there is no mention of a bishop being even a member of the households of these three important monasteries, and by the tenth century the primitive abbot-bishop relationship of the Celtic Church had become completely reversed in Morgannwg. Indeed, Bishop Gwgan of Llandaff (c. 960-982) claimed to be abbot of Llancarfan by hereditary right and there began with him a connection between Llancarfan and the bishopric which continued into Norman times. Outside Morgannwg the development of the kingdom-bishopric is far more uncertain and no clear picture emerges. Two considerations, though, suggest that in Gwynedd, Dyfed, and Ceredigion its development was not far behind Morgannwg. First, in the seventh century these places were not backwaters, out of touch with either the continent or with Ireland. The influence of continental culture, for example, is reflected in Gwynedd in the Llangadwaladr stone near Aberffraw and there were contacts with the most learned elements of Ireland and the Merovingian court. Indeed, Aberffraw was on a main route from Ireland to the continent. Likewise in Dyfed the peninsula on which St. David's was founded was a natural point of departure for Ireland, and the large Irish population of Dyfed witnessed to the contact between south Wales and Ireland. Medieval tradition makes Llanbadarn Fawr the centre of another kingdom-bishopric. Founded by St. Padarn, it was ruled by a *clas* and, as with Dyfed, the Celtic saints of Ceredigion looked towards Ireland, Llanbadarn maintaining its Irish interests into the Norman period. Secondly, there was a parallel development of kingdom-bishoprics in Anglo-Saxon England where well defined dioceses after the continental pattern were as slow to evolve as in Wales. This may have been due at least in part to the strongly Celtic influence on its early history.

Moving on to Brycheiniog and Powys, their position in the system of kingdom-bishoprics is far more conjectural. The *Book of Llandaff* implies an early ecclesiastical connection between Llandaff and Brycheiniog which is supported by dedication patterns. This connection was still intact at the beginning of the eighth century and even in the tenth century, at least according to the *Book of Llandaff*, the bishops of Llandaff were still active in Brycheiniog. The episcopal position in Powys is no clearer. When, in the first half of the seventh century, Cynddylan raided the borders of modern Staffordshire 'bishops and monks, despite their books, were not immune.' Though its eastern border then reached much further into the

Midlands than it has since the setting up of Offa's Dyke, Powys had no kingdom-bishopric. Its episcopal centre has been traditionally regarded as being at St. Asaph, though this is being disputed more and more and many regard this see as a purely Norman foundation.[3]

The Welsh pedigrees have it that St. Asaph was the cousin of Deiniol and Tysilio and his historicity is imprinted upon the place-names of Tegeingl, perhaps his native cantref. According to Jocelyn's *Life* of St. Kentigern, St. Asaph succeeded Kentigern as head of the monastic *clas* at Llanelwy which had been founded by the patron of Glasgow while he was in exile in north Wales. Unfortunately, the existence of this short-lived Celtic bishopric centred upon Llanelwy is no evidence for the existence of a kingdom-bishopric. Llanelwy had a limited *parochia*, for St. Asaph was a purely local saint whose dedications are confined to the northern parts of Flintshire, and though the boundaries of the Norman diocese of St. Asaph coincided roughly with those of twelfth-century Powys, at the time of its foundation, in the sixth century, Llanelwy was in Gwynedd. There the principal saint was Deiniol, St. Asaph's cousin. It is interesting that the foundation of one of the principal Celtic monasteries in Powys is, in fact, ascribed to St. Deiniol. He is the patron of Bangor-is-coed whose monks were massacred at the battle of Chester. At the time of the massacre the abbot of the monastery was Dinoot, a name which has linguistic connections with Dunaut Bwr, of the line of Coel Hen and Deiniol's father. The recurrence of this name and the well-established hereditary principle in Celtic monasticism have led to the suggestion that Dinoot was also related to Deiniol. Bangor-is-coed, as a daughter house of Bangor Fawr, with two other nearby Deiniol dedications, would have been part of the *parochia* of St. Deiniol whom tradition remembers as a bishop. This makes it unlikely that Bangor-is-coed had its own episcopal succession, though, despite its perilous border position it survived long enough to be celebrated in the Welsh triads as one of the major Celtic monasteries in Wales. If Powys was to produce its own bishopric, its natural centre would have been neither Llanelwy nor Bangor-is-coed, but Meifod, 'the premier church of Powys' closely linked with St. Tysilio, cousin to Deiniol and Asaph, and a member of the local ruling dynasty. Meifod's pre-eminence, like that of its royal patron, is reflected in Powys in its pattern of Tysilio dedications, and though it maintained this position throughout the Celtic period, it failed to evolve into the centre of a kingdom-bishopric. Tradition commemorates Tysilio as an abbot, not as a bishop. His nearest rival in Powys was his kinsman and contemporary, St. Beuno, whose principal church at Berriew is a mere ten miles from Meifod. It was either rivalry between these two monasteries and their founders which had political overtones, or the arrival of the Mercians on the other side of the Severn which forced Beuno to leave Berriew precipitately and to establish Clynnog Fawr as his principal church. But whatever the cause, Beuno's removal prevented Berriew from evolving, at the expense of Meifod, into the principal ecclesiastical centre of Powys from which a kingdom-bishopric could have eventually sprung.

The English bishops were presided over by an archbishop, whereas metropolitans were still unknown in the Celtic Church, but the archiepiscopal control exercised through the synod, held to be a late seventh-century innovation in England by Archbishop Theodore, was paralleled in Wales where synods were in use much earlier. They were convened by the ecclesiastic who in his day wielded most spiritual influence. The *Life* of St. David contains accounts of two sixth-century general synods of the Welsh Church, and in Morgannwg, at least, the kingdom-bishop presided over his diocese in synod from the days of Oudoceus (Euddogwy). The Laws of Hywel Dda, codifying earlier traditions, gave the synod legal sanction.

By the beginning of the seventh century the monastic life was the basis of Celtic Christianity. The Celtic abbot exercised an overall authority over his own abbey and all its daughter houses. Superiors were appointed for every daughter house, but the abbot visited them periodically himself and his authority was never relaxed by distance. When St. Cadoc retired from Llancarfan, Elli, his disciple and successor there, had to visit him once a year at the mysterious Beneventum to report what was happening. The abbot's authority was absolute: St. Cadoc had the powers of life and death over his monks and all and everything within the Celtic monastery was under the abbot's control, even strangers being admitted or excluded as he thought fit. He exercised a similar primacy in the affairs of the tribe and the local kingdom, and much of his power and authority within and without the monastery was derived from his royal pedigree and the tribal system. Consequently, he inherited the patriarchal outlook of the society in which he lived. He was not elected by his brethren but nominated by his predecessor. In many cases the abbots, whilst not in strict line of descent, were frequently drawn from the founder's family. In Wales a Celtic monastery could only be founded in accordance with tribal land-law which forbade any alienation of tribal land. Tribal patronage was necessary before a monastery could be established, especially if its founder was a stranger to the region. Thus, when St. Teilo, who was not a native of the Llandeilo district where he founded his principal monastery, died, his nephew Oudoceus is not heard of there at all. Instead he appears at Llandaff in Glamorgan which now became the permanent home of St. Teilo's community and traditions. Oudoceus and his companions would have been given the alternatives of either submitting to the local nominee as abbot in Teilo's place or of departing.

The Irish rule of St. Columba advised those seeking perfection that a fast place with one gate should enclose them. This advice was followed by many, for Celtic monasticism dominates Welsh place-names; many *llans* and *bangors* commemorate the enclosures of the Celtic saints. The function of the Celtic monastery approximated to that of the Saxon minster and by the seventh century both had a dual purpose. They were communities worshipping God which served as the religious centres of their areas. The earliest Celtic monasteries had been founded in desert places and evangelisation was not seen as one of their duties. The eighth century, however, saw the emergence of larger Welsh monasteries which appear to have replaced a number of smaller ones. These monasteries which were also the mother churches of the areas they served seem to have been located nearer contemporary settlements than their predecessors. In Anglesey the large monasteries of Caergybi and Penmon were near large villages inhabited in the immediate post-Roman centuries. Llangaffo was another large Anglesey monastery and a concentration of similar settlement remains occurs nearby. In the south, Llancarfan and Llantwit Major must have been very important centres and settlements of some size. Thus, the larger monastic establishments were not located in such desert places as those so eagerly sought after by the anchorites. Once acquired, the discharge of pastoral responsibilities was not without its difficulties. Celtic free tribesmen were pastoralists who practised a semi-nomadic life. Originally the Celtic monks also lived by the work of their own hands and St. David's monks drew the plough themselves like oxen. Their ideal was abandoned with the passing of the Age of the Saints. Like their Saxon counterparts, Celtic monks began to be endowed with land from which they were mainly supported. Slaves also played an important part in the monastic economy. The spiritually ex-curricular activities of the monastery tended to make it a centre of population. Monks were recognised agricultural specialists and long before the Cistercians developed the keeping of sheep upon the Welsh mountains, the monks of St. Beuno were shepherding. The monks also had some success as medical practitioners which, no doubt, gave rise to accounts of miracles of healing, all part of the hagiographer's stock-in-trade. The

PLATE 1.   Aerial view of St. David's
(*Studio Jon*)

monks practised other crafts, too. Schools of sculpture were attached to some monasteries, like those which evolved at Margam and Llantwit Major, and from their earliest days the monasteries were centres of learning attracting large numbers of students. Llancarfan had its *magister* and Llandaff its *scolasticus*. St. Samson was taken to Llanilltud Fawr when he was five.

Welsh learning was largely derived from Irish sources and was probably somewhat out-dated in comparison. Its Irish flavour is illustrated by the probability that the cat in the famous Irish poem about the scribe and his cat was Welsh. Though vernacular poetry was written in Welsh monasteries, they appear to have produced no Caedmons. All the same, of the many monasteries in Wales, only a handful are remembered as centres of learning, St. David's, Llanbadarn Fawr, Llantwit Major, Llancarfan, Bangor, and perhaps Llandaff, and it has to be remembered that many Celtic monasteries were so sited that the very processes of living would have occupied all the time the monks were not engaged in worship. The siting of the Celtic monastery was to some extent dependent upon the local chieftain who made initial grants of land. Larger monasteries, as they developed, were often sited near roads which not only facilitated the journeys of the monks but also made the monasteries themselves more readily accessible. St. Dyfrig built Hentland near two important Roman roads; Llandaff and Llancarfan have Roman roads passing by; and St. David's was an important point of departure for travellers to Ireland.

It is suspected that the size of some Celtic monasteries has been exaggerated. Bangor-is-coed, it is said, had over two thousand monks, and according to the *Life* of St. Padarn there were eight hundred and forty-seven monks at Llanbadarn Fawr. The Celtic Church, like the Rule of St. Benedict, saw the solitary life as an advanced form of monasticism. Not for the beginner, it marked the individual's progress towards spiritual perfection. It was taken up, with the consent of the abbot and the brethren, at the end of a monk's life.

It seems that the written charter was introduced into England by Theodore and Wilfrid in the second half of the seventh century, but some churches were already recording their possessions in written documents. The Llancarfan charters contain such written references in three documents going back to *c.* 600. The Celtic saints were invariably men of noble lineage, which may be a consequence of tribal law forbidding the alienation of tribal land. The *clas* system tended to make the monastery itself tribal so that at Llancarfan, Paul of Penychen, the local ruler, was eventually remembered as an abbot of the monastery. In a revival of the tribe's political fortunes, the abbot's office became identified with the chieftainship of the clan. The social background of the rank and file monks is illustrated by the probability that they had to pay an admission fee when they joined the monastery. There was no objection to laymen becoming abbots and when an abbot died an *ebediw* or heriot was payable by his successor. If the new abbot was unacceptable the king could reject his *ebediw*. It was not until the tenth century that, in Glamorgan at least, the bishop successfully established the principle that land given to the Church was given in perpetuity. When a fine was payable to a monastic *clas* for misdemeanours committed within its precincts, it was shared equally between the abbot and the community. This strong portionary interest of the *clas* prevented the monastery it served, or its abbot, from going against the interests of the tribe it represented.

The predominant characteristic of Celtic monasticism was its asceticism and St. David himself, for example, was referred to as David *aquaticus* because he lived only on bread and water. All his successors are said to have been content with water until the time of Morgeneu. He broke the tradition and was slain by Norse pirates in 999, a divine punishment, as it was believed, for his laxity. Celtic asceticism, however, was more than abstinence. St. Samson would pray through the night naked in the winter cold; some believe that this kind of austerity and asceticism was more characteristic of west Wales than of the Welsh saints as a whole. The emphasis of St. Gildas and St. Illtud was probably more intellectual than ascetic. This discrepancy is due possibly to the fact that no general rule was followed by all Celtic monks. Each house had its own which reflected the ideals of its founder.

Women were not conspicuous in Welsh ecclesiastical life and apart from St. Winifred no outstanding Welsh females adorned the Age of the Saints nor does the religious life appear to have been accessible to Welsh women.

The most obvious difference between the Celtic and Anglo-Saxon Churches was neither a matter of liturgy nor of order but of architecture. The Celts were not great architects and buildings in stone were not part of their artistic tradition. Through the centuries an awareness of their modest achievements in ecclesiastical architecture has inflated the defensive argument that the Welsh Church was essentially different from its English counterpart. Conservative and antiquarian by nature and poor through economic circumstances, it failed to move with the times, but it was never essentially different from the rest of western Christendom: it was merely rather old-fashioned. Like the Saxon minster, the Celtic monastery was enclosed by a hedge or palisade, commemorated by the words *llan* and *bangor* which, besides marking the monastery's separation from the world, afforded a place of physical refuge. Sometimes deserted hill forts were taken over for monasteries. The area embraced by the *llan* varied in size. At Ynys Seiriol it is some three hundred by one hundred and fifty feet, while at Llancarfan and Llantwit it must have been far larger, judging from the accounts in the *Lives* of their founders of the numerous buildings contained in these monastic establishments. Once enclosed by a *llan* the monastery had to be consecrated which in the Celtic world normally took the form of a forty-day fast. The plan of the monastery's scattered groups of buildings was haphazard and largely determined by the topography of the site. The buildings themselves were constructed of timber, or wattle, or of dry stone, the choice being determined by what was locally and readily available. Unlike the medieval church-builders they did not select materials from great distances for special ornamental or functional purposes. Churches were small and of simple design and they were built by the monks themselves with the occasional assistance of travelling craftsmen. At times there seems to have been more than one church within the monastery and the archaeological evidence suggests that they could accommodate no more than the altar with sufficient space for the celebration of the liturgy and a small congregation.

The monks' cells resembled the dwellings in civil settlements in Wales. The rectangular cells on Ynys Seiriol are some twelve feet wide, varying in length from ten to twenty-five feet. Celtic architecture was not static though its development was slow and the later, improved churches, like that excavated at Dyrysgol, were primitive in comparison with many of their Saxon counterparts.

The liturgy celebrated at Celtic altars was either identical with or very like the Gallican liturgy. The eucharist was seen as a sacrifice, a sacred offering, a concept stamped upon Welsh liturgical terminology. It seems to have been celebrated on Sundays and holy days rather than daily and the sacrament was received in both kinds. The viaticum was the normal preparation for death: St. Beuno's father 'after receiving communion and after confession, and a perfect ending, died.' The collection of relics did not become established in the Celtic Church until the eighth century, a by-product of accepting the Roman Easter. Worship, despite its modest architectural setting, was not without its glory. While there has always been something of the Calvinistic Methodist in the Welshman's theology from the days of Gildas, when it comes to ritual expression of his theology, he is a consistent high churchman. When Samson saw three bishops in a vision, not only did they wear 'golden crowns on their heads, they were clothed with vestments of pure silk and most beautiful.' The altars were decked with purple palls and the beauty of the sacred vessels and the gospel books used for the liturgy was almost proverbial. The ministry was itinerant and this is reflected in the relationship between some Welsh Celtic monuments and nearby Roman roads. Little is heard of any church except the monastery and in the *Lives* of the saints there are no references to churches being built except for monastic communities. The Welsh laws, however, do distinguish between mother churches and those of less importance. These mother churches had a *clas* of clergy headed by an abbot and their distribution seems to be connected with the cantrefs. In some cases, a smaller unit, the commote, had its own *clas*. Lesser churches were probably set up in the vicinity of old-established bond hamlets which were thought to be as numerous in the Dark Ages as churches with Celtic dedications. Kings and princes, at least by the time of Hywel Dda, had their own chapels and chaplains.

The development of the Church in the seventh and eighth centuries was, paradoxically, accompanied by some measure of decay. The Age of the Saints came to an end and this in itself suggests a deterioration in the standards and ideals of the Welsh Church. There is, however, little documentary evidence of decline, and it is the relapse into silence and anonymity which suggests that the enthusiasm and virility of the Age of the Saints had worked itself out. It may be that tribal society was unable to give the Welsh Church sufficient stability for it to mature. There was no law of primogeniture so that on the father's death his possessions and inheritance were shared out equally amongst his sons. In the case of a prince this involved the subdivision of his realm built up in his life-time by war and marriage. At the same time the Celtic practice of fosterage meant that the several sons of one father were strangers to one another, for their father had fostered them out amongst his lords and they grew up without developing the normal bonds of fraternal affection. Brothers who did not know each other were more ready to fight for territorial supremacy and could be exploited by ambitious foster-fathers. The poverty of Welsh society also made it aggressive. More land and more cattle meant a higher standard of living for the prince, even if it had to be won by force and eventual retaliation was inevitable. In such conditions it was difficult for scholars and artists to flourish and it is significant that what is believed to be the earliest mention of St. David, the fragmentary Idnert stone at Llanddewibrefi, refers to the stresses and violence with which the maturing Church had to contend in Wales. The *Book of Llandaff* also contains records of the violation of ecclesiastical property and persons.

The picture, happily, is not all gloom. There was compensation in the closer involvement of the Welsh Church with English and continental Christianity. We have seen how the *Annales Cambriae* described Elbo-dugus of Gwynedd as an archbishop[4] and how this development reflects Nennius's awareness of what was happening at that time in England. The *Annales* also record for 768 the change in the date of Easter in Wales through the influence of Elbodugus and it is thought that Nennius, who compiled his *History* as a manifesto in favour of changing the date of Easter, was his disciple. Both the Irish and the English played a large part in the change. Moreover, the confused traditions about St. Germanus and his alleged connection with Powys and the tyrant Vortigern were included by Nennius in the *History* to uphold Roman orthodoxy against Celtic deviation, and this has been seen as part of a general eighth-century movement. Another suggestion is that when the papal legate George investigated the Northumbrian Church in 786, Elbodugus of Gwynedd was represented, at the council he convened, by the Irishman, Aldwulf of Mayo, one of the signatories to its resolutions.

Dedications to St. Michael the Archangel appeared in the eighth century on the Welsh Marches and for the Welsh this represented a departure from their earlier practice of commemorating the founder of their churches in ecclesiastical place-names. The cult of St. Michael was introduced to the Marches by St. Chad who died at Lichfield in 672. There is evidence, too, that Bede and his *Ecclesiastical History* were known and respected in Wales. The animosity between Celt and Saxon, of which Bede himself was so conscious, had disappeared. Commercial relations with England developed. There was a timber trade and Welsh ale was esteemed among the English. Indeed, it seems that traders were protected by treaty and that the Marches were no longer considered a place to be avoided by ambitious English ecclesiastics. There was cultural exchange, too. For example, there is a well-known similarity between the twin crosses at Sandbach, near Crewe, and the Penally cross in Dyfed, and the ninth-century Pillar of Eliseg in Powys has English counterparts.

Irish influence in Wales remained strong even on the Marches where the impact of Irish anchorites was felt. These anchorites were spiritual heirs of the seventh-century pilgrims who found that the continent had become less accessible and less attractive on account of the growth in Anglo-Saxon influence and the Viking raids. This may account for the arrival of the cult of St. Brigid on the Marches. Besides sculptural evidence on Welsh monuments for continuing Irish influence, the close association between the two countries is also reflected in the manuscripts produced in Welsh monasteries. The best-known of these are the *St. Chad's Gospels* which came by a devious route from south Wales to Lichfield in the tenth century. Wales was much poorer than either Ireland or Northumbria, so its *scriptoria* were fewer, though the production of manuscripts was part of the tradition of the larger Welsh monasteries. Another example of the persistence of Irish influence in Welsh ecclesiastical affairs lies in the inclusion of a visit to Ireland as a matter of course for the Welsh saints as recorded in their *Lives*. Cadoc, David, Padarn, Finnian, and Gildas are all credited with at least one visit to Ireland, and from the eighth century the names of leading Welsh saints appear in Irish documents.

Closer relations with England and the continent and the maintenance of the long-established connection with Ireland must inevitably have brought the Welsh Church to the attention of Rome. Yet there is no record of undue Roman concern about either its faith or its order. The popes have no place in the Welsh annals and their appearances in the *Lives* of the Welsh saints are few and unhistorical; St. Cadoc was said to have visited a Pope Alexander in the sixth century though no such pontiff ever existed. Similarly, there is no record of any Welsh bishop having sought the *pallium* in Rome. The exact relationship between Wales and the Roman see at this period is still obscure but it seems that the pope considered Wales to be safely within his sphere of papal authority when Leo III addressed himself in 789 to all the people dwelling in the island of Britain. At the same time he carefully defined the jurisdiction of the archbishop of Canterbury as limited to England and the English. Whilst successive archbishops felt some kind of general oversight of the Welsh Church to be within their brief, the Welsh seem to have enjoyed a special relationship with the Holy See which paid due respect to their independent Celtic traditions and their geographical remoteness from Rome.

[1] This essay owes much to the following works:
    M. W. Barley and R. P. C. Hanson, *Christianity in Britain 300–700*, Leicester, 1968.
    E. G. Bowen, *The Settlements of the Celtic Saints in Wales*, Cardiff, 1954.
        Saints, Seaways, and Settlements, Cardiff, 1969.
    N. K. Chadwick, *The Age of the Saints in the early Celtic Church*, Oxford, 1961.
        Celtic Britain, London, 1965.
        ed., *Studies in the early British Church*, Cambridge, 1958; Archon, 1973.
        ed., *Studies in early British History*, Cambridge, 1959.
        ed., *Celt and Saxon, Studies in the early British Border*, Cambridge, 1963.

G. H. Doble, *St. Illtut*, Cardiff, 1944.
    St. Patern, Lampeter, 1940.
    St. Dubricius, Guildford, 1943.
H. P. R. Finberg, *Lucerna*, London, 1965.
I. Ll. Foster and G. E. Daniel, *Prehistoric and Early Wales*, London, 1965.
J. E. Lloyd, *A History of Wales from the earliest times to the Edwardian Conquest*, 2 vols., 3rd. ed., London, 1939.
V. E. Nash-Williams, *The early Christian Monuments of Wales*, Cardiff, 1950.
R. Rees, *An Essay on the Welsh Saints*, London, 1836.
A. W. Wade-Evans, *The Emergence of England and Wales*, 2nd. ed., Cambridge, 1954.
    Welsh Christian Origins, Oxford, 1934.
H. Williams, *Christianity in early Britain*, Oxford, 1912.
    Angles and Britons, Cardiff, 1963.
Dictionary of Welsh Biography, London, 1959.
The following articles are also valuable:
J.W.James,'The excommunications in the Book of Llan Dâv', *J.H.S.C.W.*, VIII, 1958.
    'The Book of Llan Dâv: The Church and See of Llan Dâv and their critics', *J.H.S.C.W.*, IX, 1959.
    'The 'Concen Charters' and the 'Book of Llan Dâv , *Trans. Cymm.*, 1963.
    'The Book of Llan Dâv and Canon G. H. Doble', *N.L.W.J.*, XVIII, 1973.
C. A. R. Radford, 'The Celtic Monastery in Britain', *Arch. Camb.*, CXI, 1962.
M. Richards, 'The 'Lichfield' Gospels (Book of St. Chad)', *N.L.W.J.*, XVIII, 1973.
Bede's *Ecclesiastical History of the English People* has been used in the edition by B. Colgrave and R. A. B. Mynors, Oxford, 1969.
The *Lives* of the Welsh saints can be examined in A. W. Wade-Evans's edition, *Vitae Sanctorum Britanniae et Genealogiae*, Cardiff, 1944.
[2] There is much debate about the origins of Llandaff. For a different view see below, p. 29.
[3] For the history of St. Asaph after the Norman Conquest see below, p. 27.
[4] See above, p. 11.

CHAPTER 2

THE WELSH CHURCH IN THE MIDDLE AGES

by

David Walker

THE Norman incursions into Wales brought about major changes in the
Welsh Church.[1] Even before the Conqueror's hold on England was
secure, Norman knights had begun to penetrate beyond the borders into
Wales. William fitz Osbern, earl of Hereford, was dead by the spring of
1071, but already his men had ringed the southern frontier with castles,
from Chepstow, on the coast, through Monmouth to Wigmore. They had
begun the slow, inexorable advance of the Norman invaders into Gwent.
In the north, Hugh d'Avranches, earl of Chester, was to spend twenty
years attacking Welsh territory. He secured Tegeingl, while his kinsman,
Robert of Rhuddlan, made Rhuddlan itself a centre of Norman domination and built at Degannwy an impressive and dangerous outpost. Before
the end of the eleventh century, Norman forces from the earldom of
Chester would move further west, to Bangor and Caernarfon and the
Llŷn, and from Bangor across to Anglesey. Meanwhile, in the middle
section of the border, Roger of Montgomery, earl of Shrewsbury, was
consolidating Norman power along the frontier, and moving firmly into
Welsh territory, in Iâl, Edeyrnion, Cynllaith, Ceri, Cydewain, and
Arwystli. His forces made daring sweeps through mid-Wales to Dyfed
and Ceredigion, and foreshadowed the future significance of Pembroke
and Cardigan. The 1080s were years of renewed activity in the south,
with Bernard of Neufmarché beginning to infiltrate into Brycheiniog,
where he and his men were firmly established by 1093. The death of the
Welsh ruler, Rhys ap Tewdwr, at Aberhonddu in that year paved the way
for the consolidation of the Norman hold on Brycheiniog, and for further
attacks in south Wales. Philip de Braiose, first of a famous marcher family
to appear in Wales, secured territory in Builth and Radnor. A little while
later, Robert fitz Hamo gained his initial success in his attack on the
kingdom of Morgannwg and began the process of building up the Norman
lordship of Glamorgan.

A Welsh revival checked the Norman advance in north Wales and thrust the invaders back towards Tegeingl. In west Wales, Ceredigion and most of Dyfed were recovered. But in the south the process of conquest continued into the early decades of the twelfth century. The boundaries of the lordship of Glamorgan were pushed westwards. The lordships of Gower and Kidwelly were created. Carmarthen became a stronghold of the English king, and remained a centre of royal influence throughout the later middle ages. The reconquest of Dyfed was attempted, and fresh efforts were made to establish Norman power in Ceredigion. The fortunes of war might vary, but the Norman presence in Wales, and especially in the south, was a fact of life.

When they invaded England the Normans found in the English Church two obvious points of contact. The Rule of St. Benedict set the pattern for organised monastic life in England as in the rest of western Europe. English and Norman monasticism had been much affected by Cluniac influence, and although the reforming impetus in England had reached a low ebb by 1066 there was still much common to both countries. A Norman abbot, introduced into an English monastery, might find his monks backward and ignorant, but they shared the same ideals and ethos. In England, too, the diocesan structure of the Church was identical with that which the Normans took for granted in France. They might have strong objections to individual bishops, but they had no need to make over in new guise the institution of the Church as they found it.

The Normans were often pious and they could be very superstitious. They were anxious to make amends for the evil which had accompanied their military conquests, and which, as their spiritual advisers told them in uncompromising terms, might endanger their eternal salvation. They were generous benefactors to the Church, seeking, especially through their gifts to monastic houses, to be associated in the spiritual benefits which derived from the life of prayer in the cloister. At first they gave lands, churches and tithes to the monasteries with which they were associated in Normandy or elsewhere in northern France. Soon they began to make gifts to the monasteries already existing in England, and like King William himself, they founded religious houses in their newly-conquered territories. Estates and churches in Wales enriched French and English monasteries. William fitz Osbern was generous to the houses which he and his wife had founded at Cormeilles and Lyre. Wihenoc, the Breton lord of Monmouth, added to the endowments of St. Florent of Saumur, while a little later, the lord of Gower gave Llangennith to St. Taurin of Evreux. Robert of Montgomery founded a monastery at

Shrewsbury, and Hugh d'Avranches was patron and benefactor of St. Werburgh's, Chester. Robert fitz Hamo founded Tewkesbury abbey and was keenly interested in the neighbouring monastery of St. Peter at Gloucester; both houses acquired rich possessions in Glamorgan.

The Church as it was in Wales on the eve of the Norman invasions afforded no such common ground and called forth no parallel gifts to indigenous foundations in Wales. The Normans found nothing which they could recognise as a monastic church, and this in spite of the long-standing monastic tradition of the Celtic Church. The *clas* church struck no chord and aroused no sympathy. Its affinities seemed to be with communities of secular clerks who served in cathedral and collegiate churches, or who were organised as the twelfth century advanced into effective orders of canons, like the Augustinians. There was little attempt to transfer Norman patronage and generosity to Welsh monasteries, and the native institutions which had flourished in the Dark Ages could not survive. Great *clas* churches like Llancarfan and Llanbadarn Fawr were used to enrich a Benedictine house outside Wales. A small number were deliberately transformed into secular communities on the European mould. The *claswyr* serving the cathedral church of St. David's became the nucleus of the cathedral chapter under a Norman bishop. The transition at Llandaff was considerably more complex, but something of the same sort appears to have happened there. Similar communities in Welsh Wales, at Bardsey, Penmon, and Beddgelert, became houses of Augustinian canons. Even the new foundations which began to appear in the Norman lordships of Wales served to emphasise the contrast between old Welsh and new Norman monasticism. A castle provided protection for a Benedictine priory where organised monastic life could be maintained on the European pattern. At such places as Kidwelly, Cardigan, and Carmarthen, or at Brecon and Abergavenny, small houses of Black monks were established. They recruited largely from settler stock, and they were associated particularly with castle and borough. If they belonged to an English monastery, as Carmarthen and Brecon belonged to Battle abbey, they looked to England for direction and control. The settlers were generous after their fashion, but these Welsh priories could never be described as wealthy. While Brecon priory was secure and well-endowed, it took three generations before the cell at Ewyas Harold was established as its founder intended; even then its existence remained precarious until, in 1358, it was suppressed and its possessions absorbed by its parent house, St. Peter's, Gloucester.

The Welsh Church was diocesan in structure, but the bishoprics were ill-defined. Their affinities lay with the Celtic Church in Ireland and Scotland rather than with continental Europe, and for the first Norman bishops in Wales change and reconstruction were the keynotes. In the north, an initial attempt at change was violent and caused much bitterness. At the end of the eleventh century, Bangor was under Norman control for a brief span, and in 1092 the invaders appointed as bishop a Breton, Hervé. Was it a stroke of imagination or a mere accident that he was a Breton who might find accord with the Welsh people of his new diocese? His time in Wales was too short to provide an answer to that question, for when the Normans were driven back towards the Clwyd, Hervé took refuge in England. He found a new sphere of activity at the abbey of Ely, and when Henry I founded the diocese of Ely in 1109, Hervé became its first bishop. During the interval Hervé and his supporters used bitter language to describe his experiences at the hands of the 'barbarians' who had driven him from Bangor, and the bitterness is reflected in the terms in which twelfth-century historians wrote about this episode. There was a long vacancy before a new bishop was appointed to Bangor in 1120 and by then Welsh control of the bishopric had long been re-established. The new bishop, David, known as 'the Scot', was certainly a Celt and probably a Welshman.

He and his successor, Meurig, might owe their first loyalty to the prince of Gwynedd but they were closely linked with the English king and the English Church and they had to live with the strains of a double allegiance. Owain Gwynedd resented this, and when Meurig died in 1161 he delayed the appointment of a new bishop for sixteen years, holding at bay King Henry II, Archbishop Thomas Becket (while he was an effective force in England), and Pope Alexander III. He caused great apprehension by threats to have a bishop consecrated in Ireland. The diocese found a resourceful and persistent spokesman in Dafydd, archdeacon of Bangor, who drove Becket to bitter anger and recrimination by a mixture of wiliness and impudence. At one point the archbishop castigated Dafydd as the forerunner and standard-bearer of the enemies of the diocese of Bangor by whose deeds the miseries of the church groaned aloud. But Owain and Dafydd were not to be browbeaten, and in the end, in 1177, a Welsh bishop, Gwion, was consecrated for Bangor.

The early history of St. Asaph, or Llanelwy, is obscure. Though the Normans had been in firm control of the eastern part of this area for seventy years, no bishop was appointed until 1143, and even then the sequence of bishops is obscure. The first Norman bishop is now believed to have been Bishop Richard,[2] but he and his successors, who included the author of *The History of the Kings of Britain*, Geoffrey of Monmouth, had short episcopates and could make little of their diocese. Another Geoffrey, bishop between 1160 and 1175, was the only twelfth-century bishop to hold the see for any length of time, but he never rose to the measure of his opportunities. He was subject to many conflicting pressures. As Owain Gwynedd established his authority in north Wales the chances that a bishop nominated by the English king could survive at St. Asaph were slight, but Geoffrey showed no inclination to make the attempt. He was happier exercising his episcopal office somewhat mischievously in England, to the great annoyance of Archbishop Thomas Becket. For many years he lived at Abingdon where he was virtually abbot and the attractions of remaining there were strong. There were persistent attempts to oblige him to return to St. Asaph or to resign, and finally, in 1175, he gave way, resigning his bishopric in hope of securing on a permanent basis the abbacy of Abingdon. Alas for his hopes, Henry II had withdrawn his favour and the abbacy went to another man. After two brief episcopates St. Asaph passed to Bishop Reinier in 1186 and he gave the diocese a measure of stability until his death in 1224.

Norman settlement in the south was the occasion of major changes in the Church. Two bishops were particularly influential, Urban of Llandaff, 1107-1133/4, and Bernard of St. David's, 1115-1148. Although they were rivals, their work as diocesan bishops was complementary. The diocese in south-east Wales to which Urban was appointed was more susceptible than any other part of Wales to English influence. His predecessor, Herewald, consecrated in 1055, was bishop for fifty-two years. At his best he was an active and forward-looking diocesan. There seems to be no reason to question the assertion that he was served by two archdeacons, which implies that he was aware of current developments in the European Church. He faced the first attacks of the Normans in Gwent and ensured that churches were consecrated and endowed and that a normal pattern of ministry and care could be maintained. The second wave of invasion which reduced Brycheiniog and Morgannwg to Norman lordships seems to have been too much for his failing powers and when Urban became bishop one of his first tasks was to repair the damage caused by an aged and ineffective bishop. There were other problems of the first magnitude. One was the despoliation of church lands by the Norman invaders. At Urban's request prominent lay magnates, men like William fitz Baderon, Payn fitz John, Brian fitz Count and Bernard of Neufmarché, were reprimanded by Pope Calixtus II because 'the complaint of their mother church of Llandaff had reached him, that its goods were despoiled by them and that it was reduced almost to nothing.' In this sphere Urban's most successful achievement was an agreement which he reached with the greatest secular magnate in south Wales, Robert, earl of Gloucester and lord of Glamorgan. It was drawn up in 1126 in the presence of King Henry I and it was attested by many of the leading barons of the kingdom.[3]

The second problem facing Urban was to define and defend his diocese. He styled himself bishop of Glamorgan, but he made vigorous attempts to extend his diocese by claiming churches to the east which had certainly been subject to Bishop Herewald's jurisdiction but were now under the control of the bishop of Hereford, and churches to the west associated with St. Teilo and claimed by the bishop of St. David's. Urban was indefatigable in building up and presenting his case. Before his death in 1134 he had travelled to Rome on three occasions to seek favourable judgment at the curia. It is not clear whether he died at Rome or on the return journey after his third visit. In the long run his successors did not regain the churches and territory which he claimed. At the end of his life the diocese of Llandaff was, for the first time, a clearly defined unit. To state the current orthodoxy, Urban created the medieval diocese of Llandaff. The evidence on which his case could be adjudged still exists but unfortunately it does not enable us to define with certainty what the diocese in south-east Wales was like before Urban became bishop. It exists in the *Book of Llandaff* which is part history, made up of lives of early saints, and part cartulary, made up of a collection of formal documents purporting to date back in some instances to the sixth century. That there is a basis of genuine, early material in the *Book of Llandaff* is not in dispute. But since the work of five successive editors can be discerned in the text, the problem is to remove the overlay of later editing and to identify what is, or is not, genuine. The result is that this collection of material 'bristles with difficulties' and raises many technical problems. For the present the view which holds the field is that the geographical diocese of Llandaff was the creation of Bishop Urban and that under his aegis the material in the *Book of Llandaff* was edited to establish the case he wished to argue for its extension.[4]

The difficulties multiply when the question is extended to cover the early history of the cathedral church of Llandaff. Did Urban also create a new centre for his diocese of Llandaff when he built his cathedral there? Or was Llandaff already the ancient centre of the bishopric? That Urban built himself a new cathedral is quite clear. He found a small church at Llandaff 'but twenty-eight feet in length, fifteen wide and twenty high, with two aisles on either side of but a small size and height, and with a porch twelve feet long.' One historian has been prompted to say, 'The church of Llandaff was a chapel when he found it, and he left it a cathedral.'[5] The dedication of the new cathedral was in one sense a proclamation of Urban's hopes for his diocese. He dedicated it to St. Peter and St. Euddogwy and he added the names of St. Dyfrig, whose cult was concentrated in Erging, the area which Urban claimed in the east of his diocese, and St. Teilo, whose churches he wished to claim in the west. The crucial problem centres on the connection of Llandaff with St. Teilo. Was Llandaff an ancient centre of his cult? Or was the association newly forged in the twelfth century? The evidence does not establish an answer clear beyond all doubt. For the present the orthodox view is that Llandaff was a new site for the cathedral. If that is the case a further question arises. Where did Urban find the men to serve in his new cathedral church? The answer which has been put forward is that he made common cause with the *claswyr* of Llancarfan who transferred their allegiance and their traditions to Llandaff, finding there a new home where they might themselves survive the era of conquest and maintain the scholarly activities of which Llancarfan had been a centre. To summarise in such brief compass is to present as certainties what are in fact reasonable explanations of the evidence. The establishment of the authority of documents in the *Book of Llandaff* and the interpretation of that difficult source are still matters under discussion. Critics of the orthodox view are re-examining documentary and topographical evidence and are concentrating attention on those features which point to an ancient foundation for the diocese and the cathedral. The last word has not yet been said, but for the present both look like Urban's work.

While Urban was establishing his diocese in south-east Wales, Bishop Bernard was reorganising the diocese of St. David's. He gave formal confirmation to many grants of lands and churches made to religious houses, and he was active in protecting the interests of monastic foundations in his own diocese. When Fulchard was enthroned as first abbot of St. Dogmael's in 1121 he brought together in one document a statement of all the grants which had been made to his monastery. Bernard presided at the ceremony and on that occasion he confirmed all these grants. He gave support to the monks of Brecon when there was a dispute about their church of Llangors and gave them a chapel within their own parish of St. John of Brecon 'favouring that church by counsel and aid and promoting its welfare in every benefit.' Carmarthen priory, too, had cause to be grateful for his support and generosity. It may be that he sanctioned despoliation in this way; certainly Gerald of Wales criticised him because 'he alienated many lands of his church unfruitfully almost and uselessly.'⁶ Bishop Bernard's constructive abilities were to be seen in the organisation of his diocese. He provided an administration based on four archdeaconries, each with its rural deaneries. He was sympathetic in his dispositions, using the ancient kingdoms of Dyfed, Brycheiniog, and Ceredigion to form the archdeaconries of St. David's, Brecon, and Cardigan, while individual commotes were used to provide the limits of rural deaneries. It is said that he was careful not to offend Welsh sentiment by injudicious interference in the Welsh areas of his bishopric. His cathedral church was served by a group of *claswyr* which included the sons of Bishop Sulien, and Bernard made this group the nucleus of the new cathedral chapter at St. David's. One son of Sulien, Ieuan, was arch-priest of Llanbadarn, and may have been archdeacon of Cardigan. Another, Daniel, was styled archdeacon of Powys, and it is possible that he exercised authority over Powys in the absence of a bishop of St. Asaph at that time. Bernard's gift for combining Norman and Welsh elements resulted in the formal canonisation of St. David. In 1119, a Norman bishop secured from the papal curia the full recognition of a Celtic saint. All told, Bernard's work at St. David's was sensitive and imaginative, and it produced a clearly-defined and capably organised diocese. With good cause he has been described as 'one of the greatest ecclesiastical statesmen that Wales has ever seen.'

Urban and Bernard have a further significance in the story of the Welsh Church. In 1107, Anselm, archbishop of Canterbury, found himself in the exceptional position of having to consecrate five new bishops on one occasion, four for English sees, and the fifth one, Urban, for Llandaff. It had been customary since the Norman Conquest for bishops in England to make a promise of obedience to their archbishop. In 1107 the new bishops of Winchester, Salisbury, Exeter and Hereford made their promise of obedience to Anselm as they were in duty bound to do. So, too, did Urban, but for a Welsh bishop this was a new departure. It does not seem to have been due to any preconceived plan on Anselm's part but it had far-reaching results. Henceforth, it became customary and Welsh bishops were clearly identifiable as suffragans of the archbishop of Canterbury. English bishops were also required to do homage to the English king, and this, too, created new and often acute problems for the bishops of Wales. The Welsh dioceses remained part of the province of Canterbury until 1920; bishops and clergy were subject to discipline and direction from Canterbury, and the archbishop had the formal right of visitation if he chose to exercise it. So, in 1188, when Archbishop Baldwin travelled around Wales preaching the crusade, he took the opportunity to celebrate mass in each of the four Welsh cathedrals, and this has been interpreted as an assertion of his authority as metropolitan. A century later, Archbishop John Pecham carried out a thorough and far-reaching visitation of the Welsh Church in 1284.

The remarkable thing is that it was a bishop nominated and appointed by the English king who first challenged the supremacy of Canterbury in Wales, Bernard of St. David's. During the 1120's he argued boldly for the independence of the Welsh Church. What he wanted to see was an independent archbishop at St. David's presiding over a separate province of the Church. He must have learned of the tradition of independence from the Welsh clerics who served his cathedral. Rhigyfarch's *Life of St. David* had been written only a generation earlier, and his brothers were still among the bishop's close advisers. The advocates of St. David's looked back to Dewi Sant and saw him as an archbishop whose successors could claim the prestige of his office. They also recalled that the bishop of St. David's had consecrated bishops for other Welsh sees as recently as the eleventh century. Bernard took up this case and pressed it forcibly. At the end of his life he was still concerned with this problem, seeking to win a favourable decision from the pope. He was not alone, for there were other bishops in Britain and in Europe anxious to enhance their standing and to secure papal recognition of claims to metropolitical status. In 1144 the archbishop of Tours had been confirmed as metropolitan of the Breton Church. A decade later, in 1152, the pope removed the Irish Church from the control of the archbishop of Canterbury and established four archbishoprics in Ireland. The bishop of Winchester, Henry of Blois, wished to have his see recognised as an archbishopric, though he failed in his attempt. At Lyons, Bourges, and Vienne, prelates were seeking to extend their authority, and they, like Henry of Blois, were unsuccessful. The critical occasion for St. David's and for four other claimants was the council held at Rheims in 1148, but that assembly was not called on to adjudicate the cause of St. David's for Bishop Bernard died before the Council was convened.[7]

Bernard's efforts on behalf of his see were to be important chiefly as the precedent on which the next phase of the struggle for the independence of St. David's could be fought, a phase linked inextricably with the name of Gerald of Wales. His task was the more difficult because the spectre of independence had alarmed the king of England and the archbishop of Canterbury. It was believed that, in addition to their normal promise of

PLATE 3. Neath Abbey
(*Stewart Williams, Glamorgan Historian*)

PLATE 4. Wrexham Church, *c*. 1830-1850
(*Wrexham Public Library*)

obedience, two bishops of St. David's had been obliged to pledge themselves to maintain their connection with Canterbury and to eschew any hope of independence. The traditions of independence were then fostered by the canons of St. David's, among whom Gerald came to play an increasingly influential rôle. In 1176, when the see was vacant, Gerald was one of four local candidates and he might well have been appointed. Henry II preferred a safer man and Peter de Leia became bishop. In 1198, when Peter died, Gerald became the leading challenger for the bishopric. He was elected in circumstances which were open to criticism and a rival candidate, Walter, abbot of St. Dogmael's, acquired a strong claim to the see. Gerald had to fight for recognition as bishop-elect. He was also determined to plead for the independent status of the bishopric. From 1199 until 1203 he used all his considerable powers to persuade Innocent III to give judgments in his favour in both causes. Innocent was impressed by Gerald's case, but there was at hand an experienced and dangerous opponent, Hubert Walter, archbishop of Canterbury, who had no intention of losing the Welsh bishoprics. At the end of the conflict Hubert claimed success. In 1203 Innocent III decided against Gerald and ruled his election out of order. It was a major set-back, and it paved the way for the defeat of his efforts to establish metropolitical authority for St. David's. Within a few months a new bishop had been elected to St. David's, Geoffrey of Henlaw, prior of Llanthony, and Gerald had withdrawn from the struggle, promising eventually not to raise the question of independence at any future time. A stormy episode in the history of the Welsh Church was over.[8] When the same issue of the metropolitical authority of St. David's was raised again very briefly in 1284 by Thomas Bek, bishop of St. David's, it was part of a personal conflict between Bek and his archbishop, John Pecham, and it was soon quashed.

Gerald of Wales pinpointed the basic problem of the Welsh Church at the beginning of the thirteenth century. It was a Church serving a multi-racial society, and bishops and clergy alike were drawn from two cultures. On the one hand there were the Anglo-Norman settlers, with the aristocracy of the marcher lordships dominating the scene, largely French in culture and language. On the other hand there were the Welsh, speaking their own tongue, many of them monoglot, many of them fiercely proud of their language and culture. In many parts of Wales the Welsh aristocracy had been dispossessed or depressed in standing and influence. In the higher echelons of the Church prominent families of both races might provide dignitaries, canons and administrators, while in the lower echelons, at the level of the rural deanery and parish, Welsh-speaking clergy were essential if they were to reach their people and make the faith a reality.

The surprising thing is the extent to which the men appointed to Welsh bishoprics were drawn from families associated with Wales and the Marches. It has been estimated that between 1066 and 1272 thirty-two out of forty-six bishops appointed in Wales 'were certainly Welsh by blood, birth, or association.'[9] In the diocese of Bangor, Robert of Shrewsbury, bishop from 1197 to 1213, is the most notable exception in a succession of predominantly Welsh bishops. When his predecessor, Bishop Alan, died in 1196, there was strong local support for a Welsh candidate, Roland sub-prior of Aberconwy, but his election was set aside and Robert of Shrewsbury became bishop. At first Llywelyn ab Iorwerth, prince of Gwynedd, resented this intrusion, but he and the new bishop soon came to appreciate each other's qualities and worked harmoniously together. At St. Asaph, where a Welsh succession might have been expected, there was a large Anglo-Norman element, especially in the twelfth century. The exception was Geoffrey of Monmouth, but for all his connection with the Marches and his interest in Celtic folk-lore, he was an absentee bishop who left no mark on his diocese. At St. David's an Anglo-Norman culture is represented by bishops such as Bernard (1115-1148), Peter de Leia (1176-98) and, much later, Thomas Bek (1280-93); Iorwerth, or Gervase as he was also called (1215-29), and Thomas Wallensis (1248-55) were Welshmen, while David fitz Gerald (1148-76), Anselm le Gras (1231-47), and Richard of Carew (1256-80) were men of the Marches. Even Gerald's supplanter, Geoffrey of Henlaw (1203-14), was prior of the border monastery of Llanthony. Gerald insisted that the right bishop for St. David's should have sympathy and understanding for the Welsh people of his diocese and for their language and culture. At least it could be said that strangers to Wales and the Marches were rarely appointed to the see in the twelfth and thirteenth centuries. Finally, at Llandaff, a number of Welsh bishops were appointed in the twelfth century but they were succeeded by Anglo-Norman marcher bishops, or by men associated with local religious houses. Bishop Urban (1107-33/4) may have been Welsh; Uchtred (1140?-1148) and Nicholas ap Gwrgan (1148-83) were certainly Welshmen. Two bishops who took their names from religious houses where they had served as prior were Henry of Abergavenny (1193-1218) and William of Goldcliff (1219-29). John de Ware (1254-56) had been abbot of Margam before he became bishop. In the thirteenth century Elias of Radnor (1230-40), William of Radnor

(1257-66) and John of Monmouth (1297-1323) were all men with strong local connections. William de Burgh (1245-53) held a name familiar enough on the March but he was a royal administrator who owed his appointment to Llandaff to the influence of Henry III.[10]

There was a similar mixture of Anglo-Norman and Welsh among the higher clergy, though the nature of the evidence makes it possible only to form impressions. The chapter at Bangor cannot be seen clearly before 1249, and at St. Asaph the formal organisation of the cathedral clergy does not emerge until even later. In English dioceses it was common from the early decades of the twelfth century to find a bishop supported by members of the chapter, sometimes by the whole chapter, in the performance of diocesan business. None of the documents which survive show a bishop of Bangor or St. Asaph acting in this way. In south Wales the story is different. The chapter at Llandaff, already discernible in embryo, was put on to a formal basis by Bishop Henry of Abergavenny.The evidence relating to St. David's is much richer, and there the chapter can be seen clearly from the time of Bishop Bernard (1115-48), though formal definition came later. The office of precentor was created in 1224, and throughout the later Middle Ages, as, indeed, until the first decades of the nineteenth century, the precentor was the senior dignitary of the cathedral chapter. St. David's had no dean, but the office of treasurer can be traced from the 1250s and the chancellorship was instituted in 1287. The origins of the chapter at St. David's in a *clas* community left its mark on the future development of the chapter, for hereditary tenure of prebends and canonries and the existence of a strong group of Welsh canons were clearly marked features of the chapter throughout the twelfth and thirteenth centuries. In 1148 it was said that the Welsh canons desired to have a Welshman as their bishop but they had to be content with David fitz Gerald, a man sprung from both races. In 1215, the Welsh canons were said to have approached their new bishop, Iorwerth, with a request that he would ensure promotion for their sons. Welsh names point to the strength of the Welsh element in the chapter: among the archdeacons, Cadifor ap Daniel, Maredudd ap Rhys and his son Gruffydd, and Meurig; among the canons, Cadwgan, Meiler, Elidor son of Elidor, Asser, John son of Asser, and Walter son of Eynon. The Norman element was drawn largely from marcher stock. David fitz Gerald, archdeacon of Cardigan before he became bishop, and Gerald himself would stand as typical examples. They are also a reminder that keeping the property in the family was by no means an exclusively Welsh prerogative! Gerald owed his advancement to the archdeaconry of

Brecon to his uncle, David fitz Gerald, and he in turn handed on his canonry and archdeaconry to his own nephew, Gerald. At Llandaff Anglo-Norman names predominate, but, again, there was a succession of Welsh canons and, more rarely, dignitaries, which points to the origins of the chapter in a *clas* community.

Below the level of the cathedral chapter there is ample evidence that many of the clergy were Welsh. In his archdeaconry of Brecon, Gerald of Wales was served by agents whom he called officials, one of whom, Ithenard, was particularly active on his behalf. A few years later Gerald tried to ensure that his nephew would govern the archdeaconry of Brecon effectively, and he appointed Thomas of Hay as an official to serve the young archdeacon.[11] Such men, and the parish clergy over whom they exercised supervision, must have had some Welsh in order to do their work properly, and many of the clergy must have been more fluent in Welsh than in English, French or Latin.

It is almost unavoidable that we should see the Welsh Church in the twelfth and thirteenth centuries through the eyes of one man, Gerald of Wales, if only because he was such a prolific writer. Had he been merely an observer, he would have stamped his mark on the ecclesiastical history of Wales. But he was also a principal actor in the drama; his changing fortunes, his close involvement in great affairs, his confidence in his own abilities, and the urge to commit to writing every facet of the struggles in which he was engaged, make him an indispensable authority. He was never an impartial witness and historians have reacted violently to him, just as contemporaries did.[12] His *Itinerarium Cambriae* described the journey around Wales which he made with Baldwin, archbishop of Canterbury, in 1188. The *Descriptio Cambriae* is a deliberate attempt to study in depth Welsh culture and the Welsh character. In the *Speculum Ecclesiae* he presented a mirror in which the image of the Church might be seen. It contains some vitriolic writing about the monastic church; for abbots and priors in Wales and the Marches it must have seemed a mirror capable of savage distortion. The *Gemma Ecclesiastica* describes many aspects of church life in Wales; it has been compared with the comment and instruction an archdeacon might give his clergy at a visitation. In varying degrees these were all scholarly works reflecting Gerald's training in the schools of Paris. He was also responsible for a series of polemical works which sprang from the conflicts in which he was engaged. An autobiographical book, the *De Rebus a se Gestis*, and a formal account of the struggle for the independence of St. David's, the *De Iure et Statu Menevensis Ecclesiae*, the *De Invectionibus*, a sharp, angry book, and a series of *Retractiones* in which he withdrew some of the worst accusations which he had made in the heat of controversy: these provide one man's view of his own life. It is scarcely surprising if he sees himself as hero and defender, nor if he exaggerates his own gifts and the unworthiness of his opponents. Even at the end of his life the habit of stating his case in writing, and stating it in fierce, partisan terms, did not desert him. He was involved in a family quarrel. Gerald, the nephew to whom he had transferred his canonry of Mathry and his archdeaconry of Brecon, showed an unexpected streak of independence, fostered by an enterprising and perhaps unscrupulous tutor, William de Capella. They infuriated the old man, wasting Llanddew where he had a favourite residence, and beating him in the arena of ecclesiastical politics where he had so much enjoyed the cut and thrust of battle. In the *Speculum Duorum* he presented a mirror in which they could see their villainy. The writing is repetitive and the line of thought confused at times, but his spirit and his gift for vituperation were still strong within him.[13]

As he looked at the Welsh Church, Gerald did not have much sympathy for its bishops whose actions he was prone to condemn without searching for underlying causes. Monks rarely gained his approval, and those who had responsibility as abbots and priors were often vilified and ridiculed. He was aware of the weaknesses and shortcomings of the Welsh clergy, though he could treat them with some sympathy. The most revealing of his books in this context is the *Gemma Ecclesiastica*.[14] While much of its contents may be exaggerated for effect, it affords a clear indication of what he believed to be the real weaknesses of the clergy of his archdeaconry. He did not write for scholars on this occasion; the work was 'intended exclusively for my own country of Wales.' He knew that the country could be called barbarous, lacking many of the finer elements of civilized life, and that there were few books, if any, in Wales. As he told his clergy, 'So that you may imitate them, I have brought together some things which will not be without value for you.' Gerald was concerned that the sacrament of the mass should be celebrated with dignity and decency, and he laid down basic directions for ensuring the security of the sacred elements. Cautionary tales of abuse of the sacrament by recipients added point to his instructions. He had practical advice on how to deal with wine which had been polluted, and indicated the conditions under which the sacrament should be taken outside the church. He suggested proper times for celebrations, and restricted the number of masses a priest should say during the day. He attacked particularly the practice of including additional gospels at the request of individual worshippers who gave alms the more readily if their favourite gospels were included. He was anxious to prevent abuse of the ministrations of the Church to ensure freedom from future punishment; the practice was evidently common of celebrating the anniversary of a death before the person had died, and this he deprecated in strong terms. He had clear, simple advice about baptism: in time of necessity a layman could baptise; he must do so in the name of the Father, Son, and Holy Spirit, but the words must be said clearly and could be said *vel Latina vel barbara*, in Latin or in the vernacular. He reminded his clergy that those who acted as godparents for a child were henceforth barred from marriage with one another, and that the wise course of action in a small community was to limit the number of godparents at each baptism. He had useful advice about confession and the efficacy of absolution. He wrote wisely about the problems raised by exorcism. On most of these issues Gerald wrote in general terms which could apply as easily to England as to Wales, but he noted one offence which was widespread in Wales. Welshmen took oaths too lightly; in doing so, he said, they 'have less respect for the New Testament than for the relics of saints, such as bells, sticks and the like.' In Wales, too, excommunication had fallen into discredit and should be used sparingly.

Practical matters were not the whole of Gerald's book, for he was deeply concerned about clerical morals, and here the most common offence was clerical marriage. Gerald's attitude was curious. He considered that celibacy for the clergy was not the practice of the early Church, and that its imposition was a dangerous prohibition from which much evil had sprung. He asserted that Pope Alexander III was ready to remove altogether the requirement of celibacy, and he was kindly in his attitude towards marriage by men in minor orders. But when it came to the priesthood Gerald was inflexible: celibacy was essential. He could not find a generous word for the women who, in all but name, were married to clerics. As a young man he had hounded Jordan, archdeacon of Brecon, from office because he lived in concubinage with a woman. As he grew older Gerald's hatred of clerical marriage remained as strong as ever. His warnings were as vivid as they were uncompromising.

Writing to clerics whom he believed to be without books, he had advice to offer on the thorny question of illiteracy. He had obviously built up a collection of stories about clerics, abbots and bishops who mangled the Latin language in their attempts at formal speech or preaching. The priest who, by a simple confusion between Barnabas and Barrabus, identified St. Barnabas as 'a good and holy man though he was a robber': the cleric who considered that the feast of St. John *ante portam Latinam* was in honour of St. John the first man to bring Latin to England: such howlers gave him some pain and much delight. Yet he could be generous and understanding when he dealt with Whethelen, the hermit of Llowes, whose Latin was acquired, as he claimed, by divine revelation and who relied exclusively on infinitives whenever a verb was needed! Gerald had to coax the clergy of his archdeaconry to a minimum standard of competence and to provide them with elementary training. It does not suggest a high quality of ministry at parish level.

Gerald's dislike of the religious orders was profound and it is often difficult to determine when he was borrowing from a common stock of critical, and sometimes scabrous, stories or when he was drawing upon his own experience. He disliked the practice, which he found particularly objectionable among the Cluniacs, of setting up in Wales small cells served by two or three monks. He believed that thirteen was the sensible establishment, a prior and twelve monks. When monks were few in number they fell into evil ways with little hope of correction. As a result, he feared that life in a distant cell was preferable to life in the parent house. The prior and monks of Llangennith, far removed from the surveillance of their abbot in Evreux, found the women of Gower very attractive. The Cistercians were Gerald's primary target. They were gluttonous and greedy, enjoying in private a standard of living which was little short of scandalous. In Wales they bought up lands, and gathered into their possession parish churches and tithes, and they added to their offence by expelling the clerics who had been caring for their people. Perhaps the venom which marks so much of his writing may owe something to a sad episode which many scholars would find distressing and disastrous. In the course of his struggle for the supremacy of St. David's, Gerald handed his books to a Cistercian abbot for safekeeping. They were, he said, the books which he had collected in painstaking fashion from boyhood to maturity. Then he had to borrow money and use his theological books as security. Whether through misunderstanding or by malice, the abbot interpreted this loan as an outright sale and Gerald never recovered his books. It must be said that Gerald consistently under-rated the value of the monastic plantation which occurred in Wales during the twelfth century. The variety of orders established in Wales enriched the Welsh Church. Cistercians and Augustinians abandoned the security of the Norman borough and set up houses in remote places where survival depended upon the protection of Welsh princes and the toleration of the Welsh peasantry. The Augustinians were to achieve a high proportion of

Welsh recruits, while those Cistercian houses colonised from Whitland were to be distinctively Welsh in character and loyalty. The contribution which they made to the cause of the Welsh princes is nowhere more obvious than in the records which they preserved and which were incorporated into the *Brut y Tywysogyon* at the end of the thirteenth century.

One consequence of the domination which Gerald of Wales exerts over the history of the Welsh Church is that the thirteenth century appears as something of an anti-climax. The men were not so influential in their activities, nor perhaps so outstanding in personality as the leading figures of the twelfth century. The problems they faced were more obviously local in their impact. As elsewhere in Europe, the coming of the friars introduced a new factor into Wales, though here again the effect which these new orders could have on Wales was limited. They were rarely influential in a rural society but made their mark especially in the cities and towns of Europe. Welsh towns were small, and the opportunities open to the friars were small compared with those which they found in England and France.

Two issues stand out in thirteenth-century Wales. One was the brilliant though unsuccessful attempt by Dafydd ap Llywelyn to enlist the authority of the papacy in support of his Welsh principality. Throughout the thirteenth century the rulers of north Wales were anxious to extend their authority and to secure recognition of their dominion over a substantial part of Wales. Their aim is best seen in the contrast between the title of prince of Gwynedd and the title of prince of Wales. Llywelyn ab Iorwerth built up a formidable power in north and mid-Wales which, for him, was indicated by his style as prince of Aberffraw and lord of Snowdon, a title at once local yet one which reflected the expansionist policy he had pursued so successfully. His successor, Dafydd, was the first Welsh ruler to use the title prince of Wales. In 1244 he persuaded Pope Innocent IV to accept Wales as a papal fief and to recognise himself as prince of Wales. It was a diplomatic move which promised well, for it gave Dafydd international recognition and it made the papacy a potential ally of great value. Within a matter of months Henry III and his advisers had caused the pope to reverse his decision. The English king exercised too much influence at the papal curia for Innocent IV to risk any breach with England. Historians have in the past condemned Dafydd for attempting a useless scheme which demonstrated his ineptitude as a national ruler, but that is to do less than justice to him. He had no means of holding Innocent IV to his undertaking to recognise the Welsh prince as an independent ruler, and when papal policy changed Dafydd was left weak and exposed. The attempt was well worth making.[15]

The second major feature was a sharp conflict between prince and bishop in Wales, a fight over comparatively trivial issues which brought grave political weakness in its train. Llywelyn the Last was a dangerous man to cross, and in Anian, bishop of Bangor (1267-1305), he met an opponent of similar temperament. Llywelyn was also at odds with the bishop of St. Asaph, another Anian (1268-93). Each bishop found useful allies in England, invoking the authority of the archbishop of Canterbury and working, however uneasily, with Edward I. Llywelyn could ill afford to lose friends and supporters in what was to be a life-and-death struggle in the 1270s and 1280s, nor could he give the tactical advantage to the English king with impunity. The conflict between Church and State may have been local and the issues over which it was fought may not have been very significant, but in terms of the struggle for power between English and Welsh it was both dangerous and costly.

Two landmarks dominate the history of the Welsh Church in the later Middle Ages.[16] One was the Edwardian Conquest with all its far-reaching consequences for Welsh society. The other was the resort to arms by Owain Glyn Dŵr, regarded by the English government at the time as a most dangerous rebellion, and seen by Welshmen in retrospect as a last throw for independence. While these were unique to Wales, the Welsh Church was also affected by long-term economic, social and cultural changes which could be matched in England and other European countries.

In terms of secular society the Edwardian Conquest brought many changes to Wales. The northern principalities were annexed by Edward I and protected by the massive castles which he built from Flint to Harlech. They were also reorganised into shires on the English pattern. This newly acquired territory was administered by rigorous and often ruthless officials whose demands pressed heavily on the Welsh people. Conquest meant suppression and exploitation. In the Marches, the balance of forces between crown, marcher lords and Welsh princes was disturbed. Already the crown had made use of lordships in royal hands to exert a stronger influence in the Marches. Now, to destroy Llywelyn the Last and to eliminate altogether the power which he had exercised was to remove an effective check on the powers and pretensions of the lords of the March. In the north, churchmen, lay and cleric alike, felt the heavy hand of Edward I's new officials and had some cause for complaint, if only because of their zeal and efficiency, but the Church was not oppressed, nor was it made, as it might have been, an instrument of royal domination. The bishop of Bangor received valuable augmentation of his income as Edward I deliberately sought to hold him as an ally. St. Asaph was less fortunate, for at the time of the conquest the bishop was at odds with Edward I, but peace was established between them, the bishop was restored to favour, and the fortunes of the see took a turn for the better.

By a curious chance, the Church was more obviously affected in the south. Marcher lords were anxious to assert claims against the crown and the king was obliged to fight with determination to prevent any movement towards greater independence in the Marches. Questions affecting the Church could easily become critical issues. The bishopric of St. David's was little affected. Edward I made lavish gifts to the bishop and this had the long-term effect of making St. David's a comparatively lucrative and desirable bishopric to which a succession of distinguished bishops was drawn in the later middle ages. In the short term, the bishop remained loyal to the king and was not diverted towards the marcher lords who controlled so much of his diocese.[17] Throughout Wales the extent of Edward I's royal authority was severely tested. The Clare lord of Glamorgan made a sustained attempt to claim full rights over the bishopric of Llandaff, and, in particular, the right to administer the see during a vacancy and to nominate a bishop for election. There was some precedent for these claims; as far back as 1186, for example, the lord of Glamorgan had attempted to intervene in an episcopal appointment. Edward I's officers opposed such claims very strongly, and eventually with success, for in 1290 Richard of Clare was forced to accept the king's interpretation of the case. Meanwhile, his contemporary, Humphrey de Bohun, earl of Hereford was claiming similar rights over the estates of the diocese of St. David's lying within his lordship of Brecknock, another claim which Edward I strenuously resisted. In central Wales Edmund Mortimer was making life unpleasant for the monks of Strata Florida in his eagerness to control their lands, while further north, in the diocese of St. Asaph, John de Warenne, earl of Surrey, was making a similar bid for power. In each case Edward I refused to acknowledge the limitation of his own authority, and by 1290-91 he had defeated these lords of the March. The Welsh dioceses were to be directly subject to the English king; they were not to lie within the sphere of any magnate, however powerful he might be.

This did not mean that the Welsh Church was immediately anglicised. With rare exceptions, Edward I and his successor continued to appoint the same type of bishop as those who had been characteristic for more than a century, Welshmen in the north, and men with strong local connections in the south. The critical change came at a later date. In 1323 there was a vacancy at Llandaff and the pope appointed John of Eaglescliffe who was translated by papal provision from the Irish see of Connor.[18] As the fourteenth century advanced, papal provision became the normal method of appointment, with the change occurring at St. David's from the 1340s and at Bangor from the 1370s. Henceforth, the appointment of Welsh bishops to Welsh sees became the exception rather than the rule as local men were squeezed out in favour of papal or royal nominees. With the final decision made at Rome, appointments now became the subject of intense diplomatic activity which sometimes degenerated into an unseemly scramble for place. Local interests were often the most difficult to defend.

For St. David's this meant that the diocese was used to reward a succession of able royal servants. Chancellor James could speak with pride of a golden age of the diocese between 1280 and 1414. Thomas Bek, appointed by Edward I in 1280, had been keeper of the wardrobe. John Thoresby (1347-49) was keeper of the privy seal and later chancellor. Adam Houghton (1362-89) was chancellor, and his successor, John Gilbert (1389-97) in addition to being a royal confessor served as treasurer. Guy Mone (1397-1407) was a very experienced royal servant as keeper of the privy seal and later treasurer, while Reginald Brian (1350-52) had been a royal clerk and Thomas Fastolf (1352-61) had served as an ambassador. When Henry Chichele became bishop in 1408 he took his place in a line of distinguished bishops. But by the beginning of the fifteenth century the effects of economic decline were very marked and the diocese no longer had the same attraction for royal servants. The bishops needed additional appointments to hold *in commendam* in order to increase their income to a reasonable level. William Lyndwood, who was keeper of the privy seal, was bishop from 1442 to 1446, and he is a reminder that the tradition did not disappear altogether. The other Welsh sees were rarely considered adequate reward for a leading royal administrator. More characteristic was the appointment at a less important level in the royal service, such as the king's confessor; Alexander Bache, for example, was made bishop of St. Asaph in 1390 and John de Burghill bishop of Llandaff in 1396. Occasionally a papal administrator or diplomat was appointed to a Welsh bishopric. The most notable examples are two men of the same name, John Trefor I appointed to St. Asaph in 1352 and John Trefor II appointed the the same see in 1395. Papal pressure lay behind an earlier attempt to secure the election of John Trefor II in 1389 and an equally unsuccessful bid to obtain the bishopric of Bangor for Lewis Aber in 1398.

What was the state of the church which such bishops governed? The condition of the Welsh Church at the end of the thirteenth century can best be seen through the sharp, critical eyes of John Pecham, the austere Franciscan friar who was archbishop of Canterbury from 1279 to 1292. With tremendous energy he succeeded in visiting every diocese in his province in the comparatively short space of eight years and by 1286 he was already looking forward to undertaking the whole formidable process for a second time. He certainly carried out a second formal visitation of Canterbury and London, and perhaps of Exeter and Worcester. He could, as a result, claim a quite exceptional knowledge of the condition of his province. He was not greatly impressed by what he found. After his second visitation of Canterbury he still had much about which to complain, for the diocese was greatly weakened by non-resident clerics, by livings held in plurality, and by sheer neglect. He urged his clergy that if, through ignorance, they could not hear confession or preach they should call on the friars to make good their deficiencies. The laity did not impress him, for he described them as 'a stiff-necked people, kicking against the pricks and determined to resist all exhortations to obey the word of God.'[19] In his attempts to define the qualities he expected to find in a priest Pecham laid great emphasis on the proper celebration of the sacrament and on the need to read the regular offices with reverence. He required priests to be generous in their charity and urged that churches and parsonages should be kept in good repair.

Pecham had considerable sympathy for Wales and for the Welsh Church and he valued particularly the greater measure of freedom from the control of a secular ruler when he discerned in Wales. He was aware of the problems created by the use of the Welsh language. When he carried out his formal visitation of the western part of the diocese of Coventry and Lichfield — the part which extended to the borderland between Chester and Powys — he ordered that a Welsh-speaking suffragan should be appointed to deal with the problems of that area. Before the Welsh war of 1282 Pecham had been in Wales seeking to act as a mediator between Llywelyn the Last and Edward I, pressing the official English case vigorously and perhaps tactlessly but, at the same time, responding to the force of complaints and arguments put forward by the Welsh prince. When he returned to Wales for his formal visitation of the four Welsh dioceses in 1284 he was no stranger to the country and its problems. He was deeply disturbed by the condition of the Welsh Church. The colourful and thoroughly unorthodox appearance of the Welsh clergy offended his sense of propriety, while their loose living appalled him. Concubinage, which he could not dignify with the name of clerical marriage, and drunkenness were common causes of offence. Quite as bad, if not worse in his estimation, was the ignorance which marred so many of the Welsh clergy. He declared that he could never remember having seen such illiterate priests and clerics as he had found in Wales. Set against his view of the clergy throughout his province, his strictures on the Welsh clergy were severe. His remedies were those which he thought useful in England: an emphasis on the importance of the proper administration of the sacrament and urgent advice to call in the friars to make good the deficiencies of the local clergy. To compare Pecham's injunctions for the Welsh bishoprics with those he issued for other dioceses is to see that the archbishop was not prejudiced or biased against Wales. It has been said that 'in him the Welsh found a just and considerate arbiter'[20], and the same qualities marked his approach to the shortcomings of the Welsh Church.

Merely to examine the state of a diocese and to issue injunctions for its reform was no guarantee of improvement. Pecham laid down that in St. Asaph his injunctions should be read each year as a reminder of what needed to be done. By the 1290s the combined effect of royal policy and Pecham's influence could be seen to have brought about a change, especially in the northern bishoprics. There had been a considerable amount of rebuilding of churches pillaged and ravaged during the Welsh wars. Elsewhere, there were risings against English power, one led by Rhys ap Maredudd in 1287 and another by Madog ap Llywelyn in 1294-5. In each case the Welsh clergy were not seriously involved. Nor do the clergy of the diocese of Llandaff appear to have been prominent in the local but dangerous revolt of Llywelyn Bren in 1316, even though Llywelyn placed his small collection of books and his other valuables in the safekeeping of the canons of Llandaff. As the fourteenth century advanced the Welsh clergy ceased to be quiescent. Savage increases in the weight of taxation after the Edwardian Conquest, the impact of bad harvests and economic decline, and increasing dissatisfaction under English rule created an uglier mood and Welsh clerics took their place among the opponents of English domination.

Permanent improvement in the quality of the clergy could not be secured by injunctions and directives. The answer to the problem lay in education. In Wales, as in England, the competence of the local clergy was improved because of the concern which learned bishops showed and was achieved through the provision of simple exposition and practical guidance in the vernacular. The Welsh bench was enhanced by the appointment of John of Monmouth as bishop of Llandaff in 1297. He was a leading figure in scholarly circles and had been chancellor of Oxford University before his consecration. He encouraged the appointment of scholars to his cathedral chapter at Llandaff, exactly as his contemporary Simon of Ghent, bishop of Salisbury, was doing. In each case the intention seems to have been the same, to make the cathedral a centre for scholarship and, so far as was possible, for the training of clergy working in the diocese. Henry Gower, bishop of St. David's (1328-47) was another chancellor of Oxford and his taste and skill in architecture have left their mark on the bishop's palaces at St. David's and Lamphey and on Swansea castle. Two disputatious friars, Thomas Waleys and Roger of Conwy, were much involved in controversy. Roger, who became provincial of the order of preachers in England, was a sharp critic of Richard fitz Ralph, archbishop of Armagh, himself an influential and controversial writer.

At home the chief contribution of Welsh scholars and writers was to provide a wide range of religious and devotional writing in Welsh, ranging from translations of sections of the Bible to formal *gwengerdd*, religious poetry. Passages from the canonical scriptures were matched by the popular but apocryphal *Efengyl Nicodemus*, the *Gospel of Nicodemus*, and the equally popular compilation, the *Breuddwyd Pawl*, the *Dream of Paul*. A manual of instruction was an invaluable aid for the parish priest, and in England a number of manuals were widely used. The *Oculus Sacerdotis*, attributed to William of Pagula, offered extensive guidance on the practical and spirtual problems of confession and preaching, together with an exposition of the seven sacraments. The *Oculus* had a number of derivatives including the *Regimen Animarum* which drew heavily upon the works of the Spanish Dominican, Raymond of Penaforte. Such material was available in Welsh, including a work on confession, the *Penityas*, which owed much to Raymond of Penaforte and to contemporary English manuals. A book widely used in Wales was *Y Gysegrlan Fuchedd*, *The Consecrated Life*, which has been called 'easily the most original and interesting piece of Welsh medieval religious literature.' A lay patron, Gruffydd ap Llywelyn ap Philip ap Trahaearn, was responsible for the most ambitious collection of medieval religious writing in Wales, *Y Llyfr Ancr*, *The Book of the Anchorite*, compiled by an anchorite living at the ancient centre of Christian activity in Wales, Llanddewibrefi. He has never been identified.

Where borrowing occurred it was generally borrowing from English exemplars by Welsh writers, but there is one notable exception. John Thoresby, who was bishop of St. David's from 1347 to 1349, was much concerned with the state of learning among his clergy. He seems to have adopted an approach common somewhat earlier in the thirteenth century, by issuing simple instructions for the guidance of his clergy. As a practical measure he ordered the chancellor of St. David's cathedral, David Baret, to lecture on the 'sacred page' to the cathedral clergy. After a brief sojourn at Worcester, Thoresby went on to become archbishop of York in 1352 and there, in the northern province, he expanded the guidance which he thought his clergy might need. In 1357 he issued a set of instructions for the priests of his diocese to be used for teaching their parishioners the basic elements of their faith. Not content with issuing this in Latin, he arranged for it to be issued in an English text, written in verse. It became known as his catechism.[21]

The revolt of Owain Glyn Dŵr brought much destruction to Wales and achieved very little but it has struck a chord in the national consciousness of Wales which guarantees it a unique place in Welsh history.[22] Richard II, a popular figure in Wales, had been overthrown by Henry IV, scion of the house of Lancaster, a dynasty which never attracted wide loyalty from the Welsh. Owain Glyn Dŵr had personal reasons for feeling aggrieved, none more irksome than his unhappy experience in conflict with a powerful English enemy, Lord Grey of Ruthin, who used his influence with the king to good advantage in a private quarrel. In 1402 Owain was an obscure Welsh landowner of distinguished ancestry in rebellion against the king. Within two years he was the head of a national revolt which was to have wide repercussions throughout Wales for a decade, and which was to affect the political and social life of Wales long after Owain himself had left the scene. Styling himself prince of Wales, he could call a parliament at Machynlleth and introduce imaginative legislation for his principality. In the end the royalist forces were successful and put down the insurgents. Glyn Dŵr retired into obscurity, his hour of glory past, and the Lancastrian king put into effect a savage penal policy of oppression and containment which left the Welsh humiliated and powerless.

In terms of the Welsh Church the Glyn Dŵr revolt merits comment in three respects. The first is the influence which prominent churchmen exercised during the revolt. The second, closely related, is the extensive scheme for the reorganisation of the Welsh Church put forward by Glyn Dŵr. The third is the sad effect which the revolt had upon the Church throughout the fifteenth century.

There were clerics in Wales whose hopes of preferment were checked if not blighted. Some had reached the eminence of a deanery or an archdeaconry, but further advancement to the episcopate was denied to them. Lewis Aber, provided to Bangor in 1398, but excluded by royal influence, is a classic example. In the early years of the revolt Owain Glyn Dŵr's cause attracted a number of such clerics, men of greater ability and promise than their limited opportunities could satisfy. They worked behind the scenes and it seems fair to assume that they formed an influential group of advisers whose deliberations are probably the source of Owain's ecclesiastical policies. The figure about whom most is known is Gruffydd Young who served Owain as chancellor and who was a belligerent advocate of Owain's cause in Europe. He had served Richard II without securing the rewards he considered appropriate for his work and he transferred his allegiance to Henry IV only to be disappointed again at his hands. He was eventually appointed archdeacon of Meirionnydd, but by then, a frustrated and embittered man, he had thrown in his lot with Glyn Dŵr. Before long he was bishop of Bangor and in 1407 he was translated to St. David's.

Gruffydd Young's name has been identified with the impressive scheme promulgated by Glyn Dŵr for the reorganisation of the Welsh Church, the Pennal scheme. This envisaged an independent province for Wales with an archbishop at St. David's. It was not conceived solely as a defensive measure, designed to seal off Wales from the English Church behind a national frontier. Instead, it was proposed that the English dioceses of Exeter, Bath and Wells, Hereford, Coventry and Lichfield, and Worcester should be included in the Welsh province. The finances of the Welsh bishoprics were to be restored to a sound condition by a policy of expropriation: all the ecclesiastical possessions in Welsh which had been granted to English religious foundations were to be given up so that they could revert to local use. The national identity of the Welsh Church was to be preserved by ensuring that appointments to high office should be limited to those who spoke Welsh. Closely linked with this scheme was the proposal that Wales should have two universities. That this was no dream, incapable of realisation, is clearly indicated by the fact that all this was to hinge on a diplomatic decision of the first importance. At the beginning of the fifteenth century the European Church was still bedevilled by the Great Schism, with one pope established at Rome, and his rival ensconced at Avignon. The English kingdom supported the Roman pontiff, while France continued its long-standing support for the Avignonese papacy. It was probably important for Glyn Dŵr's advisers that the Scots also supported Avignon. In 1404 Gruffydd Young was in France negotiating a treaty of alliance with Charles VI and a key feature of this alliance was that Wales should give its allegiance to the papacy at Avignon. Benedict XIII was no doubt glad to have this augmentation of his power, and he used his authority to make possible the appointments which Owain Glyn Dŵr desired to make in the Welsh Church. The threat to the English kingdom was unmistakable: an independent principality of Wales, with an independent Church, linked on the one hand with the papacy at Avignon and on the other with France, its independence acknowledged as a fact of European diplomacy. Young and his associates were clever men with more than ordinary political skill who understood well how to exploit the international situation to their own advantage. It has been suggested that their grasp of political realities in terms of domestic policies was equally sure. A state without an adequate civil service was unthinkable, and civil servants must be paid. A Welsh prince would need the means of training a literate class: hence the need for universities in Wales. He would also need a full range of ecclesiastical preferment to reward those who served him well: hence the need for an independent province of the Church in which the Welsh prince would have a dominant voice, and from which the influence of the English ruler would be excluded.[23]

It was a bold and imaginative plan which has inspired Welsh educationists and Welsh churchmen in subsequent ages. But there was one prerequisite on which everything depended: the power of the secular prince must be maintained. Owain Glyn Dŵr survived as a dangerous force in Anglo-Welsh politics for a decade but permanent success was denied him. As his influence declined the structure of power built up by his supporters began to collapse. That fact was underlined in signal fashion in 1408 when Henry Chichele was appointed as bishop of St. David's with the specific commission to reconcile the schismatics of his new diocese. St. David's was brought back into close association with Canterbury and to its Roman allegiance, and the see was once again held by a man trusted by the English king. Chichele was to move to greater things, as a leading diplomat, as archbishop of Canterbury, and as a cardinal. Meanwhile, the man he had replaced was in virtual eclipse. Young was forced to abandon the Avignonese papacy, and in 1418 he was provided to the remote Scottish diocese of Ross, and five years later he was given the titular see of Hippo *in partibus infidelium*. In his last years he was only able to support himself from the revenues of benefices which he had been given in France. The Welsh Church, from which he was an exile, fell into a sad state of decline.

Glyn Dŵr's particular targets were the English and anglicised communities of Wales and he struck hard in a series of raids into the marcher lordships as well as into the royal shires of the north. His forces showed little regard for churches or church property. St. Asaph cathedral was destroyed in 1402 and was said to be a roofless ruin still eighty years later when Bishop Redman began to restore it. A tradition, stemming from the Elizabethan antiquary William Camden, asserts that Bangor suffered a similar fate, though here damage rather than destruction seems more likely. As early as 1409 Bishop Benedict Nicholls was enthroned with all due ceremony, apparently in a cathedral fit to be used for the purpose. When Thomas Skeffington became bishop a century later the nave was said to be ruinous and overgrown with grass, but this appears to be the consequence of neglect during the latter part of the fifteenth century.[24] A sweep through Gwent and Glamorgan brought havoc to a number of monastic foundations including Ewenni, Cardiff, Monmouth and Abergavenny. Llandaff cathedral is said to have suffered, and certainly the bishop's palace at Llandaff was left in ruins. Bishop Peverell had little choice but to move to his palace at Mathern which remained the formal residence of the bishops of Llandaff until the nineteenth century. Reprisals by royalist troops added to the general count of churches damaged or destroyed. The friars of Llanfaes, to cite the most glaring example, were staunch in their support of Owain Glyn Dŵr and their house was devastated by the king's men, while Strata Florida and Conwy were among the monasteries which paid heavily for their Welsh loyalties.

The trail of destruction left the Welsh Church with a heavy burden of responsibility for churches to be repaired or rebuilt, and this at a time when damage to estates and loss of normal revenues were resulting in poverty which could be crippling in its effects. The remarkable thing is that there was a substantial recovery attested by building activity in Welsh cathedrals and in parish churches. Two phases of repair produced changes at Bangor, with the second phase under Bishop Henry Dean (1496-1500) and Bishop Thomas Skeffington (1509-33) resulting in extensive restorations. At St. Asaph Bishop Richard Redman (1471-95) began the rebuilding of the cathedral while Bishop Dafydd ab Iorwerth (1500-1503) rebuilt the bishop's palace. At Llandaff a similar rôle was played by Bishop John Marshall (1478-96) who left his mark on the fabric of the cathedral. There still remain in Wales a number of churches built in the fifteenth century, some of them on a substantial scale, and there are examples of church-furnishings provided at the end of the Middle Ages.

In the fifteenth century Wales was dominated by a small but changing group of great magnates, the composition of which reflected the changing fortunes of rival English dynasties, Lancastrian and Yorkist, and their supporters. The administration of their estates fell increasingly into the hands of agents, a fortuitous circumstance which enabled a small number of Welshmen to secure lucrative offices and to rise in the social scale. In the reign of Edward IV, to cite the most famous example, William Herbert built up in a comparatively short space of time an impressive structure of power and fully merited the description as 'King Edward's master lock' in Wales. Few men acquired greater authority in Wales than the duke of Buckingham to whom Richard III made grants of sweeping powers in May, 1483. Few men hold their power for so brief a spell: by the autumn Buckingham was deeply suspect and had been brought to trial and to execution. The large number of lordships in which the king could not exercise sovereign rights meant that the power of the crown was weak, and only with the emergence of conciliar government in Wales and the Marches during the reigns of Edward IV and Henry VII did the position begin to improve. Welsh churchmen played very little part in the government of Wales. Some, like Robert Tully of St. David's, John Hunden of Llandaff, and Thomas Knight of St. Asaph, paid the price of failing to walk the political tight-rope securely. In 1471 they supported the restoration of Henry VI, and when, after a brief eclipse, Edward IV re-established his authority, they were forced in varying degrees to suffer the consequences of their misjudgment.[25]

Men of great distinction were not generally appointed to Welsh sees, though Richard Martin of St. David's was an able and experienced royal servant. St. David's had the misfortune of having no fewer than fifteen bishops between 1408 and 1509. The more able the bishop, the less likely was he to spare time for the needs of his diocese. Even more ennervating was the fact that Welshmen were not appointed to Welsh bishoprics. In part this was a continuation of a practice which had been evident since the early decades of the fourteenth century. In part it was a direct result of the fears inspired by Glyn Dŵr's revolt. No Welshman held St. David's between 1389 and 1496, nor Bangor between 1408 and 1500. St. Asaph was in a curious position since Reginald Pecock, bishop between 1444 and 1450, is claimed as a bishop with Welsh connections. There might be links with a Carmarthenshire family, though on balance the connection does not seem very likely. Llandaff represents an older tradition, for there bishops with local connections were rare after 1323 and no Welshman was appointed to the see between that date and 1566.

In the fifteenth century the Welsh Church was sadly lacking in character and leadership. Not until the accession of the Tudor king, Henry VII, would Welshmen again be appointed to the Welsh dioceses and strong, committed personalities once more begin to dominate the Church in the principality.

---

[1] The classical modern study of the Welsh Church during this period is that of James Conway Davies, *Episcopal Acts and Cognate Documents relating to Welsh Dioceses, 1066–1272*, 2 vols. Historical Society of the Church in Wales, 1946, 1948. In his introductions to these volumes Conway Davies examined a wide number of controversial issues in great detail. For the secular history of the period Sir John Lloyd's *History of Wales from the earliest times to the Edwardian Conquest* (2 vols., 3rd. ed., 1939) remains a fundamental work. I have surveyed the impact of the Normans in Wales in *The Norman Conquerors, A Students' History of Wales*, 1976.

[2] D. M. Smith, 'The Episcopate of Richard, Bishop of St. Asaph: A Problem of Twelfth-century Chronology', *J.H.S.C.W.*, XXIV, 9–12.

[3] *Ep. Acts.*, ii, 616, no. L. 30; 620, no. L. 45.

[4] There is an extensive literature on the *Book of Llandaff*. For a summary of recent views see especially Wendy Davies, 'Liber Landavensis: its construction and credibility', *English Historical Review*, lxxxviii, 335–351, one of a number of important articles on this text by Dr. Davies. The defence of the older date for the appearance of the diocese of Llandaff is argued strongly by Chancellor J.W. James in a number of essays. See especially, '*The Book of Llandâv*: The Church and See of Llandâv and its Critics', *J.H.S.C.W.*, XIV, 5–22. Mr. R. W. D. Fenn accepts the antiquity of the diocese, see above, p. 12.

[5] C. N. L. Brooke, 'The Archbishops of St. David's, Llandaff, and Caerleon-on-Usk', *Studies in the Early British Church*, ed. Nora K. Chadwick, 218.

[6] We hear little about the depredations of the Normans. It was said that Bishop David fitz Gerald, Bernard's successor, was so disseised of his possessions, lands and men by Mahel, son of Miles, earl of Hereford, 'that he could not dwell within the boundaries of Brycheiniog, but as an exile, had to dwell in England and in other parts of his diocese.' Mahel may have been exceptional in the vigour of his attacks, but he was by no means an isolated example. If he was unusual it was because of the restitution which he made. (*Ep. Acts.*, i, 269, no. D.153; 284, no. D.206.)

[7] *Ep. Acts.*, i, 200; A. Saltman, *Theobald Archbishop of Canterbury*, 21–2, 134. The archbishop of Canterbury was concerned to carry the long conflict with York a stage further during the early part of Bishop Bernard's episcopate.

[8] For Gerald see David Walker, 'Gerald of Wales, Archdeacon of Brecon', *Links with the Past: Swansea and Brecon Historical Essays*, ed. O. W. Jones and David Walker, (Llandybie, 1974), 67–87, and David Walker, 'Gerald of Wales: a Review of Recent Work', *J.H.S.C.W.*, XXIV, 13–26. A number of important articles by Michael Richter include those which he reprinted in his *Giraldus Cambrensis*, and 'Professions of Obedience and the Metropolitan claim of St. David's', *N.L.W.J.*, XV, 197–214, 'Canterbury's Primacy in Wales and the first stage of Bishop Bernard's opposition', *Journal of Ecclesiastical History*, 22, 171–189. See also his *Canterbury Professions*, Canterbury and York Society, LXVII, part CXL, issued for 1972–3.

[9] *Ep. Acts.*, ii, 538.

[10] David Walker, 'The Medieval Bishops of Llandaff', *Morgannwg*, vi (1962), 5–32; F. G. Cowley, 'The Church in Medieval Glamorgan', *Glamorgan County History*, iii (1971), 105–6, 693–4.

[11] A second official, Llywelyn, was also named in documents issued early in the thirteenth century. Their activities can be seen in the *Brecon Cartulary* (1884), 52, 119, 120. For Thomas of Hay see *Speculum Duorum*, ed. M. Richter, Y. Lefèvre and R. B. C. Huygens (Cardiff, 1974), xxxi, xlvi, 1, 248. An Ithenard who was active in Gerald's interests was made canon of St.David's when Gerald was bishop-elect and administrator of St. David's. His appointment was confirmed by Innocent III. (*Ep. Acts.*, i, 307, no. D.304; 327, no. D.372.)

[12] For Chancellor James, Gerald was a self-seeking churchman solely concerned with his own advancement; the interests of Wales and the Welsh Church were no more than useful weapons in his search for place. (James, *Church History*, 80–81.) Dr. Richter and I see him in kinder terms.

[13] For Gerald's works see Eileen A. Williams, 'A Bibliography of Giraldus Cambrensis, *c.* 1147–*c.* 1223', *N.L.W.J.*, XII (1961–2), 97–140. I have confined attention here to those of Gerald's works which are immediately relevant to the history of the Welsh Church. The *Symbolum Electorum*, is a collection of passages from his own books which had especially pleased him.

[14] The *Gemma Ecclesiastica* was edited for the Rolls Series by J. S. Brewer, *Opera*, II (1862). Brewer gives a detailed analysis in his preface and is followed closely by E. J. Newell in his chapter on 'The Church in the Age of Gerald de Barri' which is an extended paraphrase of the *Gemma*. (*A History of the Welsh Church to the Dissolution of the Monasteries*, 238–274.)

[15] The recent study of this episode is by Michael Richter, 'David ap Llywelyn, the First Prince of Wales', *W.H.R.*, 5 (1970–71), 205–219.

[16] The seminal study of this period is Glanmor Williams, *The Welsh Church from Conquest to Reformation* (Cardiff, 1962), on which I have drawn heavily.

[17] Some sixty years later, in 1347, Edward the Black Prince and his advisers made a serious attempt to claim St. David's as part of his principality of Wales, but Edward III was adamant that the bishopric should not be removed from his own sphere of influence. The bishop came to be recognised as a marcher lord.

[18] John de Eaglescliffe had the distinction of serving as bishop in Wales, Ireland and Scotland. He had been consecrated as bishop of Glasgow in 1318.

[19] D. L. Douie, *Archbishop Pecham* (Oxford, 1952), 155. Miss Douie's work is the indispensable study of Pecham's career. This and the following paragraph owe much to her chapters on 'Archiepiscopal Visitations and Relations with the Cathedral Priory of Canterbury', 143–191, and 'Wales', 235–271. Glanmor Williams considers Pecham's visitation of Wales in detail, *Welsh Church*, 35–80.

[20] ib., 36.

[21] For manuals of instruction available in England see W. A. Pantin, *The English Church in the Fourteenth Century* (Cambridge, 1955), 189–219. The *Oculus Sacerdotis* and its derivatives are the subject of research at present in progress. For the material available in Wales the papers written by J. E. Caerwyn Williams are fundamental. For a valuable summary see Glanmor Williams, *Welsh Church*, 81–113. Where the *Gemma Ecclesiastica* of Gerald of Wales, clearly intended as a book of instruction for Welsh clergy, survives in only one manuscript, 24 manuscripts of the *Breuddwyd Pawl* and 22 of the *Llyfr Ancr* have survived.

[22] The classic study of Owain's career is Sir John Lloyd's *Owen Glendower* (Oxford, 1931), from which all recent studies of the revolt stem. There is a brief but perceptive study by Glanmor Williams, *Owen Glendower* (Clarendon Biographies, 1966), and a bilingual essay by G. A. Jones, *Owain Glyndwr c. 1354–1416*, published in Cardiff, 1962. For an extended treatment of the consequences of the revolt for the Welsh Church see Glanmor Williams, *Welsh Church*, 210–243.

[23] This aspect of the scheme is brought out very clearly by Glanmor Williams, op. cit., 223.

[24] The classic studies are by Browne Willis who produced *Surveys* of Bangor (1721) and St. Asaph (which was not published until 1801). See also M. L. Clarke, *Bangor Cathedral* (Cardiff, 1969).

[25] The best accounts of political conditions in Wales in the fifteenth century are to be found in R. A. Griffiths, 'Wales and the Marches' in *Fifteenth-century England, 1399–1509*, ed. S. B. Chrimes, C. D. Ross and R. A. Griffiths (Manchester, 1972); C. D. Ross, *Edward IV* (1975), and S. B. Chrimes, *Henry VII* (1972).

CHAPTER 3

THE REFORMATION IN WALES

by

David Walker

THE sixteenth century was an age of religious revolution, and in Wales, as elsewhere in Europe, the Reformation was a major upheaval. Increasingly in the field of Reformation history the importance of regional studies has been recognised and Wales has characteristics which make it a valuable case-history. A poor and comparatively backward area was suddenly affected by changes in religion which were revolutionary for society and government as well as for the Church. But how sudden was the onslaught? Wales was essentially rural and the Reformation was very much an urban phenomenon. How far did this contrast affect the course of events in Wales? Again, Wales was a land of two languages with English taken for granted in the towns and among the county gentry, and Welsh as the language of a peasantry still largely monoglot. How did that affect the course of the Reformation in Wales? How far was this linguistic pattern altered because of the Reformation?[1]

There were ample signs that all was not well with the Church in the fifteenth century and the early decades of the sixteenth. Poverty was the hall-mark of the majority of the Welsh clergy. Only 6% of the Welsh benefices listed in the *Valor Ecclesiasticus* in 1535 were worth more than £20 a year; 23.5% were worth between £10 and £20; 46% were worth £5-£10, and 24% were worth less than £5. That is to say that 60% of the Welsh livings were worth £10 or less; the comparable estimate for England is 50%. To see this as it affected one rural deanery, Abergavenny, is to give greater point to the bare statistics. There were thirty-three benefices in the deanery; one, Llanwenarth, was worth £26 16s. 9d., six more had incomes of more than £10, and twelve were worth less than £5.[2] It was a depressing picture. The price of poverty was two-fold: an ill-educated, and sometimes illiterate clergy, and inadequate pastoral and spiritual direction for the country people. In an English context the level of parish clergy was low indeed. Local studies for such areas as Essex, Yorkshire,

Lincolnshire and Lancashire point to the fact that only a minority of parish clergy were graduates. While the universities and the inns of court were producing an educated laity the standard of the parish clergy remained sadly deficient. Men of ability and training served elsewhere in cathedral chapters, collegiate churches, and in administration. In Lancashire which, like Wales, was remote from the mainstream of political and intellectual activity and conservative in outlook, it has been noted that 'the educational standards of the Lancashire clergy were too low for the major task the Reformation was to impose on them.' Many clergy may have been without books altogether, often apparently without even a Bible, though there can be little doubt that the printing press gradually made available a supply of useful and inexpensive books from which, in England though not in Wales, the literate parish priest might profit.[3] Traditional books of piety and instruction continued to be popular and it has been suggested that insufficient material was available from orthodox sources to satisfy the needs of the better-equipped clergy. There was, however, little reason why standard works should be supplemented or replaced. Until the European Church had seen the real nature of the threat of protestantism and had begun belatedly to respond to the dangers of division and heresy, there was nothing to stimulate the production of new statements of orthodoxy. In the same way, until the anglican Church of the Elizabethan settlement had experienced attack from papist and puritan there was little occasion to reorganise on any large scale the rôle, education, and function of the average parish priest. Only under attack did he become an apologist.

The printing press brought to these islands copies of new books, some like the writings of Erasmus calculated to arouse the critical qualities of scholars, and others, like the writings of Luther and his contemporaries, designed to translate criticism into a movement for change. In the transmission of these new ideas and of books which, by the standards of the medieval Church were heretical, the importance of long-distance trade and of the major sea-ports can scarcely be over-stated. There can be little doubt that a small minority of the clergy in England acquired these works, nor that such men played a rôle quite disproportionately large in comparison with their numbers during the religious upheavals of the sixteenth century. Nor can the crucial importance of towns and merchants be doubted. Shrewd and literate, the men of the towns could respond to new ideas and new teaching. In this context the importance for Wales of such places as Carmarthen, Haverfordwest and Swansea must be determined. In an urban setting, a man like William Barlow could exert a very powerful influence. The provision of English scriptures and of sermons and pamphlets in English could have only a limited effect in Wales, for in the towns alone was there an English-speaking population to which such writings could have any appeal.

Much of the success which attended Henry VIII's religious policy was due to anti-clericalism, as sharp in Wales as it was in England. Dislike of the priestly order strengthened often into hatred. Financial exactions were a primary cause of this widespread anti-clericalism, but there were other contributory factors such as dislike of ecclesiastical jurisdiction and church courts, criticism of the quality of life of individual clerics, absentee rectors, and pluralists enjoying the revenues of a number of benefices at the same time. The monastic orders incurred a large share of this hostility. They had little zeal and provided a comfortable, even a cosseted, life for the members of their houses.

In England and Wales the Reformation was linked at every stage with royal policy. When, in 1527, Henry VIII began the process of securing the annulment of his marriage to Catherine of Aragon diplomacy and threats failed and the king turned to a policy of separating the English Church from the jurisdiction of the papacy. Thereafter, doctrinal changes were controlled by the crown. Changes of religious policy under Edward VI, Mary and Elizabeth were acts of state as the royal will was imposed upon the kingdom. Throughout, it was difficult to draw a sharp distinction between treason and religious dissent. For Wales this aspect of the Reformation had particular significance. The Council of Wales and the Marches had been used as an instrument of government since the days of Edward IV, and the Act of Union of 1536 made one integrated kingdom of England, the Marches, and Wales. The Tudor dynasty drew strong loyalty from Wales and Welshmen, and policies inaugurated by Henry VII and his successors met with little opposition from their Welsh subjects.

So much for the background against which the progress of the Reformation in Wales must be assessed. The immediate cause of the Henrician Reformation was Henry VIII's lack of a legitimate male heir. Catherine of Aragon had married Arthur, eldest son of Henry VII, in 1501, and when he died in the following year she remained in England. It was her father-in-law's intention that she should marry his second son, Henry, now heir to the throne, but there were financial and diplomatic issues which cast doubts on the value of the match, and which delayed the marriage until 1509, when Henry VIII had already become king. Catherine failed to provide a son to ensure the succession. Indeed, with one exception, she was denied healthy children. She had a number of miscarriages; three children were still-born or died soon after birth. A son was born in 1511 and lived for seven weeks; another daughter died early in infancy. Only one, the Princess Mary, survived to adult life. As Henry's hopes for a son were frustrated, so were his fears aroused that the lack of healthy children was a punishment for marrying his brother's widow. From the mid-1520s Henry was anxious for an annulment of his marriage, and his anxiety was given a fresh note of urgency when he became deeply infatuated with Anne Boleyn. Cardinal Wolsey failed to obtain the annulment and was discarded, eventually to be replaced by Thomas Cromwell, the royal servant who deserves to be regarded as the architect of the English Reformation. A Parliament had been summoned in 1529, and in the critical years from 1532 to 1536 Cromwell mobilised the strongly anti-clerical sentiment of this Parliament to break the ties between England and Rome, and so to make possible the release of Henry VIII from his unwanted queen. Threats were used in the Act of Conditional Restraint of Annates of 1532 as a means of bringing pressure to bear on the pope. The threat was imposed in the following year, and was made absolute in 1534. At the same time, the pope's jurisdiction was attacked. An Act in Restraint of Appeals, passed in 1533, laid down that all spiritual cases should be completed in England and this effectively excluded the papal curia as a court of appeal. In 1534 the Act of Supremacy declared the crown's authority 'over all persons and all causes within the realm', and Henry VIII became Supreme Head of the Church of England. The pope's authority was finally and completely extinguished in 1536. Meanwhile, the bishops and clergy of England and Wales were brought to heel with the submission of the clergy in their convocations in 1532. Fortunately for the king, Archbishop Warham died in the same year and Thomas Cranmer was appointed and recognised as archbishop of Canterbury in his place. From Cranmer Henry secured the declaration that his marriage with Catherine of Aragon was null and void, and in May, 1533, he married Anne Boleyn, already carrying his child, the future Queen Elizabeth I. 'The king's great matter' made little impact on Wales. The Princess Mary, daughter of Catherine of Aragon, was sent to Ludlow in 1525, when she was only ten years old, and she lived there for a brief period. Perhaps some local sympathy for the child and her unfortunate mother may have been engendered. One unwise cleric in north Wales ventured to say publicly that were Henry VIII but in Snowdon 'he would souse the king about the ears till he had made his head soft enough.'[4] That was in 1533, but how widespread such feelings may have been cannot be estimated.

The first stirrings of the religious revolution in Wales came in 1534 in the lordship of Pembroke, then held by Anne Boleyn. Under her patronage a new prior was appointed to the Augustinian priory at Haverfordwest, William Barlow, a convinced and belligerent exponent of new ideas in religion and a violent opponent of papal authority. His condemnation of the old order did not extend to the time-honoured practice of nepotism, for he established three brothers very successfully in the diocese of St. David's, and together they formed an influential and vocal pressure group fulminating against the lack of response from Bishop Rawlins and the conservative clergy among whom they had settled. Barlow did not remain long at Haverfordwest, for he was appointed prior of Bisham in 1535 and bishop of St. Asaph in January, 1536. Within a few weeks of his appointment, Rawlins of St. David's was dead, and Barlow was translated to the southern see which he was to rule until 1548. In the search for greater efficiency he was anxious to transfer his cathedral from its ancient site at St. David's and to establish his seat at St. Peter's, Carmarthen. He claimed wider powers over the cathedral chapter than could be justified by any appeal to precedent, and he made an unscrupulous but unsuccessful attempt to discredit the leading figure in the chapter, Thomas Lloyd the precentor. Barlow survived the fall of two patrons, each influential but each, in the end, dangerous company for an ambitious man. He remained bishop, though somewhat subdued, until he was translated to Bath and Wells in 1548.

Apart from establishing his brothers in Pembrokeshire, Barlow encouraged a group of able and contentious radicals in his diocese, George Constantine and Robert Barnes, who had already played some part in the production and dissemination of protestant books, Thomas Young, Rowland Meyrick, and Stephen Green. Much of Barlow's strength lay in two things, his uncompromisingly protestant views which he held with firmness and consistency, and his association with two boroughs in south Wales, Brecon and Carmarthen. He transferred to Brecon the collegiate community which had previously served his church at Abergwili, and he associated with this college a newly-established grammar school. Here the sons of Welshmen could acquire education and, especially, 'skill in the English tongue' so that, among other things, they could understand and keep the enactments of the king's government. It is a powerful reminder that the policy of Henry VIII in Wales was one of anglicisation; the Church was expected to play its part in enforcing this policy upon the Welsh people. Barlow himself was in close contact with Carmarthen, the largest and most important borough in south Wales, where there was an educated circle capable of discussing critically the doctrines propounded by their bishop. The indications are that some of the merchants of Carmarthen were ready to respond and needed little persuasion to implement the protestant teachings of their able but difficult father-in-God.

If the problem of St. David's at this stage was too vigorous a bishop, the problem for Llandaff over the critical years of the Henrician Reformation was an absentee bishop. George de Athequa, bishop of Llandaff since 1517, was a Spaniard who served Catherine of Aragon as confessor. He was her constant companion until her death in 1536, and though he was held in contempt by the king's officials he was courageous in his loyalty to the discarded queen. So far as the government was concerned, his chief offence as a diocesan was that he allowed priests to preach against the king and made no attempt to encourage preachers to defend Henry's policy. Eventually he tried to escape from England 'but managed it so badly that he was taken prisoner and put in the tower.' Diplomatic pressure secured his release and he was allowed to leave the kingdom.

One of the first major effects of the religious changes in England and Wales was the disappearance of the religious houses which had been a principal feature of religious and social life for so many centuries. The orders were conservative and international, and there may have been some genuine fear that their continued existence would produce a reaction in favour of the papacy. But their chief attraction for Henry VIII and Cromwell was their wealth. There was some precedent for this policy, notably in the suppression of a small number of houses by Cardinal Wolsey to provide endowments for his new foundations at Ipswich and Oxford. In 1534 commissioners travelled around the country to receive the oath of supremacy, and the response to their demand was some indication of whether particular houses or individuals might prove stubborn. There is no evidence that any Welsh monk refused the oath. The subscriptions to the oath of supremacy on this occasion are a valuable guide to the size of religious communities. Then, in 1535-6, Cromwell sent out commissioners to enquire into the condition of monastic houses, and in 1536 it was decided that the property of all religious houses with an income of less than £200 a year should be surrendered. The dissolution of the greater monasteries was ordered in 1539. All the Welsh houses fell within the terms of reference of the earlier suppression. Reports on their condition ranged from sharp and sweeping condemnation at Monmouth to approval and commendation of Carmarthen priory. But, favourable or unfavourable, the report made little difference to the fate of the house. Some priories were dependencies of large English monasteries, and they were allowed to continue in existence in 1536. Ewenni priory, for example, was a dependency of St. Peter's, Gloucester, and Brecon and Carmarthen were daughter houses of Battle. They gained, as it were, a stay of execution. A small number of abbeys attempted to purchase a reprieve. Whitland paid a heavy fine of £400 for the privilege of continued existence; Neath paid £150, and Strata Florida, £66. They could not know it, but in the event they paid dear for a brief respite.

The dissolution of the Welsh monasteries has a direct bearing on the larger issue: how sudden was the onslaught of the Reformation? The steady flow of grants to monastic houses had dried up, though benefactors were leaving sums of money to the religious, and especially to the friars, in the sixteenth century. The clearest indication that there might be valuable pickings from monastic lands in the near future is to be found when a local magnate acting as steward of a monastery thought it useful to increase his hold over the house and its lands. The monks of Pill were constrained by their steward, Sir John Wogan, only to lease their lands with his permission. After the dissolution the bulk of their estates were in his hand.[5] On the other hand, as late as 1535 there was still some jockeying for place and on occasions substantial investment in attempts to secure Welsh abbacies. The future might be uncertain, but it did not yet appear to be without promise. The visitation of Cromwell's commissioners in 1535-6 seems to have been the clearest indication that monks should take thought for the future, and in a number of Welsh monasteries there was a sudden spate of leases which committed the use of monastic lands for substantial periods of time ahead. Glanmor Williams has emphasised especially the evidence relating to Neath, Whitland, and Strata Florida. At Neath, 71 of the surviving leases relating to the abbey's estates are datable, and of these 51 were issued after the end of 1535. At Whitland, 138 leases were issued at the eleventh hour. So successful were the lessees in this case that the earl of Essex was to complain many years later that he had no profit from the abbey's lands because these leases ran for so long.[6] At Strata Florida, the evidence is not so clear, but it looks as if there was some move to issue new leases in the last months of the life of the community. Elsewhere, such forethought may not have been necessary. To cite evidence of transactions of a slightly different nature, the nine principal churches of Brecon priory had been held at farm since the fourteenth century, and no special arrangement was necessary to safeguard them for the future.[7]

The lands which the Tudors gained through the dissolution of the monasteries were at first leased for short terms, and later many of them were sold by the crown. The beneficiaries varied widely in origin and background. Two of the English dioceses created by Henry VIII, Gloucester and Chester, retained lands and revenues formerly held in Wales by the abbot and convent of each church. Many of the greater magnates of Wales gained new estates from houses with which they had been associated. The commissioners who visited the Welsh monasteries in 1535-6 made valuable acquisitions. Sir John Pryce, who secured the estates of St. Guthlac's, Hereford, also obtained Brecon priory and lands in and around Brecon. His colleague, John Vaughan, profited substantially from Grace Dieu, Whitland, and Pembroke. Sir Edward Carne of Nash obtained Ewenni priory. Elsewhere family influence might be valuable; Roger Barlow, brother of the turbulent bishop of St. David's, secured the commandery of Slebech and added materially to his stake in west Wales. In the north the greater part of the monastic lands was acquired by the local gentry. The Owens of Plas Du secured Bardsey; Bangor friary went to the Griffiths of Penrhyn, and after an interval to Geoffrey Glynne. Richard Bulkeley laid claim to Penmon. He was urgent in his request to Thomas Cromwell 'that I may have it to farm according to the king's books, for it lieth hard at my nose.'[8] Rice Mansel, by shrewd and persistent investment, obtained Margam abbey and its estates. In four separate transactions, each of which was a major speculation involving high risk, he spent some £2,482 for these rich pickings. The aristocracy and gentry of Wales gained enormously in lands and wealth as a result of the fall of the Welsh monasteries.

The dispossessed religious were treated with some generosity, many of them being given pensions or livings. Many were also allowed to continue wearing their monastic habit beneath that of a secular priest. Throughout 1537, monks of Margam, Tintern, Llanthony, Conwy, Clifford, Grace Dieu and Talley, and other Welsh houses received such dispensations, and in 1540 they were joined by former monks from Whitland and Strata Florida. Nuns were released from the obligations of the religious life, though there was little they could do by way of alternative.

A few years later, in 1547, it was the turn of the chantries to be suppressed. These ranged from the establishment of masses at a particular altar to elaborate foundations like the Mathew chantry at Llandaff or the Kyffin chantry at Bangor. They remained popular throughout the later Middle Ages and well into the sixteenth century. In 1532, for example, James Walbeuf set up a chantry in the church at Llanhamlach, while right on the border between Wales and Herefordshire in Welsh Newton a chantry was founded as late as 1547. Their resources were another target which could be plundered and their function ran counter to fundamental protestant teachings.

So long as he lived, Henry VIII kept firm control over religious change, restraining the radicals eager for the introduction of protestant teaching, yet checking the conservatives who were ready to use religion as a means of extending their political influence. His death in 1547 opened the way for a violent swing towards protestantism which character-ised the reign of Edward VI, and the equally violent catholic reaction under Mary Tudor. Wales did not escape the consequences of these fluctuations in religious policy. The centre of conflict was the diocese of St. David's where William Barlow had secured the succession of Robert Ferrar to the see when he himself went to Bath and Wells in 1548. Ferrar was a Yorkshireman, shrewd and astute enough, a staunch protestant, but basically unsound in his judgment of men. The early years of his episcopate were taken up with a series of bitter quarrels between himself and the canons of St. David's who included in their ranks a number of leading protestants, men who by conviction and belief should have been counted among Ferrar's supporters. The bishop and his unsavoury com-panions were no match for such able lawyers and administrators as Thomas Young, Rowland Meyrick, and, in the later stages of the quarrel, George Constantine. Ferrar also alienated the leading citizens of Carmarthen and created much bad feeling by his dealings with the rural tenants of St. David's. In 1552 his enemies brought him to book and he was im-prisoned. While he languished in prison, Mary became queen. In the eyes of the new régime Ferrar was a man of deeply suspect views, and Carmarthen was a hot-bed of protestant teaching. In 1555 he was sent back to Wales and at Carmarthen he was burned at the stake. His death may have been intended as a salutary warning to his former friends and enemies alike that Mary would have no heretics in her kingdom. Where the danger was already great a summary execution might be a valuable deterrent. If Ferrar was unscrupulous and questionable in his earlier dealings with his diocese, he made amends in the dignified manner of his death.

Tudor bishops were to find that even the most loyal of service might not save them from the rapacity of the crown. The dissolution of the monasteries and the suppression of the chantries were total and perman-ent in effect but there were other targets, and the spoliation of the Church was by no means at an end. The ancient endowments of cathedrals and parishes might provide lucrative posts for royal nominees and their estates and revenues were much sought after. Above all the ancient endowments of the medieval bishoprics were viewed with covetous eyes. The fate of the northern archbishopric of York may stand for the danger in which all the dioceses of England and Wales found themselves. In 1542 Archbishop Edward Lee was obliged to sell to the crown five large and profitable manors. Three years later, in 1545, Robert Holgate was translated from Llandaff to York, and there followed what has been called 'a mammoth alienation of ancient archiepiscopal lands.' On March 14th, 1545, Holgate surrendered to Henry VIII some fifty-one ancient manors and other more recent acquisitions in exchange for rectories and revenues from former monastic possessions. It has been estimated that these two successive archbishops handed to the crown lands which produced an income of £1,563 a year. When the compensation paid to them is taken into account this represented the forfeiture of about half of the annual income of the medieval archbishopric. By the end of the sixteenth century there had been some recovery, and the plight of the northern archbishopric was not so grave as it had been in the middle decades of the century.[9]

One radical suggestion made in Henry VIII's reign was that all the episcopal estates of the kingdom should be surrendered to the king and the bishops be paid salaries. In Edward VI's reign this radical expedient was forced upon the bishop of Winchester, but it was never taken-up as a general policy. Elizabeth was a hard and astute patron for the English Church, and she, too, obliged bishops to surrender valuable estates in exchange for other types of property and less reliable sources of income. At the beginning of her reign she ordered her bishops not to lease their lands on long leases: three lives or twenty-one years was to be the norm. Nor must they offer preferential rents except to the queen herself. She also asserted the right of the crown to alienate estates during a vacancy, and when Oxford was left vacant for forty-one years or Ely for nineteen, the consequences could be disastrous. Under cover of legality the queen and her courtiers could plunder the Church at will.[10] Sometimes the crown profited directly, and at other times a great magnate was the beneficiary. Bishop Barlow of St. David's had much to fear from Lord Ferrers and his son, Richard Devereux. In 1546 Barlow alienated the rich manor of Lamphey to Richard Devereux for which he received the advowson of the rectory and the vicarage of Carew, but slight compensation for such a prize. A little later, in 1553, Anthony Kitchen, bishop of Llandaff, leased the manor of Llandaff to Sir George Matthew, client of William Herbert, earl of Pembroke. Kitchen's predecessors had drawn about one third of their annual income from this one manor, but it was leased in perpetuity to Matthew at an accustomed rent and all chance of making future revenues from an economic rent or from entry fines was lost. Kitchen has a bad reputation as the bishop who reduced his diocese to extreme poverty, but at least one of his successors could not resist royal pressure. In 1581-2 Bishop William Bleddyn was obliged to lease the manor and rectory of Bassaleg to the queen for 100 years. Nor was this an isolated occasion, for he was also responsible for leasing on long terms the manors of Machen, Mynyddislwyn, Bedwellty, Henllys, Risca, St Bride's and Coedkerniew. Elsewhere in Wales the rapacity of William Herbert was matched by that of the earl of Leicester. Together they secured the rich estates of Clynnog Fawr and Llanddewibrefi. In the diocese of Bangor, the rivalry of Glyn and Bulkeley shaped the fortunes of the bishopric and dominated the local politics of the area. Overall, the effects of despoliation on the Welsh bishoprics was very marked. Exact figures and reliable comparisons are not, however, easy to obtain. The *Valor Ecclesiasticus* of 1535 provides a useful index with St. David's valued at £457, Bangor at £131, St. Asaph at £187 and Llandaff at £144. These are net annual values; gross income, temporal and spiritual, produce markedly higher figures. The extent to which it was thought that income had declined can be gauged from the assertion, made in 1583, that St. David's produced 'not £263 clear', while Llandaff was said to have declined to £130 annual value by the early decades of the seventeenth century.[11] Bangor was 'impoverished by so many long leases'.

Scarcely less dangerous for the economic security of the Welsh dioceses was the blatant nepotism of the Tudor bishops. They were not exceptional; like all bishops they needed local support and one of the easy ways of securing this was to install relatives and dependants in the prebends, churches, manors and other possessions of their sees. Early in the story of the religious upheavals in Wales, William Barlow established his kin very handsomely in west Wales, while at the end of the sixteenth century Bishop William Hughes of St. Asaph (1573-1600) had leased episcopal manors to his wife and children, and also to his sisters and cousins. Even Richard Davies, the outstanding member of the Welsh episcopate in the sixteenth century, provided on a splendid scale for his family.

For individual bishops the solution to such poverty was to hold other benefices *in commendam*. Economic necessity forced them to be pluralists. Hughes of St. Asaph is probably the arch-offender. He held the valuable archdeaconry of St. Asaph and, at different times, sixteen benefices from which he drew a substantial income. Each was neglected in varying degree and many were served by ill-paid deputies. When Archbishop Laud began the Herculean task of restoring stability and strength to the Church he considered the only solution to this particular problem was to recognise long-standing tenure of benefices *in commendam* as a necessary part of the bishop's income. Hughes's successors at St. Asaph regularly held the archdeaconry with the bishopric, and this was one diocese in which Laud was able to standardise the position to his own satisfaction.

Until 1563 the progress of the Reformation in Wales was linked with the use of English as a prescribed language. It was in keeping with long-term Tudor practice that this should be so, for the dynasty was concerned with the maintenance of law and order, and the unification of their kingdom was served and symbolised by the use of a single language. With the Act of Union of 1536 this principle was written into the Welsh policy of Henry VIII and his advisers. English became the formal language of official business. So, too, with the provision of scriptures in the vernacular and the imposition of successive Prayer Books from 1549 to 1559, the vernacular for the whole of England and Wales was English. In Cornwall and the south west, where a Celtic language had survived in use, the first English Prayer Book gave great offence and provoked a rising in 1549.

Few decisions had more far-reaching consequences than the decision to abandon this principle so far as religion was concerned in Wales. There had been some attempts to provide material in Welsh for worship and devotion. Welsh versions of parts of the Bible and paraphrases of parts of the Old Testament were current in the Middle Ages. The impact of the Henrician Reformation on Wales prompted Sir John Pryce of Brecon to publish in 1547 his *Prymer, Yn y Llyvyr Hwnn*, which included Welsh versions of the Ten Commandments, the Lord's Prayer, and the Creed. Four years later a more ambitious book appeared, the *Kynniver Llith a Ban o'r Ysgrythur Lan* by William Salesbury. This provided Welsh translations of the epistles and gospels for Sundays and holy days. Within a decade, this collection had gained both currency and fame. In 1561 the bishop of St. Asaph ordered that 'After the pistyll and gospell, yn Englyshe, the same to be red also in Welshe.' The texts in the *Kynniver Llith a Ban* were used for this purpose.

How the local demand for Welsh scriptures and Welsh services was brought to the notice of Elizabeth I and her advisers, and how they were persuaded to respond to it cannot be known. William Cecil, at the very centre of power, and Archbishop Matthew Parker, undoubtedly exercised great influence. The two leading figures in Wales were Richard Davies, bishop of St. Asaph from 1560 to 1561 and of St. David's from 1561 to 1581, and William Salesbury himself. Both had some access to powerful men in government circles and could have played the decisive part. It is generally assumed that Davies was the prime mover. He was clearly Salesbury's patron during the actual work of translating the New Testament. He was the only Welsh bishop to be present at all three readings of the Act of 1563 in the House of Lords, and the inference is that he had some special interest in the Act. It laid down that the four Welsh bishops and the bishop of Hereford were to ensure that Welsh scriptures and a Welsh Prayer Book were to be provided within three years. Salesbury was mainly responsible for the Prayer Book and much of the New Testament but in preparing them he unfortunately adopted a Latinized and archaic orthography which made his prose difficult. It might appeal to a small learned circle, but it would not become a popular work. Richard Davies translated a group of letters, I Timothy, Hebrews, I and II Peter, and James. Thomas Huet, precentor of St. David's, was responsible for the Book of Revelations. Altogether, it was a major achievement. It seems that the original intention of the translators was to produce a Welsh Old Testament but this eluded them. For a full Welsh version of the Bible it was necessary to wait until 1588 when William Morgan produced his translation. Morgan was not cut off from the active life of the Church while he was preparing his translation. He was, for a few years, vicar of Welshpool, but most of the work was done while he was vicar of Llanrhaeadr-ym-Mochnant. There was, it is true, criticism that he was neglecting his parish duties, but his bishop was able to give him protection and support. He was also involved in bitter and time-consuming quarrels with his leading parishioners which resulted in resort to the Court of Star Chamber and the Council in the Marches. Once the translation was completed there was still the formidable task of setting the Bible up in type and seeing it through the press. Happily, a London-Welsh divine came to Morgan's aid. He was Gabriel Goodman who founded Christ's Hospital at his native town of Ruthin and who had served William Cecil (later Lord Burghley) as chaplain. Goodman was dean of Westminster from 1561 to 1601, and he had the doubtful distinction of being considered and passed over for no fewer than seven bishoprics! He provided Morgan with a place to live at Westminster in 1587-8 so that he could supervise the printing of his Bible. The new Welsh version quickly became popular and influential. In 1620 a revised edition appeared, comparable with the Authorised Version of the English

Bible of 1611, and in 1630 for the first time an inexpensive edition was published. Worship in Welsh made the anglican Church an acceptable institution in Wales, while the popularity of the Welsh scriptures became one of the formative influences on the development of the Welsh language and on Welsh popular piety.

Before long the Bible and the Prayer Book were buttressed by the publication of metrical versions of the psalms in Welsh, first by William Middleton and, later by Edmwnd Prys, archdeacon of Meirionnydd, and by Welsh translations of standard theological works by such men as Maurice Kyffin, Huw Lewis, Rowland Vaughan, and Robert Llwyd. The Church of the Elizabethan settlement could take firm hold on the Welsh gentry and, increasingly, on the Welsh peasantry for it was no longer separated from them by the barrier of language. The Act of 1563 required that the Welsh versions should be provided within three years, and there is some evidence to show that once texts were available they were purchased and used. The Tudor records of St. Mary's, Swansea, show that in 1563 the churchwardens bought 'a Welsh booke of sarvys', probably a copy of the Litany in Welsh, published in 1562. In 1569 they acquired 'a Whellch boke ffor the cominion', which was clearly the Welsh Book of Common Prayer published in 1567. Morgan's Bible was published in 1588 and it is possible, though not certain, that the parish had already bought its copy by 1589. St. Mary's had 'the ould Wellshe bybell' among its books thirty years later and the purchase of 'the Weshe booke' in 1589 may refer to Morgan's Bible.¹²

The maintenance of the Elizabethan settlement depended upon firm discipline. The queen gave a lead with the royal visitation and injunctions of 1559. A commission of royal visitors travelled around the Welsh dioceses to examine the state of the Church. The active members included three men soon to be bishops, Richard Davies, Thomas Young and Rowland Meyrick. Their first duty was to secure from the clergy recognition of the royal supremacy and of the form of worship laid down in the Act of Uniformity. Those who held out against this policy were deprived, and a small number of influential clerics paid the price of their convictions. The commissioners also made sure of the election, in accordance with royal policy, of three new bishops, Meyrick for Bangor, Davies for St. Asaph and Young for St. David's. Once the initial impact had been made, Elizabeth left her archbishop of Canterbury, Matthew Parker, to impose his own discipline, though she was ready to bring pressure to bear on him and on other bishops if she thought the occasion demanded it. Early in 1563 she issued orders to the archbishops of Canterbury and

York 'to take effective measure that an exact order and uniformity be maintained in all external rites and ceremonies'. They were to insist that clerics newly appointed to benefices should bind themselves in advance to maintain 'common order'. Parker himself laid down a series of requirements in his *Book of Advertisements* in 1566 which provided a standard of obligation. In England, though not in Wales, the *Advertisements* were received with strong and vocal opposition from the Puritans. Individual bishops carried out visitations of their sees and issued injunctions to correct what they found amiss. In Wales the general tone of the injunctions reflects the deep-seated conservatism of the Welsh Church, a conservatism which the Elizabethan bishops were anxious to reform. In Bangor the attempt had begun while Arthur Bulkeley was still bishop. In 1551 he issued articles of enquiry which demanded whether by preaching, writing, word or deed any clerics maintained the usurped power of the bishop of Rome, whether there was an English Bible and a copy of the *Paraphrases* of Erasmus in each church, whether any prayed on beads, or had masses said contrary to the form and order of the Prayer Book, and whether there were any images, tabernacles, shrines, or feigned miracles in their churches. A dozen years later, Bishop Robinson wrote to Cecil in terms which showed that very little headway had yet been made:[13]

> But, touching the Welsh people's receaving of the gospell, I find by my small experience among them here that ignorance contineweth many in the dregs of superstition which did grew chefly upon the blindness of the clergie, joined with the grediness of getting in so bare a country, and also upon the closing up of God's worde from them in an unknown tongue, of the which harmes, though the one be remedied by the great benefite of our graciouse Quene and Parleament, yet the other remayneth without hope of redresse: for the most part of the priests are too olde (they saye) to be put to schole. Upon this inabilitie to teache God's worde (for there are not six that can preach in these three shierres) I have found since I came to this countrey images and aulters standing in churches undefaced, lewde and indecent vigils and watches observed, much pilgrimage goying, many candels sett up to the honour of saintes, some reliques yet carried about, and all the countries full of bedes and knotts, besides diverse other monuments of wilfull serving of God. Of the which abuses some (I thank God) are reformed, and other, my hope is, wyll dayly decaye by the helpe of the worshipfull of the countries who show some better countenance to the Gospel . . .

Whatever the worshipful of the country might do, the people still clung
to the old ways.

Richard Davies found in St. Asaph and in St. David's that the same
problems had to be faced. In his view only sound preaching would win
over the people, but there was a desperate shortage of preachers. In St.
Asaph there were five men fit to preach the gospel effectively. In St.
David's he found nine such men. His contemporaries were in no better
state: in Llandaff there were but five men fit to preach, while in Bangor
there were only two. Bishop Meyrick gave hope that the position might
improve, for he could list the names of thirty more who were capable of
preaching 'and may do goode', but they were not apparently in the same
class as the dean of Bangor and the vicar of Llangurig, his two reputable
preachers. In the absence of persuasion, the insistence upon discipline
was all the more imperative, but clearly it was not very effective. When
Marmaduke Middleton became bishop of St. David's in 1582 he had
hard things to say about his illustrious predecessor and about the condition of his diocese. He saw too many signs of Roman survivals which
he condemned in round terms. His visitation of 1583 embodied enquiries
as to whether traditional rites were being maintained; he prohibited the
elevation of the host at the service of holy communion; he repeated the
instruction that images, pictures, and rood-lofts must be destroyed, and
that holy days should not be observed as once they were. Protestant
ideas and ways of worship had made little headway in the rural areas of
his diocese. In the towns things were different. This continual insistence
on the importance of establishing the new ways obscures the quiet but
real concern which episcopal visitations demonstrated for the routine
business of parish life. Middleton wished to know, for example, whether
the queen's injunctions were read every quarter, and whether the *Homilies*
were delivered in a clear voice. Did the church have the *Paraphrases* of
Erasmus, or Bullinger's *Decades in English*? Did the church keep a
register as the vicar was required to do?[14] By slow and steady process
standards of practice and behaviour might be built up. By the same means
the Elizabethan bishops might hope to change the religious habits of the
Welsh people. What had begun as a violent change in the middle decades
of the sixteenth century gave way to slower and more gentle change
under Elizabeth.

Violent changes could produce violent reactions, and in Wales as in
England, there were those who were anxious to restore the old structure
and to keep the old habits. There were also those for whom the pace and
scale of reform were not radical enough. Wales was known to be a very

conservative part of the Tudor kingdom and there was some expectation, unfounded in fact, that the Welsh would rise against the overthrow of their faith. True, Wales produced some notable and influential Catholics. Morris Clynnog, elected bishop of Bangor at the end of Mary's reign but not consecrated, was a leading figure among the catholic exiles. He became warden of the English College established at Rome in 1578. Morgan Phillips, precentor of St. David's, and Owen Lewis were associated with William Allen as founders of the College at Douai. The hope that Wales might be won back prompted Morgan Phillips to produce his *Athravaeth Gristnogawl*, while Gruffydd Roberts, the Marian archdeacon of Anglesey, produced *Y Drych Cristionogawl*. The same hope prompted missionary priests under Jesuit influence and control to undertake the dangerous work of re-conversion in Wales as the reign of Elizabeth advanced.

It is a curious fact that, despite the bishops' animadversions, recusancy in Wales was recorded on only a small scale in the first decades of the reign, whether from lack of information or from a policy of acquiescence. A larger number of recusants was recorded towards the end of the sixteenth century. The majority were found near the English border. There was certainly a sharpening of the fear of hidden Catholics in the 1570s and 1580s, and there may well have been some hardening of old loyalties during this period. Local justices were on the alert and the chances that catholic families might practise their faith discreetly were decreasing. In 1603 there were only 32 recusants identified in Bangor; there were 145 in St. David's. St. Asaph had 250, and Llandaff the high figure of 381. The greatest concentration of catholic families was in Monmouthshire, with 336 names listed. The priests who ministered to them were the principal targets for Burghley and Walsingham and the administrators who, like Whitgift, governed Wales through the Council of the Marches. Few enjoyed a longer career than Walter Powell who was still active in 1604 and who had been 'a priest ordered in Queen Mary's days'. For more than thirty years he had 'been accounted a common massmonger.'[15] Many Catholics suffered hardship and lived in fear, and some were put to death for their activities. The first to be executed in Wales, in 1584, was Richard Gwyn of Llanidloes. William Davies was hanged in 1593 and John Jones of Clynnog was executed five years later. The story continued well into the seventeenth century.

The puritan reaction to the Elizabethan settlement was less marked in Wales than in England, and the outstanding men appear at the end of the sixteenth century and the beginning of the seventeenth. None is more important in his influence nor more intriguing for the problems his life presents than John Penry. He was born at Cefn Brith near Llangamarch, and as a young man he studied at both Cambridge and Oxford. He acquired advanced views for which he found little sympathy or support in Wales. He first came to prominence in 1587 and 1588 by addressing exhortations to Parliament. The first, *A Treatise containing the Aeqvity of a Humble Supplication*, was published in 1587, and this was followed in 1588 by *An Exhortation vnto the Gouernours and people of hir Maiesties countrie of Wales*. There were more to come in the few short years left to Penry, including his *Defence* published in 1588. He was a fervent opponent of those who had 'abandoned the Gospel', as he believed the queen and her advisers to have done in formulating their religious policy. The logic of his argument drove him outside the established Church, a lonely eminence where few Welshmen of his day would join him. The crucial issue, on which no firm agreement has yet been reached, is to determine what share he had in the production of a series of virulent attacks on episcopacy, the *Marprelate Tracts*. They were produced by the same secret press which published Penry's *Treatise*, *Exhortation*, and *Defence*. The government believed him to be the author and he was arrested, tried, and executed in 1593. Modern opinion holds that he played a leading part in producing the *Tracts* but that he was not himself the author.[16]

A man who was more influential in his own day, and whose posthumous reputation as a Puritan was very considerable, was Rhys Prichard, 'Yr Hen Ficer', vicar of Llandovery from 1602 until 1644. He was a Llandovery boy who had been educated locally, a phrase which has been taken to mean either Christ College, Brecon, or Queen Elizabeth Grammar School, Carmarthen. He went on to Jesus College, Oxford, and was ordained in 1602, the year of his appointment to Llandovery. In view of his subsequent practice, it would be particularly interesting to know what influences shaped his outlook. If his habits derived from his 'local' education they would imply a strong puritan tradition in Brecon or Carmarthen. He preached to large crowds, often in the open graveyard of his church. He encouraged a piety which was distinctively puritan in tone: he wanted people to read the Bible regularly, and he was a strong advocate of regular family devotions and of strict observance of Sunday worship. All this he did from within the establishment. Not only did he hold other livings in the diocese, but he was for some eighteen years chancellor of St. David's. He also composed and made use of Welsh religious songs, and in the second half of the seventeenth century these were published by Stephen Hughes in a collection called *Canwyll y Cymry*,

The Welshman's Candle. They ensured the continuation of his influence in puritan circles long after his memory had begun to fade in his native town.[17]

While Vicar Prichard was implementing puritan ideals through his ministry within the established Church, others were beginning to move away from its security and its restrictions. In Wales the process seems to have been slow and limited in scale, and, as elsewhere in the kingdom, it was marked by discipline for those clergy who went beyond the bounds of conformity and by repression of those who sought independence in gathered churches. Increasingly, the archbishop of Canterbury, and through him the king's government, were becoming well-informed about the state of the whole province. In his canons of 1603, Archbishop Bancroft issued regulations which looked back to the firm suppression of Puritans in the last years of Elizabeth's reign and looked forward to the 'thorough' administration of Laud. The activities of the Court of High Commission provided another check on what was happening locally. Whether it was the high-handed action of powerful secular figures, the undue leniency which Bishop Edmund Griffith of Bangor showed to well-born offenders, or the number of leases for terms of lives which the bishop of Bangor had issued, the archbishop of Canterbury wished to be kept informed. News of disaffected clergy or of gathered churches and conventicles could be included in the same reports. Laud made a determined attempt to control and suppress the means by which radical views could be expressed within the Church. The control of the pulpit was the critical issue, for good, informed preaching did much to mould men's opinions. The Stuarts, like Elizabeth, were anxious that sermons should be used as an instrument of propaganda to disseminate royal policy, and they were concerned that preaching should not be the means of spreading dangerous or nonconformist views. One device used by Puritans in order to secure a safe pulpit was to buy up impropriations and to install in a well-endowed church a capable preacher. Laud feared their success, and went far to circumvent them, but he approved their methods and made them his own. Another device was the use of endowed lectureships in parish churches. Those who were appointed might strengthen the establishment against catholic teachings and practice; that, certainly, was the purpose of establishing them in the diocese of St. Asaph. But lectureships could also be used to spread advanced doctrine, and the Puritans made good use of them for this purpose. In the 1620s and 1630s these lectureships were made subject to control designed to restrict the range of Christian teaching which might be covered. It was laid down that such lecturers must limit their preaching to matters arising from the Catechism, the Creed, the Lord's Prayer, and the Ten Commandments. As the official pressure increased, so the effectiveness of the lectureships declined, until by 1633 Laud could feel that he had brought this danger under control. The suspension of a lecturer in the diocese of St. David's in 1634 for 'inconformity' belongs clearly in this national pattern. He was probably Evan Roberts who was appointed in 1642 to preach in the parish of Llanbadarn Fawr after the monarchy and the established Church had been overthrown.

The man chiefly responsible for setting the anglican Church on so markedly an anti-puritan course, William Laud was for five years bishop of St. David's. He was consecrated in 1621 and translated, first to Bath and Wells in 1626, and then to London in 1628. When Archbishop Abbot died in 1633, Laud succeeded him as archbishop of Canterbury. In view of his reputation and the zeal with which he prosecuted his aims elsewhere, Laud left remarkably little impression on St. David's. At Oxford he was frequently at the centre of controversy. As a client of the duke of Buckingham he was involved in intrigue and rivalry, especially with John Williams, the cleric from north Wales with a sharp mind and flexible conscience who finally became archbishop of York. At Gloucester, when he became dean, Laud introduced his own arminian ideals at the cathedral, bringing strife and discord in his wake. The bishop, deeply wounded by Laud's policy, refused to set foot in his cathedral church again. Laud was essentially a partisan who needed a cause and an enemy. He flourished in a fight. James I knew his man well. 'He hath,' he said, 'a restless spirit and cannot see when matters are well but loves to toss and change and bring things to a pitch of reformation floating in his own brain.' Laud did not show much interest in St. David's, perhaps because he was fully occupied in the corridors of power, seeking influence with the duke of Buckingham and the future Charles I. He visited the diocese twice in the five years of his episcopate. A set of orders issued after a visitation in 1622 laid down the proper rites and ceremonies with which he expected services to be conducted in the cathedral.

The first stirrings of religious conflict in Wales occurred in the diocese of Llandaff. William Erbury, vicar of St. Mary's, Cardiff, and his curate, Walter Cradock, came under suspicion, and in 1634 Bishop Murray warned Erbury of his dangerous schismatical tendencies. In the following year Erbury was hauled before the Court of High Commission, and Cradock's licence was withdrawn. On this occasion they were associated with William Wroth, vicar of Llanfaches, an Oxford graduate who came under strong puritan influence and experienced a clear, if not a violent, conversion, probably in 1630. The three men had very different careers ahead of them. Erbury showed the same independence after he had left St. Mary's as he had displayed while he was vicar, and was often at odds with his fellow-puritans. He was no man's lackey, and refused simply to move from one orthodoxy to another. Wroth held the living at Llanfaches, but he was much influenced by Puritans from Bristol, and particularly by William Yeamans the rebellious vicar of St. Philip's, who was prominent for his rejection of the Prayer Book. Wroth gave much of his time in the 1630s to St. Philip's where he continued Yeaman's tradition. He had resigned Llanfaches by 1639 and, with Erbury, he began to build up a separatist church at Llanfaches. His wish was to die before he saw his country reduced to war, and apparently he was spared that sorrow, for he was dead by 1641. Cradock travelled north after being dismissed from St. Mary's and was instrumental in winning over two notable recruits. One was Vavasor Powell, the Radnorshire Puritan who was to play an important part in the religious life of Wales during the interregnum. The other was Morgan Llwyd of Trawsfynydd, Puritan and mystic. For a few years Cradock ministered at Wrexham where he began to build up a gathered church. In 1634 the bishop of St. Asaph could report that there was no problem of nonconformity in his diocese; his difficulties were still with those who maintained catholic practices. In 1640 he had to declare the existence of 'a conventicle of mean persons' at Wrexham. There are indications that Erbury, Wroth and Cradock did not work in isolation. The Baptist church at Olchon appeared about 1633 as a group of separatists in Radnorshire, Breconshire and Herefordshire looked for a safe refuge on one side or the other of the English border. In St. David's, too, there were similar stirrings. In 1636 the bishop reported two Puritans to the Court of High Commission. He had also to take action against Marmaduke Matthews, vicar of Penmaen, who was reported to him for preaching against the observance of holy days.

The first half of the seventeenth century was a period in which both anglican and nonconformist traditions were being defined in terms which would for long hold the field. In the established Church it was not Laud's fussiness, nor his efficiency, nor his love of power, nor his political influence which were of paramount importance. It was, rather, the creation of a Laudian, or as the next generation would term it, a 'Canterburian' view of anglicanism which mattered. It was high, efficient and intolerant, moving away from the careful moderation of the Elizabethan Church and reacting sharply from the puritan tendencies apparent both inside and out of the anglican Church. After passing through the crucible of civil war it survived to dominate the restoration of monarchy and Church in the reign of Charles II. In dissent, the search for independence under social and legal handicaps led to suffering and proscription which added to the political bitterness of the civil wars and the interregnum. Despite their hopes the dissenters were to find the restoration of Charles II the occasion of harsh intolerance and a crippling penal code, and the conflict between Anglican and Nonconformist remained a deep and bitter cleavage in Stuart society.

The civil wars and the interregnum were dark days for Welsh Anglicans. The middle years of the century were dominated by powerful laymen on the parliamentary side, men like Colonel Philip Jones, Bussy Mansel and George Twistleton, while Vavasor Powell and Walter Cradock exercised great influence over ecclesiastical affairs. After the death of Charles I anglican clergy paid the price of loyalty. In 1650 an Act for the Better Propagation and Preaching of the Gospel in Wales was passed which was intended to provide for the state of religion in Wales. Seventy-one commissioners were appointed under the direction of Major-General Harrison, twenty of them for north Wales and, with some overlap, forty-three for south Wales. Many Anglicans had either withdrawn or been removed from their livings before the Act. 278 were ejected under the Act. An allowance of one-fifth of the value of their living was to be paid to their dependants. To be effective such meagre provision required prompt and regular payment and that placed a great strain on both the generosity and the efficiency of parliamentary government. In Glamorgan, thirty-five clerics were ejected before the Act and twenty under the terms of the Act. In 1650 fifths were paid in twenty-nine cases, in 1651 only in six, and in 1652 in nine.[18] In other places, as in Cardiganshire, the authorities seem to have been more generous. There is surprisingly little information as to how the ejected clergy maintained themselves. Some, like Jeremy Taylor of Golden Grove, Hugh Lloyd, archdeacon of St. David's, the future bishop of Llandaff, Nathaniel Gamage of Eglwysilan, Hugh Gore of Oxwich, and Francis Davies of Llangan, another future bishop, turned to schoolmastering. William Thomas, canon of St.David's, had 'during the term of the Great Rebellion been sequestered for his loyalty and then taught school at Laugharn, where he sometimes read the Common Prayer and preached, but not without some disturbance from ye itinerant preacher.'[19] Lloyd retained a strong interest in education in later years and showed a genuine concern for the work of free schools in his diocese. The ejected clergy were replaced by men selected for their skill as preachers, but these were not as numerous as the parliamentarians would have wished. Sixty-three preachers were appointed in Wales and some of them were inadequate for the task. They were at first an itinerant ministry responsible, like many a pluralist before them, for a number of congregations. They merited the apt but cynical comment that 'the sinecure rector makes room for the fleeting preacher'. Walter Cradock and Vavasor Powell played a large part in their selection. The experiment met with very limited success even in the eyes of those responsible for its inception and in 1653 a second attempt was made to deal with the problem. A commission for the approbation of public preachers was set up. Gradually an itinerant ministry gave way to a settled ministry with men acceptable to the new régime intruded into Welsh livings. In Swansea, for example, Marmaduke Matthews, formerly vicar of Penmaen and puritan emigré, was appointed to St. John's-iuxta-Swansea. At Meifod, Stephen Lewis was intruded, and Walter Cradock was appointed to Usk and Llangwm. Evan Roberts settled at Llanbadarn Fawr which had previously served him as a base for an intinerant ministry. The process could be illustrated from many Welsh parishes. Many of the new men stayed in office until 1662 when the passing of the Act of Uniformity confronted them with a difficult choice. Some, like Matthews, refused to conform and were ejected in their turn. He continued his nonconformist ministry until his death in 1683, and had what must have been for him a doubtful privilege of seeing three sons comfortably settled in the ministry of the established Church. The ministers of the interregnum were not free from criticism. Alexander Griffith was a most virulent and persistent critic of Vavasor Powell. He held the living of Llanwnog in the diocese of Bangor and was vicar of Glasbury, and in due course he was ejected from his livings. For Powell as 'the metropolitan of the itinerants' he had an undying hatred which found its fullest expression in his pamphlet, *Strena Vavasoriensis*. One of his indictments of Powell and his associates was that so many churches were closed and their ministers forbidden to worship or preach in them while the people of Wales stood in urgent need of their ministrations. Vavasor Powell moved steadily to a more extreme position, becoming one of the leaders of a small group of Fifth Monarchy men. His political ideas found little support among Welshmen. It would be difficult to say whether the variety of religious groups ranging from the Presbyterians to the Quakers and Anabaptists was more confusing in Wales than it was in England. Certainly there were not the obvious centres where sectarianism could flourish and equally certainly the conservatism of Wales where religion was concerned worked against the new ideas, just as earlier it had worked against the reforming zeal of Barlow and Davies. Where the new ideas took root they produced enthusiasm and loyalty which could eventually stand the strain of proscription and persecution. During the interregnum the number of gathered churches in Wales increased very substantially and these provided the basis from which nonconformity would grow in the second half of the seventeenth century. For the rest, conservatism and inertia defeated the best efforts of Powell, Cradock and the other itinerant ministers to change the face of religion in Wales on a massive scale. The old order survived the new dawn.

[1]   Glanmor Williams has written a number of important essays on the Reformation in Wales, many of them collected in his *Welsh Reformation Essays* (Cardiff, 1967). The most recent study of the period is to be found in a volume which he has edited, *Glamorgan County History*, IV, *Early Modern Glamorgan* (Cardiff, 1974), which includes essays on the ecclesiastical history of the county by Glanmor Williams, Anthony M. Johnson, E. T. Davies, and Gomer Roberts. A. H. Dodd has contributed a great deal to our knowledge of this period. The essay on 'The Church in Wales in the Age of the Reformation' which he contributed to the *Handbook* of the Welsh Church Congress held in Swansea in 1953 deserves to be more widely known. T. Lawrence, *The Reformation in the old Diocese of Llandaff* (Cardiff, 1930) remains a valuable study. Modern studies of the Reformation in an English setting are dominated by the writing of G. R. Elton and A. G. Dickens.

[2]   These figures are taken from Glanmor Williams, *Welsh Church*, 283, 284, 558. See also *The Agrarian History of England and Wales*, *IV, 1500–1640* edited by Joan Thirsk, 382.

[3]   Recent local studies of particular areas include J. E. Oxley, *The Reformation in Essex* (Manchester, 1967), Margaret Bowker, *The Secular Clergy in the Diocese of Lincoln, 1495–1520* (Cambridge, 1968), and Christopher Haigh, *Reformation and Resistance in Tudor Lancashire* (Cambridge, 1975). A. G. Dickens has examined the Yorkshire material in depth, notably in his *Lollards and Protestants in the Diocese of York* (Oxford, 1959). Peter Heath's, *The English Parish Clergy on the Eve of the Reformation* (1969), is a major study.
      The comment on the Lancashire clergy comes from Haigh, *Lancashire*, 43.

[4]   Glanmor Williams, *Welsh Ref. Essays*, 40.

[5]   Glanmor Williams, *Welsh Church*, 408.

[6]   ib., 362, 363.

[7]   David Walker, 'Brecon Priory in the Middle Ages', *Links with the Past*, especiall 56–62.

[8]   Glanmor Williams, *Welsh Church*, 407.

[9]   Claire Cross, 'The Economic Problems of the See of York: Decline and Recovery in the Sixteenth Century', *Land Church and People*, ed. Joan Thirsk (British Agricultural History Society, 1970), 64–83. The range of problem discussed by Dr. Cross is examined at length by Christopher Hill in *Economic Problems of the Church from Archbishop Whitgift to the Long Parliament* (Oxford, 1956).

[10] Hill, *Ec. Problems*, 15.

[11] ib., 26; Glanmor Williams, in *Agrarian History of England and Wales*, *IV*, 381.

[12] Margaret Walker, 'Welsh Books in St. Mary's, Swansea, 1559–1626', *Bull. Board of Celtic Studies*, 23 (1970), 397–402.

[13] The letter is often printed in whole or in part. See, for example, the texts in W. Hughes, *Bangor* (1911), 82–3; David Mathew, 'Some Elizabethan Documents', *B.B.C.S.*, 6, (1931–33), 77–8; Glanmor Williams, *Welsh Ref. Essays*, 55.

[14] Margaret Walker, 'Church Life in Sixteenth-century Swansea', *Links with the Past*, 89–116 and especially 104–107.

[15] *Glamorgan County History*, IV, 232.

[16] See John Penry, *Three Treatises concerning Wales*, ed. David Williams (Cardiff, 1960); D. J. McGinn, *John Penry and the Marprelate Controversy* (Rutgers, 1966). For an assessment of the present state of the debate, Glanmor Williams, 'John Penry: Marprelate and Patriot', *W.H.R.*, 3 (1967), 361–80.

[17] See R. Tudur Jones, below p. 83.

[18] A. M. Johnson, 'Politics and Religion in Glamorgan during the Interregnum, 1649–1660', *Glamorgan County History*, IV, 286. See also C. Hill, 'Puritans and 'the Dark Corners of the Land' ', *Trans. R. Hist. S.*, 5th series, 13 (1963), 77–102, for a general discussion of these questions.

[19] A. I. Pryce, *The Diocese of Bangor during Three Centuries* (Cardiff, 1929), xxvii.

CHAPTER 4

RELATIONS BETWEEN ANGLICANS AND
DISSENTERS:
THE PROMOTION OF PIETY, 1670-1730

by

R. Tudur Jones

IT is still tempting to think of the various religious parties of the seventeenth century as though they were Victorian denominations poised for
militant action. It seems so easy to divide them into two entrenched
armies facing each other. On the one hand we have the Anglicans forming
a solid and united body of soldiers, all dressed in the same uniform. On
the other hand, we have the puritan allies, wearing a variety of uniforms,
and led by a motley collection of generals, but united in their implacable
opposition to their religious enemies. The tide of war ebbs and flows
across the no-man's-land dividing them. In the 1630s, under the command
of William Laud, the anglican forces over-run the puritan trenches. In
the 1640s the Puritans counter-attack, having secured (rather unfairly,
their opponents would claim), the services of a real live general, Oliver
Cromwell. But his success was of no long duration. In 1660 came the
massive counter-attack of the Restoration, followed up by a long war of
attrition which culminated in the stalemate of the Toleration Act, with
both sides agreeing to abandon warfare in favour of a policy of religious
apartheid.

Such a portrayal of seventeenth-century religious history has an
obvious dramatic advantage, but it hardly does justice to the fascinating
complexity of events. Denominations in the nineteenth-century sense
did not exist in the seventeenth century. The Congregationalists had no
head office or central organisation. And that goes for the Baptists also.
Presbyterian dreams of government by a hierarchy of councils, extending
from the local congregation to a national general assembly, had evapor-
ated even before the Restoration. And the Quakers were not enamoured
of centralism, however close the personal ties between their leaders might

be. Amidst such variety, it would be surprising indeed if the Nonconformists should act and think in precisely the same way everywhere and
at all times. At first glance, the Church of England has all the appearances
of being a tightly organised body, rather like the denominations of a
later age, even in the seventeenth century. But that is not so. Anglican
history in that century is as much the story of conflicts and upheavals
within as it is the story of contentions with critics outside. Despite its
episcopal organisation, its canon law, its subjection to definition by the
law of the land, and its commitment to uniformity by means of the Book
of Common Prayer, it must be seen against the background of the seventeenth century. Large allowance must be made for the characteristics of
the age. As an institution that was specifically intended to embrace the
whole population, it could not but include amongst its communicants and
clergy a wide variety of people and views. Strict uniformity might be
defined by Parliament, but its achievement was frustrated by all kinds of
influences. The means of verbal and personal communication which are
available to a twentieth-century organisation were not available then.
The administration of law and the support of public order was far more
personal and idiosyncratic than in a society where these activities are the
responsibility of professionally trained full-time officials. Bishops varied
considerably in conviction, policy and efficiency. And anglican laymen,
whether in their role as moulders of local opinion or as magistrates, could
speak with a very different accent from that of their church leaders.
Whatever may be said of the Church in Wales in the seventeenth century,
it was not a monolithic organisation. And, as a result of all this, we come
across surprising examples of fraternisation across the frontier dividing
Anglican from Puritan—as well as vigorous and sometimes vicious
sorties.

For Nonconformists the years immediately succeeding the Restoration were difficult ones. The ministers who were ejected between 1660
and 1662 had to come to terms with the precarious existence of men who,
unless they had private resources, were faced with real hardship. Those
people who wished to avail themselves of their ministry knew, after the
passing of the First Conventicle Act, that they were liable to sharp
punishment in the courts if they were discovered worshipping illegally.
And the supreme penalty embodied in that Act was transportation.
Although William Roberts of Bangor was the only bishop who had been
elected in the age of William Laud, the episcopal bench in the post-
Restoration period was in warm sympathy with the ideal of churchmanship that had been so close to the heart of Laud. And they were happy to

implement the ecclesiastical policies of the restored Church. Men of this stamp were committed to the policy of uprooting nonconformity. They had at their disposal the machinery of the church courts. It is true that by this time that machinery was creaking ominously. The court officials were diligent enough. They listed disobedient communicants and Non-conformists in the various parishes. They went through the necessary legal motions that ended in the excommunications of the offenders. And sometimes the list of excommunicated persons would be sent down to the offenders' incumbent to be nailed up on the door of the parish church. And that was that. Very rarely did actions in the church courts lead to public punishment, as in the case of Thomas Gwyn of Pantycored, who in 1685 had to submit to the consistory court at Brecon and do public penance.

Since excommunication could hardly mean anything by way of punishment to people who did not wish to attend the parish services in any case, can it be assumed that the proceedings of the consistory court were subjects for levity amongst Nonconformists? Certainly not. As we study the surviving Act Books of the consistory courts, we notice that the cases which did not result in any public punishment far outnumber those that did. But Nonconformists could not know beforehand that the courts had largely lost the energy, if not the will, to seek the support of the secular arm to chastise the guilty. Richard Pugh, the miller of Tredwstan in Breconshire, in one of his ballads sings about the consistory court 'proclaiming the great wayward excommunication, many a time without knowing why. What injury!' And then he goes on, 'After excommuni-cation, the writ comes roaring forth into the sheriff's hand; and brutally he chases the innocent and when he lays them by the heels; off they go to ail to suffer cruelly for long days.' The poetry is not elegant but his legal knowledge was accurate enough. The church courts could not punish without authority from the court of Chancery or the court of Great Sessions and to get the necessary writs was a tiresome business fraught with not a few legal pitfalls. But for Nonconformists the possibility that the secular power might be invoked was a constant and disconcerting threat. And when the writs did come, they spelled suffering for those found guilty. And, in any case, the surviving evidence shows clearly that local magistrates' courts were ready enough to bring Nonconformists to book and to punish them sharply for infringements of the penal code. Tension was increased by the vacillations in official attitudes. In 1665, Bishop Hugh Lloyd and Archdeacon Francis Davies of Llandaff sought by persuasion to make a conformist of the distinguished Samuel Jones

(1628-97) of Brynllywarch, sometime fellow of Jesus College, Oxford. His judicious questions in reply to their overtures are to be found in the pages of Edmund Calamy's *Account*. But Jones did not receive satisfactory answers. And when Davies himself became bishop in 1667, he suffered imprisonment for his nonconformity.

Then again attitudes could vary even amongst churchmen. Stephen Hughes (1622-88), the foremost pioneer of congregationalism in Carmarthenshire, was under constant surveillance by the consistory court and was excommunicated more than once. Even so, according to Calamy, 'His Moderation and lively Preaching, recommended him to the Esteem of the sober Part of the Gentry, by whose Connivance, he often preach'd in the publick Churches . . .', that is to say, in the parish churches. And personal influence could go even further. Henry Maurice (1634-82) was to Breconshire Congregationalists what Stephen Hughes was to those of neighbouring Carmarthenshire. He was once arrested and brought before a court, but, says Calamy, he 'was discharg'd by the Favour of some Gentlemen, who were Justices of the Peace, and his Friends and Relations.' Maurice was indeed a matter of concern to the bishop, William Lucy, who complained that he preached illegally near Brecon, 'not att all checked or disturbed by the Justices of the peace.' Obviously the co-operation between clergy and gentry, upon which the maintenance of good order depended, often broke down. But then, Stephen Hughes was the son of a Carmarthen silk merchant who had been mayor of the town and Henry Maurice was a scion of the Methlan family in Caernarfonshire and linked by blood and marriage to many of the leading families of Gwynedd. Not all Nonconformists could hope to hide behind their relations in the day of distress. And even ties of blood were not infallible insurances against molestation. They could sometimes exacerbate religious animosity.

Nonconformists knew the risks they were taking by preaching and worshipping in contravention of the laws. And many of them knew the unhappiness of having to pay fines and spend long spells in prison. On the other hand, the conformists knew the risks they would be taking if they encouraged dissent in any way. The cavaliers were haunted by the possibility of another puritan rebellion and it was a simple matter for critics to represent kindness towards individual Nonconformists as sympathy with potential rebels.

And, inevitably, there were bitter feelings. If Nonconformists had cause to complain after the ejections that followed the Restoration, so Anglicans could look further back to those dark days when they had been ejected from their livings under the provisions of the Propagation Act. On both sides there were good reasons for recrimination. On both sides there were dedicated men who were prepared to pay the highest price for their convictions. All this needs to be recalled because it adds considerably to the interest and excitement of the co-operation between Anglican and Dissenter in the 1670s.

Round about 1670 a subtle change was occurring in the political and religious world. The Second Conventicle Act of 1669 was intended to be a more efficient instrument for the repression of nonconformity than the first precisely because it was less ferocious and therefore more likely to be applied by hesitant magistrates. But in addition fear of a new puritan rebellion was yielding before a greater fear of militant Roman Catholicism —a fear that was to culminate towards the end of the decade in the hysteria of the Popish Plot. It was in this new atmosphere that a remarkable experiment in religious co-operation took place.

Stephen Hughes is best known as the editor of Vicar Rhys Prichard's poetry. This in itself is worthy of comment. Prichard (1579?-1644) became vicar of Llandovery in 1602, was a protegé of William Laud's, and became chancellor of St. David's in 1626. Yet, it was the Puritan Stephen Hughes who published his manuscript poems. The first part appeared in 1659 and the task was completed with the collected edition of the poems, *Canwyll y Cymry*, in 1681. To the 1672 edition of the vicar's work, *Gwaith Mr. Rees Prichard* (1672), Hughes prefixed a letter to 'some responsible ministers in Wales'. Amongst the men to whom he was indebted he mentioned William Thomas, and it was to him that the book was dedicated. William Thomas (1613-89), although born in Bristol, had been educated at Carmarthen. After a distinguished career as an academic and churchman, he became dean of Worcester in 1665 and two years later bishop of St. David's. In 1683 he returned to Worcester to be its bishop. He was a gentle as well as a learned man and a bishop of rare quality. This comes out in his practical concern for the spiritual welfare of Wales. Hughes dedicated the 1672 book to him, he says, because, if any good had come of a previous volume that he had published in 1670, 'all Wales is indebted for that to you, the Reverend Dr. Thomas; because it was the good testimony that you gave here, in London, under your own hand, on behalf of the author and his first two books, that secured him permission to print the Third.' And it was the continued patronage of William Thomas that enabled Hughes to publish his 1672 edition of the New Testament as well as his book *Catechism Mr. Perkins*.

It is obvious that Stephen Hughes, while remaining faithful to his distinctive convictions about the nature of the Church of Christ, was eager to grasp at every opportunity to enrich the spiritual life of his countrymen and to co-operate with all men of good will in doing that. We have already seen that he was glad to avail himself of opportunities to preach in parish churches when invited to do so. Whatever differences of view there might be amongst ministers of the various religious parties, the first priority for Hughes was the preaching of the Gospel and the enrichment of the spiritual life. He writes, in his second address 'To the Reader' in *Cyfarwydd-deb i'r Anghyfarwydd* (1677) that there were, 'amongst Conformists and Nonconformists', ministers who were 'as learned, as able, as pious, as careful of Christ's sheep committed to their care, as in any place in Christendom.' Then he adds,

And God forbid that I should utter one word against their Holy Calling, or against their Persons, or make any kind of suggestion that might provoke people to find fault with such reverend ministers as are faithful to God, in accordance with their knowledge, their vocation and station, whatever may be their judgment on matters of detail that are in dispute.

This sentence breathes that conciliatoriness and tolerance which are so characteristic of Hughes and which make him one of the most winsome personalities of that age. It is not surprising that Bishop William Thomas should have found himself in close sympathy with Stephen Hughes's aspirations.

Hughes was not alone in his concern for producing 'good books' in Welsh. Charles Edwards, who was born in 1628 and died on an unknown date after 1691, had already embarked on this kind of work with the publication of the first edition of *Y Fydd Ddi-ffuant* (1667) — 'The Unfeigned Faith', as the English subtitle of the much enlarged edition of 1677 translates it. Edwards's life was a melancholy one, punctuated by personal and family troubles that drove him almost to distraction as is evident from his autobiography, *An Afflicted Man's Testimony concerning his Troubles* (1691). After a brief period as an itinerant preacher under the Propagation Act, he was appointed to the sinecure living of Llanrhaeadr-ym-Mochnant in 1653 and held it until 1659. Strictly speaking, he was not one of the ejected ministers of the Restoration but he was usually considered as one of them and late on in life, in 1691, he accepted a grant — somewhat hesitantly — from the Common Fund set up by the Congregationalists and Presbyterians to relieve distressed ministers. The details of his life after 1659 are shrouded in obscurity but it is clear that his nonconformity was of a moderate kind and that he took considerable pains not to offend the church authorities. He did however take advantage of the provisions of the Declaration of Indulgence in 1672 and took out a general licence as a presbyterian teacher at Oswestry. He says in his *Testimony* that he attended services at his parish church and but rarely joined 'in private Worship with any greater number than the Law allows of'— an allusion to the definition of an illegal congregation in the Conventicle Acts. He states his attitude clearly when he says in his *Testimony* 'My Disposition was Moderate also towards the established Ecclesiastical Government, acknowledging its usefulness in exhibiting the Scriptures and Prayers to these Nations in their vulgar Tongues.' This brings out the concern of the whole group with whom we are now dealing. They were anxious to have godly books published and they were no less anxious to have them published in Welsh. The Church of England earned their respect, as Edwards intimates, because it had adopted what would nowadays be called a bilingual policy. No doubt it was his desire to maintain the sympathy of church leaders in this matter that explains why Edwards is so tantalisingly silent about puritanism in the outline history of Christianity in Wales which he included in *Y Ffydd Ddi-ffuant*. After all, it was Dr. Michael Roberts, his old principal at Jesus College, Oxford, who read the manuscript of the book on behalf of the publishers and certified to the university authorities that it was suitable for printing at their press since it contained nothing obnoxious to the teachings of the Church of England. It would not have been granted a certificate if it had contained a laudatory treatment of puritanism.

In 1671 Edwards published *Dad-seiniad Meibion y Daran*. It contains a scholarly reprint of *Deffynniad Ffydd Eglwys Loegr*, Morris Kyffin's translation (published in 1595) of Bishop John Jewel's *Apology*. This classic of anglican apologetics was a steady favourite amongst moderate Nonconformists who approved of its Calvinistic tone. Thus Thomas Charles of Bala issued a reprint of it in 1803. Not less significant is it that *Dad-seiniad Meibion y Daran* also contains the 'Epistle' which Bishop Richard Davies prefixed to the 1567 translation of the New Testament. Edwards published this book, he says, because 'so many of the few books that are available in Welsh have all but disappeared because no new editions have appeared.' To help fill the gap, then, he published this volume in 1671 as well as a second edition of *Y Ffydd Ddi-ffuant*. Edwards's enthusiasm for evangelisation by the printed word and his faith in its efficacy is clearly manifested in his account of the growth of protestantism in Wales. He gives a full account of the translations of the

Bible and of the books published in Welsh. 'It pleased God to multiply aids to faith amongst us, and so the number of those who rightly used them increased. After He had given our country the light of the Gospel, many consciences were aroused. . . And so, not in vain did He light his lamps, since so many have worked out their salvation in their radiance.' He shows how the Church had already made a notable contribution by its production of good books, and his own labours are a testimony to his eagerness to see that contribution maintained. This, then, is the moderate position amongst Nonconformists. There is nothing approaching the indiscriminate condemnation that one finds amongst early separatists such as Henry Barrowe, or for that matter amongst nineteenth-century Nonconformists after the disestablishment campaign had got under way. Edwards is intensely appreciative of the anglican achievement in promoting piety and knowledge of the Christian faith. And there is no reason to suppose that Stephen Hughes would disagree with him. Nor will it do to dismiss these men as trimmers who spoke soothing words in order to get their names into print. That is to misunderstand completely their devotion to the evangelistic task as they understood it and their deep love — very movingly expressed by Charles Edwards — of that body of Christian tradition and wisdom enshrined in the Welsh language.

So Stephen Hughes and Charles Edwards had begun, quite independently, to produce 'good books' in Welsh. By 1674 they had joined forces with the London philanthropist, Thomas Gouge. Gouge (1609-81) had been ejected from St. Sepulchre's, London, in 1662. After reading of Joseph Alleine's unfulfilled hopes of evangelising in Wales, he began to visit the country himself in 1672. His main interest at that time was the promotion of education, but Stephen Hughes sharply disapproved of his policy of providing English schools for Welsh children. Hughes was not the man to allow the Welsh language to be set aside in the name of the Gospel. And so Gouge was soon made to realise that there was a crying need for books in Welsh. Gouge took the hint and bought up copies of the Welsh translation of The Whole Duty of Man for distribution. The Welsh version was the work of John Langford (1650?-1715/16?) who held livings in Denbighshire. The book was translated a second time by Edward Samuel (1674-1748) and became something of a best-seller after it had been issued in 1718 under the imprint of the S.P.C.K.

By 1674 Gouge had formed the Welsh Trust. It was a remarkable manifestation of co-operation between the 'men of latitude' in the Church of England and the moderate Nonconformists. The document defining the aims of the trust shows what Gouge and his associates had in mind.

The money contributed to the fund was to be used, first of all, to buy and distribute freely amongst poor people copies of *The Practice of Piety*, the Church Catechism, 'as also some thousands of other Licenced *Welch* Books'. Then, in the second place, it was to be used 'to raise and maintain several Schools for teaching the poorest of *Welch* children to read *English*, and then the boys to write and cast accompts; whereby they will be anabl'd to read our *English* Bibles, and Treatises, to be more serviceable to their Country, and to live more comfortably in the world.' Needless to say, Stephen Hughes was no party to this document. In fact there was no Welsh signatory to it. This is not to say that the signatories were not a fascinating group. The first name is that of John Tillotson, dean of Canterbury at the time, and later archbishop. The names of Benjamin Whichcote and Edward Stillingfleet also appear. And these were the distinguished protagonists of 'accommodation'. Simon Patrick, later bishop of Ely, and Simon Ford, later bishop of Gloucester, also appended their names. On the nonconformist side, we have Richard Baxter, who never gave up hope of bringing divided Christians together in a united church, William Bates and the biblical commentator Mathew Poole. The treasurer of the trust was the Socinian, Thomas Firmin, girdler and mercer in Lombard Street, London, and a generous philanthropist.

Gouge himself was the link between this group and the workers in Wales. Much as Stephen Hughes disapproved of Gouge's anglicising educational policy, he was not averse to channelling the generosity of the fund into the production and distribution of Welsh books. Sometime between 1673 and 1675 Charles Edwards moved to London where, according to his *Testimony*, 'I was busie about the Printing of *Welch* Books', supervising their progress through the press. The first book which he edited was *Yr Ymarfer o Dduwioldeb*, which was ready by November 1675. This was a translation of *The Practice of Piety*, the work that had pride of place in the stated programme of the Welsh Trust. Its author was Lewis Bayly, bishop of Bangor from 1616 until his death in 1631. Edwards now reviewed and corrected the previous Welsh translation which was the work of Rowland Fychan (Vaughan), the cavalier squire of Caer-gai, Merioneth. Here again we have an example of the way in which the desire to promote godliness linked conformist and nonconformist, cavalier and puritan. During the years 1675 and 1676 Gouge, Edwards and Hughes co-operated to bring out other translations. They were assisted in the enterprise by William Jones (died 1679), the puritan minister of Denbigh and brother-in-law to Dr. David Maurice, vicar of Llanasa, who also preached his funeral sermon. Another colleague was Richard Jones (1603?-73), an Oxford graduate and puritan schoolmaster at Denbigh until his expulsion at the Restoration. This group devoted itself to preparing translations of English books, mainly by Thomas Gouge and Richard Baxter. Richard Jones, however, had died before seeing his translations of Gouge's *Christian Directions* (*Hyfforddiadau Christianogol*) and Baxter's *Now or Never* (*Bellach neu Byth*) in print. Then in 1677-8 appeared a new issue of the Bible, including the Apocrypha, the Book of Common Prayer and the metrical Psalms of Archdeacon Edmwnd Prys (1544-1623). The man who was chiefly responsible was Stephen Hughes and there is strong reason for suspecting that 'the Welshman expert in his native tongue' who assisted him was Charles Edwards — and it is noteworthy that this edition of the Book of Common Prayer was produced by two men who had been licensed as nonconformist preachers under the terms of the 1672 Declaration of Indulgence!

Not all Anglicans were happy about the activities of Thomas Gouge and his friends. Bishop Humphrey Lloyd (1610-88/9) of Bangor wrote an excited letter to Archbishop Gilbert Sheldon, August 10th, 1676, expressing considerable alarm,

> I find that he is an itinerant emissarie entrusted by the leading sectaries, to insinuat into the affections of the credulous common people (he adventures alsoe, heere and there, vpon the weaker Gentrie) and covertly to draw them into a disaffection to the Government and liturgie of the Church. . .

He procures 'from godly and piously disposed persons summes of money', continues the bishop, which are then spent, first of all, to support schools and 'he drop's heer and there, to litle Scholemasters and scholmistresses fortie shillings in a place.' 'Secondly he carrie's vp and downe a great number of English and welsh bookes, which he partly sells, partly give's. . .' But more serious than these activities is the third, 'the great and principall pretence of his peregrination, is the collecting of subscriptions for mony towards the reprinting of the Bible in Welsh. . .' Lloyd is thoroughly perplexed by Gouge's appeals for money and begs guidance, 'I very humbly request your Grace will please to give me your good advice and direction, how farr I may complie therwith. He saieth, that he hath alreadie subscriptions for 1000 *li* and that 1400 *li* will be sufficient. . .' Obviously Bishop Lloyd was not aware of all the facts. Gouge 'an emissarie' of 'the leading sectaries'? Was this an adequate description of John Tillotson? The archbishop knew better. He advised circumspection. He was aware of the plan and Bishop Lloyd must be on his guard: 'considering the nature of the design it must receive no open discouragment from us.' He wished he could stop it. But how? Gouge was doubtless too crafty to fall foul of the law and there was no court that would take cognizance of an extraordinary case of 'sectaries' collecting money to print Bibles. But he does not inform the bishop that the 'sectaries' were working hand in glove with some very distinguished figures in the Church. Better, therefore, to leave Gouge well alone.

The activities that stemmed from the alliance between conformists and nonconformists under Thomas Gouge's banner had a two-fold significance. The English patrons of the Welsh Trust represent that latitudinarian tendency which was to become yet more influential in the eighteenth century. In due course it would be openly contemptuous of enthusiasm. Already it was showing signs of impatience with the passion-ate commitment to theological and ecclesiastical distinctions which had so occupied the minds of the men of the seventeenth century. It favoured lucidity rather than prolixity in preaching, rationality rather than passion in argument, decorum rather than unction in worship. But this can hardly be said of a man like Stephen Hughes who rarely preached without shedding tears. Nor can it be said of Charles Edwards whose elegant prose expresses rather than conceals profound emotion. Surely, what we have at the Welsh end of the movement is the emergence of a Welsh form of pietism—concurrent with the better-known movement in Germany—and a pietism nurtured at its root by the godly tradition which was to be found in the anglican Church and in the puritan sects. The emphasis on Bible-reading, the promotion of godliness by means of devotional reading, the belief in the value of education, are all characteristics of pietism. And in addition, so far as Nonconformists were concerned, the years of persecution had compelled them to make lavish use of cottage-meetings and informal gatherings of intimate neighbours. All this was not to be forgotten. It was from this type of concentration on the spiritual life and upon informal worship that the 'religious societies' were eventually to emerge, not least amongst Anglicans, and it was these, in turn, that provided the pattern for the methodist 'societies'. And so, if Thomas Gouge's activities are a reflection on the one hand of latitudinarian tendencies, on the other they patronised the pietistic concerns which would eventually nurture the enthusiasm which the spiritual heirs of Tillotson and Whichcote would find so distasteful in the following century.

But in the early 1680s the mood changed and a new and more enigmatic chapter opens in the story of the relationship between Anglicans and Nonconformists. William Lloyd (1627-1717) was a man of impeccable Welsh ancestry and a member of a family that produced an uncommon number of clerics. He became archdeacon of Merioneth in 1668, dean of Bangor in 1672 and bishop of St. Asaph in 1680. He was firmly opposed to Roman Catholicism but equally firm in resisting the claims of Nonconformists. As a bishop he was conscientious and efficient. He was a learned scholar, although he was not above being beguiled by the obscurer allusions of the prophecy of Daniel and the book of Revelation. But, all in all, a striking man. (And he must not be confused with the other William Lloyd (1637-1710), bishop of Llandaff, 1675-9, Peterborough, 1679-85, and Norwich, 1685-9. He refused to swear allegiance to William III after the Revolution and became the acknowledged leader of the non-jurors).

William Lloyd took up residence at St. Asaph in April 1681. Before the end of the year he had begun to arrange meetings with the Nonconformists in his diocese. During his first visitation, he asked the Quaker leaders, Richard Davies of Cloddiau Cochion (1635-1708), Charles Lloyd (1637-98) and his brother Thomas (1640-94), both of Dolobran, to meet him at Welshpool. Davies was unable to be present, but the bishop spent a whole day in discussion with the Lloyd brothers. They decided to hold a more public meeting at Llanfyllin on September 22nd, 1681. It was a meeting to remember with a distinguished audience present and the bishop supported by Henry Dodwell and Humphrey Humphreys (1648-1712), the new dean of Bangor. The debate lasted for two days and made a distinct impression upon Lloyd's mind. A warm personal friendship developed between the bishop and Richard Davies, the Quaker. Soon afterwards a writ *de excommunicato capiendo* was issued to apprehend Davies and other Nonconformists. Before going to prison Davies insisted on seeing William Lloyd. Davies had just returned from London and had in his pocket a letter (obtained through the good offices of William Penn) from Lord Clarendon to the bishop, asking for mercy. The bishop gave him a generous welcome and the conversation went on far into the night and dealt principally with baptism and ordination. Not only so, but it went on for the best part of the two following days. Neither yielded his position, but Richard Davies teased the bishop before leaving, 'Bishop Lloyd, if I go to prison upon this account I shall have more peace there than thou shalt have in thy palace.' And of course, it needs to be pointed out that to say *thou* to a bishop in 1681 would be as much of a discourtesy as it would be for a stranger to say *ti* to a Welsh-speaking bishop today! But there is no reason to believe that William Lloyd was offended. Now, in order to flavour the piquancy of another part of their conversation, it needs to be said that William Lloyd was one of the famous seven bishops that were brought to trial for refusing to read publicly James II's Declaration of Indulgence. Richard Davies asked him, 'Suppose another prince should arise that would impose something upon thee that thou couldest not do for conscience sake, what wouldest thou do?' The bishop's answer suggests that he had not lost that humour for which he had become well-known during his student days. 'Then,' he replied, 'I will go to Pennsylvania also.' Richard Davies himself did not emigrate, but his friend Thomas Lloyd left for Pennsylvania just two years later and became one of the most respected citizens of the colony. It says something of the nature of the personal relationship between Richard Davies and William Lloyd that their long conversation produced an immediate result. The bishop called for pen and paper and wrote a note to his chancellor, 'I desire you for the present to suspend the serving of the Writ upon Davies the ranter of Poole.'

There we have the bishop facing the extremists among Nonconformists. On September 26th, 1681 he confronted the moderates amongst them at Oswestry. Ordination was the subject for debate this time. The bishop called upon the Nonconformists to explain why they claimed to be ministers when they had not been ordained by a bishop. Debate was to commence at two o'clock in the afternoon and a large crowd gathered to listen. It went on until half past seven in the evening. The bishop was again assisted by Dodwell and Humphreys. His opponents were James Owen (1654-1706), Philip Henry (1631-96) and Jonathan Roberts (died 1664), all Presbyterians. Matthew Henry, the distinguished biblical expositor and son of Philip, testified in his father's biography that the bishop conducted the argument with calm dignity. But it was drawn to an undignified close through no fault of the bishop's. Jonathan Roberts whispered in Philip Henry's ear that it would be courteous to allow the bishop to have the last word. A foolish magistrate overheard the remark and shouted, 'you say my Lord shall have the last word; but he shall not for I will; we thank God we have the sword of power in our hands, and by the Grace of God, I will root you out of the country.' Another member of the audience rejoined with, 'Amen, throw them down stairs.' The bishop listened in silence to all this but the mayor took the Nonconformists to safety. Philip Henry made a more favourable impression upon the bishop than his assistants for in a couple of days Lloyd wrote to him, 'I was much pleased with the good temper I found in you at the conference at Oswestry, and sorry to find so little of it in those to whom you had joined yourself.' He goes on to say that he did not think it worthwhile to continue the discussion with men 'that contend, not for truth, but only for victory.' It would be interesting to know more about the bishop's reaction at this point. Had he perhaps been somewhat irked by the scholarly James Owen on this matter of ordination? Owen was not an easy man to conquer on that topic. However a friendship developed between the bishop and Henry and he wrote to him later to say that 'he did not look upon him as Schismatic, but only as a Separatist, and, if he were in his diocese, he did not question but he should find out some way to make him useful.' The bishop was anxious to have further conferences with both Quakers and Presbyterians but it is not known for certain whether the meetings were held as arranged.

Meanwhile, the scene changes to Wrexham. The leader of the Nonconformists there was John Evans (1628-1700). The bishop prepared the way for further conversation by having a private chat with Evans in August 1681. Then in December, when he was visiting Wrexham, William Lloyd took advantage of the opportunity to meet the Nonconformists face to face. He told Archbishop Sancroft about it in a letter dated December 21st, 1681,

> I conferd with divers of the Conventiclers in private, & had 2 public Conferences with them all-together ... where before a hundred other persons each time, I heard & answerd all they had to say for their separation; & as I am sure all others were fully satisfied, so I believ there was not one of the Conventiclers but was convinced they had not one Text of Scripture on their side... They were every face that I saw of them so extremely cast down, that I know they were ashamed of their Cause...

But he had to admit in a later letter, November 24th, 1682, that he was as far as ever from convincing these Nonconformists of the error of their ways,

> I am very much troubled (he confided to Sancroft) for the poor Souls at Wrexham in my Diocese. They were horribly poisoned by one Vavasor Powell in the late wretched times. The widow of Vavasor married one Evans who succeeds the other in his principles. This man (I may adde, & this woman) keep a conventicle still at Brynyffynon a house that they rent of mr. Williams the late Speaker...

The 'late Speaker' was William Williams (1634-1700), a notoriously mobile political weathercock, who was to gain a bad name in 1688 as the prosecutor of William Lloyd and the six other bishops. To return to the Wrexham Nonconformists. John Evans was obviously not a man to be trifled with and amicable conversations were not likely to make a conformist of him. And the bishop realised this. In the same letter, November 24th, he tells Sancroft that he has set the legal process in motion to apprehend Evans but complains bitterly of the dilatoriness of the law officers.

William Lloyd's readiness to engage in conversations had made a very favourable impression upon his nonconformist opponents. Charles Owen, James Owen's brother and biographer, says of him, 'That excellent and learned Prelate, being a declared Enemy to Persecution, studied to reduce the Dissenters in his Diocess, by mild and Christian Methods. . .' And again he says, 'In his pious Clemency towards the Dissenters he was singular, and had no Rivals nor Imitator. . .' Matthew Henry is slightly more guarded when he says that when Lloyd decided to put pressure on Nonconformists, 'he resolved, before he took any other methods, to reason the matter with them, and to endeavour their conviction by discourse.' But even so the bishop did create a favourable impression. What is puzzling is Charles Owen's statement that Lloyd was 'a declared Enemy to Persecution'. It seems clear from Lloyd's letters to Sancroft that he had no doubt whatsoever about the need to apply the laws against Nonconformists. And his conversations are to be understood in the context of this conviction. He would prefer to persuade them into conformity but if they were stubborn, then they must face the consequences. His letter of July 17th, 1683 to Commissary John Edwards is certainly a ferocious one,

> Let Owen the preacher (James Owen) and all the rest at Oswestry that were formerly decreed be now published, and in short every protestant-dissenter (as those bloody wretches are pleased to call themselves) that is decreed and not published . . . And get the Sheriffs to do their duties. For 'tis visible that all this while we have been treating with these Sectaries, it has been God's wonderful providence that when they mustered in their conventicles they had not come out to cut our throats. . .

As Dr.Tindal Hart says in his biography, *William Lloyd* (London, 1952), of this letter and others of the same period, 'These are certainly the letters of a very frightened man.' The reason for his fright was the discovery of the Rye House Plot to kill Charles II and his brother. When he heard of 'a most wicked and dangerous Conspiracy of Atheists and Fanatics', he wrote a letter for distribution amongst his clergy calling everyone to join in the search for the conspirators. The letter was dated July 17th, 1683. Dr. Tindal Hart has argued that there was a complete change of attitude on the part of the bishop towards Nonconformists as a result of this crisis. 'In 1683, however, Lloyd found himself compelled to sing a very different song', he says. His tone is certainly more strident. But his basic position does not seem to have changed. His readiness to talk amicably with Dissenters was certainly a new and welcome element. But, unless one assumes (as Dr. Hart tends to do) that Lloyd was throwing dust in the eyes of the archbishop with his rough talk in his letters about repressing nonconformity, one must concede that his belief that compulsion was necessary is common to his letters before and after the summer of 1683.

But the story does not end there. Fear of catholicism drove Anglicans and protestant Nonconformists closer together. There were men of influence in the Church of England who sincerely wished to win over the Dissenters. The foremost of them, perhaps, was Henry Compton, bishop of London. His views were echoed by others such as Thomas Tenison, Gilbert Burnet, John Sharp, John Tillotson and Edward Stillingfleet—some of whom we have already mentioned. When James II sought to compel the bishops to proclaim his Declaration of Indulgence from the pulpits of the parish churches, the outstanding rebel in northern Wales was none other than William Lloyd. And his stand served to transform the whole atmosphere of a predominantly pro-James II area. Strange to relate, William Lloyd whispered the secret of the invitation that had been sent to William of Holland to invade the kingdom to Richard Davies, the Quaker of Cloddiau Cochion, who had joined other Nonconformists in a visit to the prison where the bishop was held. The bishop also shared the secret with James Owen. And in the long conversation that he had with Owen that summer afternoon, Lloyd had moved very far from those days of crisis when he thought of Owen as a possible conspirator against the life of the king. By this time the bishop could say to him,

> You and we are Brethren: we have indeed been angry Brethren, but we have seen our folly: and we are resolved if ever we have it in our power again, to show that we will treat you as Brethren.

But tolerance built on momentary exhilaration and gratitude is a fragile edifice. Things did not happen quite as William Lloyd had hoped.

With the coming of legal toleration in 1689, yet a new flavour was given to the relationship between Nonconformist and Anglican. In a real sense it was the parting of the ways. Most Welsh Nonconformists were happy enough to interpret the Toleration Act as a positive measure of liberty which granted them a specified and guaranteed place in society. None of them wished to revive old puritan dreams of ascendancy. They set to it to cultivate their own patch.

There was no need to worry any more what bishops thought of them, nor to lose any sleep over the doings of courts whether ecclesiastical or secular. They set to it to build chapels, to secure licences for their preachers and buildings, and to cultivate their religious convictions. It was rather different, of course, amongst the rich Nonconformists of the big cities in England. Sir Humphrey Edwin, the well-to-do presbyterian merchant and Glamorganshire squire, was elected lord mayor of London in 1697. On October 31st he complied with the letter of the law by attending holy communion at his parish church. But the same afternoon, still dressed in his mayoral regalia and attended by his city officials, he shocked the establishment by attending his presbyterian meeting-house. And so the practice of 'occasional conformity' became a matter for public debate. Although the issue itself was of no great moment in Wales, Welshmen were given an opportunity to see the struggle from the sidelines. When the tories surged into power in the elections of 1701 and 1702, they were eager to pass legislation that would soon put a stop to occasional conformity. But their attempts were frustrated by the intransigence of whiggish peers, the tolerance of liberal bishops like Gilbert Burnet and the tortuous backstairs diplomacy of Sir Robert Harley, the member for the Radnor Boroughs and the most un-puritan grandson of the Sir Robert Harley who had made his home at Brampton Bryan a haven of refuge to such men as Walter Cradock, Morgan Llwyd and Vavasor Powell.

Amongst the first to appear in print on behalf of the repressive legislation was the M.P. for Cardiganshire, Sir Humphrey Mackworth (1657-1727) of Gnoll, Neath, with his pamphlet, *Peace at Home*. He was, of course, a pioneer industrialist. But he was also a promoter of the new pietism and one of the five founders of the S.P.C.K. And amongst those who took issue with him was none other than James Owen, the man who had been fined £20 for holding an illegal conventicle at Llangybi, Caernarfonshire, in 1676 and who had been entrusted with a momentous international secret by Bishop William Lloyd in 1688. In 1703 he published *Moderation a Virtue*. He pleaded with churchmen to consider what an advantage it was to them to have 'moderate dissenters' joining with them occasionally in holy communion. Rather curiously, he admitted that such a practice would be a disadvantage to dissent. His arguments for occasional conformity went down well and the book went to four editions. Not surprisingly he published a sequel in the following year to proclaim *Moderation Still a Virtue*. And the public was still avid to study his arguments. It went to three editions.

As far as their interest in the promotion of piety went, Mackworth and Owen might be expected to be very closely in sympathy with one another. But obviously the new circumstances were dividing promoters of piety from each other. Bishop Lewis Bayly in his book *The Practice of Piety* said, 'The Practice of Piety consists in knowing God and glorifying Him aright.' In 1670 it was possible for conformist and nonconformist to join forces on this basis. But by the end of the century, things had changed. This was partly because of the success of the pietistic movement. As it gathered momentum, its promoters came increasingly to think of 'glorifying God' in terms of the outward manifestations of piety, such as frequent attendance at holy communion, greater respect for the ordained ministry and zeal for what was conceived to be scriptural or catholic forms of church government. And this outlook was to be had amongst both conformists and nonconformists. The Act of Toleration encouraged them to concentrate more seriously on the differentia of their churchmanship. Consequently, despite the direct links between the Welsh Trust and the S.P.C.K., the one element that was not common to the two organisations was 'accommodation'. And, of course, Presbyterians and Congregationalists joined to form a Common Fund under the short-lived ecumenical experiment known as The Happy Union, and soon they were using their money not primarily to promote piety, but to consolidate their ministry. And so, the great divide widens. The S.P.C.K. was the organ of militant anglicanism, and militant anglicanism at its best and most creative. The odd story of William Evans exemplifies this. William Evans had been a student at the dissenting academy conducted by Rhys Prydderch (1620?-99) at Ystradwallter, Llandovery. In 1688 he was ordained into the congregational ministry to serve at Pencader. On September 6th, 1705 the S.P.C.K. at London received

> a letter from Mr William Evans of Carmarthen, who teaches gratis 12 poor Children, and says that they want Bibles, Catechisms, Arithmetic Books and Copy Books, whereupon the Society ordered them 6 Bibles, 12 Christian Scholars and 12 Catechisms.

One wonders what was going through William Evans's mind as he opened his 'packet' from London. Did he chuckle to himself as he meditated on the innocence of these Londoners? That hardly sounds likely in the editor of *Gemau Doethineb*. Or did he offer a fervent prayer of thanks for people whose generosity extended beyond the limits of party and church? He continued, Congregationalist that he was, to nestle under the wings of the society until November 2nd, 1710 when John Vaughan of Derllys, one of the most generous and knowledgeable patrons of the society, informed London that 'one Mr. Evans, a Dissenting Minr. did teach twelve poor children at Carmarthen' and since it was hardly becoming that such a school should appear in the society's accounts, he suggested that another school should be patronised in its place. But that is not all. On September 21st, 1710 Archdeacon Edward Tenison informed the society

> that there is a Seminary at Carmarthen in which Dissenting Preachers are trained up, which he is informed is represented in the Society's Acc[oun]ts as a private School: if it be so, he submits it to the Society whether continuing it in their accounts will not look like giving encouragement to ye Dissenters to keep up their Separation.

Surely the archdeacon's information is defective here. Certainly an academy had been opened in Carmarthen in 1704 and the principal was William Evans. It was long the tradition at Carmarthen to have a school connected with the academy. Could this have been so from the beginning? We have already heard of William Evans's school for 12 poor children, and that it enjoyed the patronage of the S.P.C.K. Could Tenison have mistaken one for the other? Or did Evans avail himself of the generosity of the society to provide books for his students as well? We have no means of knowing. But we do know that William Evans's concern for the promotion of piety was every whit as deep as that of the leaders of the S.P.C.K. In 1707 he had published his version of the catechism, *Egwyddorion y Grefydd Cristionogawl*, conveniently divided into thirty sections so that families could work their way through it once a month. Nevertheless, 1710 saw the end of the connection between William Evans and the society. It adds piquancy to his ejection from amongst the dependants of the S.P.C.K. that he secured the old anglican chapel at Llan-y-bri for use as a meeting-house by Congregationalists—the only church building in Wales to undergo such a transformation.

The last years of Queen Anne's reign were an anxious time for Dissenters generally. In 1711 the tories succeeded in passing the Occasional Conformity Act which imposed a fine not exceeding £40 for attending a conventicle after fulfilling the demands of the Corporation Act. It was this Act that gave legal standing to the outrageous practice of electing rich Dissenters to public offices from which they were debarred by reason of their nonconformity and then fining them for refusing.

More serious for Wales was the desire of the tories to close nonconformist schools. Ever since the decision in the King's Bench on the Bates Case in 1670, the law was that a bishop's licence was not required by a teacher who had been appointed by the founder of the school. Since then a vast number of schools had been set up by Dissenters—William Evans's school at Carmarthen was one example. Agitation against these schools had grown ever since the Lower House of Convocation had passed a resolution in 1704 beseeching the Upper House to take some action in the matter. The campaign culminated in the passing of the Schism Act in 1714, a measure devised by Bolingbroke who was himself an old student of the dissenting academy at Sheriffhales. It enacted that no person was to keep a private or public school unless he expressed unfeigned assent to the contents of the Prayer Book and secured a bishop's licence. No teacher was to attend nonconformist worship or teach any but the anglican catechism. It was a savage Act, and was due to come into force on August 1st, 1714. But Queen Anne died that day and the Act proved a dead letter. The reins of power fell from the hands of the tories for many a long day.

But this period provided a foretaste of a form of harassment that was to cause many anxious days and nights for Nonconformists throughout the eighteenth century. On March 24th, 1710, when news arrived of Dr. Henry Sacheverell's escape with a derisory penalty after his trial at the House of Lords, the mob at Wrexham celebrated the occasion by breaking windows at the houses of leading Dissenters and at their chapels. This behaviour was repeated on July 16th, 1715 when the chapels were attacked again and two days afterwards the New Meeting, which belonged to the Presbyterians, was virtually gutted. It was probably at this time too that Jacobite sympathisers burnt the congregational meeting-house at Llanfyllin. These buildings were rebuilt or repaired at government expense but the threat of mob violence only receded as hooligans transferred their attentions to the Methodists after the beginning of the evangelical revival or to nonconformist preachers who adopted the tactics of the Methodists and preached up and down the country in the open air.

Under the Hanoverians, the older Dissent became increasingly conscious of the effectiveness of legal methods of redress when their rights or liberties were challenged. On November 9th, 1732 the body known as the Protestant Dissenting Deputies came into existence. This was a committee of laymen drawn from the baptist, congregational and presbyterian churches of London. Its main interest throughout the years has been to champion the legal rights of Dissenters and to do so, wherever possible, by action in the courts. It soon became adept at using the most sophisticated methods for pressing its views and could command expert legal opinion on every conceivable topic. And because its members were always men of influence and distinction, it was able to gain access to the most exalted circles, not excluding the throne when necessary. So great was the reputation for legal accuracy that the Deputies won in their first few years that the mere threat that they would take up a case was often sufficient to have a wrong redressed. This was because the Deputies had always made it a policy never to take up a case unless they were virtually certain to win it. The minutes of their meetings are a mine of information about the relationships between Nonconformists and their opponents. But they lie outside the scope of the present study. Suffice it to say that a wide variety of Welsh cases was drawn to the attention of the Deputies and that some at least of the bitterness that characterised the relations between conformists and nonconformists in the nineteenth century has its origins in the numerous infringements of their legal rights suffered by Nonconformists in Wales in the second half of the eighteenth century. Many magistrates' benches (Anglesey provided some bad examples) believed that they had a discretion in the matter of granting licences under the Act of Toleration and refused applications. There was no such discretion and when cases were drawn to their notice, the Deputies without hesitation sought writs from a higher court. There were cases of clergymen refusing to bury the infants of Dissenters on the ground that they had not been baptised by an episcopally ordained minister; there were examples of citations of an irregular kind into the church courts; there were nasty examples of harassment by mobs and even of attacks by masked or armed men. Let one instance, from the second half of the century suffice, to show how the Dissenting Deputies dealt with a case. On October 13th, 1769 the Deputies were informed by the Revd. Richard Davies of Abergavenny that James Evans, vicar of Marshfield, had refused to bury the daughter of Mary Daniel, a widow and one of the parishioners. The secretary was instructed to inform Evans that he must 'make Satisfaction to the Mother of the Child' otherwise 'this Comm[itt]ee will proceed against him, as the Law directs.' On January 19th, 1770, Dr. Benjamin Davies of Abergavenny informed the committee that their letter had been delivered to the vicar of Marshfield but his reply was that 'he would make no concessions, and said he would abide by the law.' The committee, in accordance with its usual policy, resolved to appeal to the bishop of the diocese. By March 1770 a deputation had been received by the bishop of Llandaff who 'was very sorry that any clergyman in his Diocese should be so little of the Gentleman and Christian, and so Ignorant of the Laws of his Country as to be guilty of such a piece of Misbehaviour.' The bishop begged the Deputies not to proceed with the prosecution until he had had an opportunity of writing to the vicar, asking him for an acknowledgement of his error and a promise to bury Dissenters in the future. If he proved obstinate, the bishop promised to prosecute him in his own court. By May 11th, 1770, the vicar had written to the bishop to say that he would have buried the child had it 'been baptized by any regular Dissenting Minister', but this child had been baptized by a minister who had been ordained by a mason. The bishop thought this an insufficient cause for refusing burial and would write to Evans 'directing him for the future to bury all Dissenters in his Parishes without asking any Questions.' In view of the bishop's reply, the secretary was ordered to write to the aggrieved mother, Mrs. Daniel, urging her and her friends to exercise 'Candor & Moderation.' This case is typical of the methods employed by the Deputies, in its unemotional, strictly legal and pragmatic approach, and the appeal to the higher authority of the bishop. In fact, the bishops come out in rather a favourable light in these minutes. Hard things have been said about Welsh bishops of the eighteenth century, but several of them are revealed in these documents as men of tolerance and understanding in dealing with cases where the local clergy had infringed the rights of Nonconformists.

Our study ends, as it began, on a creative note. The pietism that first emerged in the joint efforts of Bishop William Thomas, Stephen Hughes, Charles Edwards, and their English patrons, Anglican and Nonconformist, continued to gather strength despite the divisions and difficulties of the years that followed. It flourished in a quiet and unobtrusive way in the dissenting churches as they settled down to their new mode of life after the passing of the Toleration Act. It flourished more vigorously in the Church of England, and especially so in the marvellous activity of the S.P.C.K.

Under the patronage of men like Bishop Humphrey Humphreys, Bishop John Evans, Sir John Philipps and John Vaughan a series of notable translations appeared from the pens of Ellis Wynne, Edward Samuel, Theophilus Evans, Moses Williams, John Morgan and others. These books filled the 'Packets' sent by the S.P.C.K. to all parts of the country. On the other hand, we have the productions of the Nonconformists. Prominent amongst them were Thomas Baddy of Denbigh, Christmas Samuel of Pant-teg, Jenkin Jones of Llwynrhydowen, Jeremy Owen, Matthias Maurice of Rothwell, Thomas Williams of Capel Isaac, William Evans of Carmarthen, Howel Powel of Bailihalog and Philip Pugh of Cardiganshire. James Davies (Iaco ab Dewi) deserves to be mentioned apart from the others. By religious affiliation he was a Congregationalist but he forms a link between the nonconformist translators and the S.P.C.K. Of the books translated by Iaco ab Dewi, four were written by distinguished Anglicans. *Llythyr y Dr. Wells at Gyfaill* (Shrewsbury, 1714) was a rendering of a *Letter to a Friend Concerning the Great Sin of Taking God's Name in Vain*, by Dr. Edward Wells (1667-1727), rector of Bletchley. In 1716 appeared his translation of *A Sermon Preach'd at Ely-House Chapel in Holbourn* with the title *Pregeth a Bregethwyd Ynghapel Ty-Ely Yn Holbourn* (Shrewsbury, 1716). The original was by William Fleetwood (1656-1723), bishop of Ely, but from 1708 to 1714 bishop of St. Asaph. Iaco ab Dewi's best-known translation was *Meddylieu Neillduol Ar Grefydd* (1717), a rendering of *Private Thoughts Upon Religion* by William Beveridge, bishop of St. Asaph from 1704 to 1708 and a leading influence upon the S.P.C.K. and allied religious movements at the beginning of the eighteenth century. Iaco ab Dewi died in September 1722 and the last translation to be mentioned appeared posthumously in 1730. It was *Yr Ymarfer o Lonyddwch*, printed at Carmarthen. The original was *The Practice of Quietness*, a popular devotional manual of a previous generation, and the work of George Webbe who became bishop of Limerick in 1624. It will be seen immediately that just as Stephen Hughes in the seventeenth century contributed to the publication of books of anglican devotion, so Iaco ab Dewi continued the tradition. And this should cause no surprise for there is strong (but not explicit) evidence that Iaco assisted Stephen Hughes in the preparation of his translation of *Pilgrim's Progress* in 1688. In any case, it cannot be doubted that Iaco had absorbed the spirit of Stephen Hughes. And the books that he translated were, needless to say, acceptable to the S.P.C.K.

Since Welsh books were few, new ones would be welcomed by the growing reading public in Wales. And such readers would not be unduly concerned to ask critical questions about the church-allegiance of their authors. Religious people, interested in the cultivation of piety, would welcome good books from whatever source they emanated. The assiduous scholar Moses Williams, vicar of Defynnog, in his editorial commendation to Iaco ab Dewi's translation of *The Practice of Quietness* writes,

If people after reading this book take it as a model by which to order their lives, and set their minds vigorously to live according to the godly intentions that they find in it, we may hope to see (through the blessing of the Lord upon the work) a better increase of piety and religion than hitherto.

These words convey with precision the motives that inspired the literary work of both the anglican and nonconformist promoters of piety extending from the age of Stephen Hughes and Dr. William Thomas to the age of Iaco ab Dewi and Ellis Wynne. And the readers of their books in parish church and meeting-house came under spiritual influences that combined the insights of Puritan and Anglican. On the one hand, it is quite striking how Dissenters in the early eighteenth century began to take a new devotional interest in holy communion. And this interest was stimulated not only by Thomas Baddy's translation of *A Treatise Concerning the Lord's Supper* (*Pasc y Christion*, 1703) by the Presbyterian Dr. Thomas Doolittle (1622?-1707) but also by such anglican books as Edward Samuel's translation of Bishop Beveridge's treatise advocating frequent communion, *Angenrhaid a Mawrlles Mynych Gymuno* (1723). On the other hand, the translations of John Bunyan's books must have had a wide readership amongst Anglicans. Another example of this cross-fertilisation is Iaco ab Dewi's translation of Matthew Henry's Catechism, *Catechism o'r Scrythur Yn Nhrefn Gwyr y Gymmanfa* (1717). John Evans (1702-82), Eglwys Gymun, a stern critic of the Methodists, finds fault with Griffith Jones, Llanddowror, because he used this catechism in his circulating schools. So, the varied work of these writers and translators penetrated the Welsh mind during the years immediately preceding the evangelical revival.

It is only in recent years that the extent of this literary and educational work has been fully appreciated. But its impact must not be exaggerated. Despite the labours of many people, Anglicans and Nonconformists, their books and schools affected but a minority of the population. Literary evangelism is valuable but limited in scope and influence. And there were immense hindrances to the work arising from an oppressive spiritual lethargy, depressing social and moral conditions, and a general spirit of opposition to Christianity. Lewis Morris vividly expresses the sceptical mood of the age when he writes,

> Religion in this country is quite out of taste, it is such an old fashioned thing. I am positive if Mahomet had any dareing fellows to preach him here, he would gain ground immediately, or any merry religion like that. And if Sadlers Wells and the play houses could be brought in as branches of a new religion, it would have abundance of converts and would take extremely well.

These words were written in London on June 18th, 1757. Morris had not appreciated that a momentous change was already under way. The evangelical revival had begun in 1735 and was gradually to transform the pattern and quality of Christian life in Wales. And in that transformation the piety of the late seventeenth century and the early eighteenth century was swept up into a dynamic religious enthusiasm that enabled it to affect the lives of many more people than the early Welsh pietists could have hoped for.

CHAPTER 5

THE WELSH CHURCH IN THE EIGHTEENTH CENTURY

by

Owain W. Jones

A T the beginning of the eighteenth century Wales was inhabited by a small, widely dispersed and almost completely rural population. Its size can only be estimated roughly but it appears to have been about 400,000. Travel was difficult; law and order not always sure; and the conditions and habits of the men of the time tended to be centred on their immediate locality where most if not all of the important events of their lives took place.

The general standard of living in the Welsh countryside was low and this was matched by the poverty of the Church in Wales. This had dated from Norman times when a considerable amount of parochial tithes and endowments were alienated for the benefit of the monasteries which the conquerors were so fond of building. The abbeys of Tewkesbury and Keynsham, for example, were given a very large number of parishes in south Wales. After the dissolution of the monasteries the monkish patrons were replaced by lay impropriators and in some cases by clerical corporations which were not lacking in rapacity. The two dioceses in south Wales suffered most. Over half the tithes in St. David's and about one third in Llandaff had been alienated.

The Welsh dioceses were poorly endowed, Llandaff and St. David's in particular. Therefore they were usually occupied by those on the lowest rungs of the episcopal ladder who left them for other and more lucrative sees as soon as the opportunity offered, sometimes moving inside Wales itself. Bishop Warren went from St. David's to Bangor in 1783, and Samuel Horsley moved from St. David's (via Rochester) to St. Asaph in 1802. The men appointed as bishops were all Englishmen, but this was only considered a fault by a later age; and Welshmen like Humphrey Humphreys of Bangor and William Lloyd of St. Asaph had little hesitation in accepting translation to English sees.

In Wales there were many poor cures—hence the tale of woe in Erasmus Saunders' *State of Religion in the Diocese of St. Davids* (1721). Saunders also thought that too many ill-qualified clergymen had been ordained either to serve these parishes or to be cheap chaplains to wealthy pluralists or rich impropriators. There was much that was wrong in this old order of society. Pluralities abounded among the beneficed and unbeneficed clergy. Property, whether secular or ecclesiastical, was sacrosanct; and monstrous inequalities were not only condoned but thought to be a necessary part of the structure of that hierarchical society which was generally thought to be divinely ordered. Yet we should beware of judging it by the standards of a later age. To describe the eighteenth-century Church as 'drowsy' or 'asleep' is to look at it through the eyes of the men of the late nineteenth century whose situation was so completely different, in size of population, urban and industrial development, modes of thought and piety and even taste in architecture, that it was difficult for them to see the development from the earlier period to their own.

It is not easy to reach a balanced assessment of the state of religion in Wales at the beginning of the eighteenth century. Many contemporary statements are highly critical. William Williams, Pantycelyn, declared in 1773 that all Wales was enveloped in thick darkness and that the ministers of all denominations were asleep before Howel Harris began to exhort, but it was one of the older Dissenters, Edmund Jones of Pontypool, who stated that this was a travesty of the truth. In 1799, an article in *Y Drysorfa* (edited by Thomas Charles of Bala) pictured Wales as sunk in superstition and vice; but it was the historian of nonconformity, Thomas Rees, who wrote that historians (including A. R. Johnes, the author of *Causes of Dissent in Wales*, 1831) one after another had been misled by this account. Erasmus Saunders paints a sombre picture of some parishes which had no service, of others served by pluralist curates who came at no set time, 'and having so little time, and so many places to attend upon, how precipitately and as if out of breath are they obliged to read the prayers, or to shorten or abridge them . . . and like hasty itinerants to hurry from place to place?' Yet there is some light amidst the shade, something, for example to appeal to the post-Tractarian looking for signs of continuity in the anglo-catholic tradition, for the people continued an ancient practice 'namely that of crossing themselves . . . with a short ejaculation that through the Cross of Christ they might be safe or saved'. They used to kneel in prayer upon the graves of relatives and friends, invoking 'not only the Deity, but the Holy Virgin and other saints; for Mair-Wen, Jago, Teilaw Mawr, Celer,

Celynog and others are often thus remembered as if they had hardly yet forgotten the use of praying to them'. There was an element of joy in their devotions for they 'frequently compose a kind of divine hymns or songs, which they call *Halfingod* or *Carolion* which generally consist either of the doctrinal, or historical parts of Scripture, or of the lives and worthy acts of some eminent Saints'. They also took pains 'by reading or discoursing to instruct one another in their houses'. Indeed the domestic element in the religion of this period is the key to our understanding of it, and this has been stressed by a recent writer, Dr. Tudur Jones.

It is this domestic orientation of eighteenth-century piety that explains the contents of so many of the 'good books' published by the S.P.C.K. and by individual authors. They were not primarily books for use in the churches—whether dissenting or anglican—but books to be used either by individuals in their private devotions or by the family groups in the homes. Indeed so strong was this tradition of family devotion that it was necessary for those who were concerned to foster church life to produce the occasional book stressing the value and importance of frequent communion in church.[1]

This tradition persisted in the earlier part of the nineteenth century. John Keble's *Christian Year*, first published in 1827 and the 'best seller' of the period, was intended for the use of individuals in the privacy of their homes. When Isaac Williams translated his *Hymns from the Parisian Breviary*, he put the hymns into harsh metres so that they would not be sung in church. The later Victorians came to think of Christianity as a mass-movement and to judge success or failure by the number of sittings which a denomination provided and by its ability to fill them with members or hearers. The men of the eighteenth century did not look at things in this way.

Since Elizabethan times Wales had possessed a reasonably well organised system of secondary education, with grammar schools established at Brecon, Abergavenny, Bangor, Beaumaris, Carmarthen, Cowbridge, Ruthin and a number of less notable establishments in the smaller towns; and there were some notable additions to the number in the seventeenth and eighteenth centuries, Haverfordwest (1614), Cardigan (1653) and Ystradmeurig (1770). Wherever possible a number of free places were kept for 'poor scholars' who were taught gratuitously on condition that the parents provided the basic necessities for schooling. Entry to these grammar schools was of necessity restricted by money and by distance; so most Welsh country folk had to rely on more local institutions. Churchmen made good use of the dissenting academies, particularly the one at Carmarthen, either to prepare their sons for the universities or for holy orders. Other schools were opened as a result of local initiative, such as the school kept by the celebrated Unitarian, David Davies of Castell Hywel. They sometimes achieved some reputation outside the local area, but they generally laboured against great difficulties. These schools had a life span of about twenty to thirty years, and they often collapsed on the death of the founder. Elementary education, by which the poorer children learned their letters, was provided either by dame schools which were independent enterprises, or by the charity schools which came into being as a result of the philanthropic impetus which inspired reform movements in the eighteenth century.

Chief among these movements, so far as Wales is concerned, was the Society for the Promotion of Christian Knowledge. Founded in 1699 it immediately began the work of providing education for the children of the poor in the charity schools which it initiated all over the kingdom. In Wales its work had been anticipated by the Welsh Trust set up by Thomas Gouge, an ejected puritan minister in London. Gouge had a good deal of support from churchmen and dissenters but his Trust was short-lived, from 1672 to 1684. That there was some continuity between the two movements is suggested by the fact that thirty of the schools set up by the S.P.C.K. were in towns or villages where Gouge had established his Welsh Trust Schools, and some of the pioneer workers for the S.P.C.K. had been associated with Gouge's Trust. Sir Erasmus Phillips of Picton Castle had been associated with the Welsh Trust, and his son, Sir John Phillips, and his son in turn, worked hard for the S.P.C.K.

The charity school movement started well. Sixty-eight schools were founded by 1715, but then it ran into difficulties. Only twenty-eight schools were set up after 1715 and none after 1727. A number of reasons contributed to this decline. It seems that 'the struggle between High and Low Church for control of the schools became so bitter that the Society abandoned them in order to avoid division within itself'. Nor did the Jacobite revolt of 1715 help matters: 'in more than one report do we hear of good schools failing owing to the anti-Hanoverian views of teacher or patron'.[2]

The language used in the schools was generally English. There are no references to the use of Welsh in the schools in south Wales. However, when Dr. John Jones, dean of Bangor, set up a chain of twelve schools in Caernarfonshire, it was specified that the Welsh language should be used. The upkeep of the schools was always a problem to the local promotors and to the central committee. They were maintained by voluntary subscriptions, some endowments and in some cases by church collections.

They received no direct help from the society except in cases of great need, but they were allowed books and materials either free or at a low price, depending on local circumstances. A greater problem was the circumstances of the people themselves. They were, Dean Jones remarked, 'too poor to learn', that is they could not afford the time for their children to be instructed.

In the next development in the charity school movement allowance was made for these particular difficulties. The result was that between 1737 and 1761, the circulating schools initiated by Griffith Jones were to be found in all the Welsh counties.

Born in 1684 Griffith Jones was educated at Carmarthen Grammar School from which he was ordained in 1708. Eight years later Sir John Phillips presented him to the parish of Llanddowror, with which his name will always be associated. His name appears frequently in the records of the S.P.C.K. in connection with appeals for Welsh Bibles and he became one of the four receivers of S.P.C.K. books for the county of Carmarthen.

The idea of using itinerant schoolmasters was not original. It had been advocated by Sir Humphrey Mackworth in 1719. Griffith Jones developed the idea in the schools he started in 1731 but which grew in numbers after 1737. The circulating schools were held for three-monthly periods, usually in the winter months when the demands of farm labour were less; lessons were conducted in Welsh and the curriculum was limited to the bare essentials of reading the Bible and the Prayer Book catechism. Children attended the day sessions, and some adults who were able to be there, and evening classes were held for the others. It is estimated that two-thirds of the pupils were adults and not a few of them advanced in age. The teachers were given some training at Llanddowror and sent out with a letter of introduction and a copy of the regulations to which they were to adhere. These documents were to be presented to the parish clergyman whose consent was required before a school was opened in any district. The system is an eloquent witness to Griffith Jones's organising ability; but he was also fortunate, both in England and Wales, in his patrons who are mentioned in the annual account of these schools known as the *Welch Piety*. In particular he owed much to the help of Madam Bridget Bevan who carried on the work after his death in 1761 until her own death in 1779. She bequeathed £10,000 for the maintenance of the schools, but the will was contested by her relatives and the money was put into chancery where it remained for some thirty years.

Griffith Jones obtained a good deal of support from the parish clergy; but he also had his opponents. There was no theory of popular education at this time, only some debate as to whether the children of the poor should be taught to read or not. The points of view of those who held that they should, and those who maintained the converse, were rooted in an identical social theory which saw society as a divinely ordered mechanism in which everyone knew his place, and the primary concern of both sides was to maintain the established order. The charitable motives of the reformers were concerned not only with the salvation of souls but also with the continuance of existing social patterns.

Some of Griffith Jones' less conventional habits brought him into conflict with the diocesan authorities. His preaching excursions, usually made between Easter and Whitsun were directed against wakes and fairs 'and other impious gatherings'. John Evans of Eglwys Gymyn irately declared that this activity 'contributed to the no small lessening of Christian love and charity and of all good neighbourhood, to which they (the wakes and fairs) very much contributed with very little or no ill consequences attending'. Some were suspicious of Jones's friendship with methodist leaders, even though methodism was still a movement inside the Church; and others thought the circulating schools were a cloak for methodist activity. There is, however, a good deal of evidence to show that Griffith Jones looked with disfavour at the uncanonical and irregular practices of his methodist friends.

Parallel with these developments in popular education went the distribution of Welsh Bibles and other 'good books'. The extent to which this presupposes a reading public is open to debate. We have Griffith Jones' testimony that many of the Welsh Bibles distributed by Gouge's Welsh Trust turned up among the pupils of the circulating schools in a very fresh and unsullied condition. Yet the pious founders of the S.P.C.K. had little doubt that amongst the humblest members of society there was an adequate reading public both in England and Wales for their productions. Were they being quixotic? Their early discussions show a lively sense of reality, and it is not likely that they would waste money which they themselves largely contributed in impractical schemes. Their attitude suggests that the printed word was already becoming increasingly important in the lives of the people.[3]

It would seem that the task of publishing and distributing books and tracts was regarded as second only to the provision of charity schools. Thousands of devotional books and tracts were distributed, either free or at a low cost, in England and in Wales. The Welsh books were chiefly translations of English writers but some of the translators were men of considerable literary ability, and the dedication of some of their works to

Humphrey Humphreys, Bishop of Bangor 1689-1701 and of Hereford till 1712, gives some indication of the influence of this staunch supporter of the work of the S.P.C.K. Ellis Wynne of Lasynys dedicated his translation of Jeremy Taylor's *Holy Living* to Bishop Humphreys, and it was published in 1701 under the title *Rheol Buchedd Sanctaidd*. Another was Samuel Williams, vicar of Llangunllo and Llandyfriog, who translated John Foxe's *Time and the End of Time*; and the dedication tells of the services rendered by the bishop to the Welsh language. Another translator of merit was Edward Samuel, rector of Llangar near Corwen, but his first work, *Bucheddau'r Apostolion a'r Efengylwyr*, was an original composition published on the advice of Humphrey Humphreys. Another translator was Joshua Thomas, curate of Llanlleonfel. The subscribers to his translation of John Scott's *Christian Life* included nineteen members of the Gwynne family of Garth House in that parish, and among these is the name of Sarah, the wife of Charles Wesley. Two editions of the Welsh Bible were produced in 1717 and in 1727 under the direction of Moses Williams, vicar of Defynnog. Ellis Wynne's edition of the Welsh Prayer Book appeared in 1709, an edition which is notable for the first inclusion of the Thirty-Nine Articles and also for Wynne's own hymn, *Myfi yw'r Adgyfodiad Mawr*. The clergy were catered for by the establishment of diocesan libraries at Cowbridge, Carmarthen, Bangor and St. Asaph, each receiving books to the value of £60. More is known of the library at Cowbridge than of the others. There the library catered for three classes of borrowers: i. any clergyman or schoolmaster living within ten miles of Cowbridge; ii. any trustee; iii. any person giving 10*s*. in cash or books. Again we see the combination of local initiative and outside help in these philanthropic activities.

No picture of the eighteenth century could be complete without some reference to the literary and antiquarian movement of the period. It may not bear directly on the life of the Church, but churchmen, from the time of Edward Lhuyd (1660-1709) onwards, were prominent in it. They include Ellis Wynne, the author of *Gweledigaethau Y Bardd Cwsc*, one of the major Welsh prose classics; John Davies the grammarian who was vicar of Mallwyd; the brothers Lewis, Richard and William Morris of Anglesey, whose circle included Goronwy Owen and Evan Evans (Ieuan Fardd); and also the exiles in London who formed patriotic societies at this time, notably the Honourable Society of Cymmrodorion founded in 1751. They include Theophilus Evans whose *Drych Y Prif Oesoedd*, first published in 1716 and reissued in 1740, propounded a romantic idea of Welsh history—one which was widely held over a century later—namely that Britain was founded by Brutus the Trojan; and Evans combined this theory with the supposition that the Welsh were the descendants of Japheth the son of Noah. He was also the author of the *History of Modern Enthusiasm*, the most vitriolic attack made on methodism judged even by the polemical standards of the day.

The methodist movement is another aspect of the general revival in religion at this period. In Wales it was also a spontaneous movement which, at least at the outset, owed nothing to its English counterpart. Howel Harris, a young man intended for holy orders, passed through the experience of conversion after hearing the vicar of Talgarth preach on Palm Sunday, 1735. Though a layman, he began to exhort in the surrounding villages and at fairs and parish wakes. He may have heard of the Oxford Methodists but he did not meet Wesley and Whitefield until 1739. Also in 1735 Daniel Rowland, already in priest's orders and a curate to his brother at Llangeitho, was converted by a sermon preached by Griffith Jones. He too began to evangelise the surrounding area and to attract a good deal of attention by his powerful preaching. Harris and Rowland met for the first time at Defynnog where the latter was preaching. For the next few years the two young leaders were busily engaged in developing the organisation of their converts.

Preaching in itself was not enough. Opportunities had to be provided for those who were touched at the heart to meet together to sustain the new enthusiasm. 'The result was that small groups of converts began to meet together for this purpose, week by week, and the generic term applied to them all was 'society'. It was quite as natural for like-minded people to join together in the eighteenth century for spiritual purposes as it is for like minded people to come together for professional or social purposes in the present day'. These societies were no new phenomenon for they had flourished in the established Church towards the end of the seventeenth century. Howel Harris stated that the societies he founded were begun 'in imitation of the Societies which Dr. Woodward gave an account of in a little treatise he wrote on that head'. Woodward's *Account of the Religious Societies in the City of London etc* was first published in 1697 and the S.P.C.K. produced *Abstracts of Dr. Woodward's Book* some time later. It could hardly be foreseen that the consequences in the eighteenth century would be quite different from those in the seventeenth, so much as to amount to a religious revolution.

In the beginning methodism was not a movement but an attitude to religion. It was, in the words of R. T. Jenkins, 'nid enwad, nid sect, nid cymdeithas hyd yn oed, yn y lle cyntaf; ond osgo, agwedd, dull, ffordd, pa air bynnag a ddewisoch' (not a denomination, not a sect, not even a society in the first place; but an attitude, a manner, a way—whatever word you choose). But as time passed, a number of differences began to appear, and members of these societies were required to make a choice, between the Calvinism of Harris and Whitefield and the Arminianism of the Wesleys, or between remaining within the Church and leaving it: 'Then and only then did Methodism become something rigid rather than fluid, a movement rather than an attitude to religion and only then did the labels begin to appear, as some members and some societies followed this leader and others that. Some became Arminian or Wesleyan, others Calvinist or Whitefieldian, while still others left Methodism and the Church and joined the ranks of Dissent'.[4]

With the exception of Howel Harris, the early methodist leaders were all in holy orders. Daniel Rowland was already in his curacy at Llangeitho when he began to preach. Howel Davies was ordained priest in 1740. He was curate to Griffith Jones for a while and his vicar was disturbed by his wild and unlawful ways. He then moved to a curacy in Pembrokeshire which he held until his death in 1770 despite his determination to 'go about'. William Williams, the poet and hymn writer of the movement was less fortunate. He was made deacon in 1740 and served his title at Llanwrtyd. His vicar, Theophilus Evans, did nothing to defend Williams when he was charged with uncanonical behaviour in the bishop's court at Brecon; it may well be that it was he who instigated the charge; and Williams, refused ordination to the priesthood, became an itinerant methodist preacher. Peter Williams, after a curacy at Eglwys Gymyn under John Evans, the old enemy of Griffith Jones and his circulating schools, joined the Methodists in 1747 and became their leading biblical scholar and commentator. It is interesting to note that two of his sons, Eleazar and Bayley, became beneficed pillars of the Church in the next generation, the one as vicar of Lampeter and the other of Llanrug.

Howel Harris, it has been said, was 'an Anglican with a difference'. In practice he was a high churchman. He made his communion frequently (in church of course) and was given to fasting three days a week. He disliked the custom of sitting at prayer, and at Trefeca he encouraged the family to turn east at the creed and to show reverence at the name of Jesus. Twice he had applied for ordination.

Although in one place Harris says expressly that his application for Holy Orders had been rejected 'for no other reason but for my preaching as a layman', in another he admits that he was 'refused ordination only because I went about, was promised ordination if I promised not to go about'. These two things—lay preaching and itinerancy—are related of course; both were contrary to the accepted usage, if not also to the law, of the Church; both would have ceased with ordination, had Harris been willing to accept a title to ordination with the settled condition implicit in a title. He was not willing.[5] When on a third occasion his ordination was mooted, Harris said: 'I could not be confined'.

Thus far the development of methodism, even of Howel Harris himself, is indicative of that revival *within* the Church which characterizes the eighteenth century. It was an evangelical reaction against many of the features of the theology of the Age of Enlightenment which tended to speak of God as a remote 'Supreme Being' who had created this best of all possible worlds, which gave first place to reason, and had a horror of enthusiasm. But increasingly the organisation of the Methodists tended towards its final development *without* the Church. The societies came to be organised into zones and associations. In the 1740s they began to acquire meeting places, 'New Rooms' they called them, designed for preaching and educational purposes. When the New Room, Alpha, was opened at Builth Wells (Llanfair-Ym-Muallt) in 1747 Howel Harris declared that 'God had never been before in Llanfair'. Even allowing for the enthusiasm of the moment, such an attitude of mind could only bode ill for the future, though Harris himself was determined not to break away from the Church. His societies were designed to work within the establishment.

Wesley and Whitefield parted company in 1741. Howel Harris was no idle spectator of the doctrinal dispute, and he and his colleagues sided with Whitefield. The result was that methodism in Wales became Calvinistic rather than Arminian or Wesleyan. There were some tensions between those who were now obliged to choose their position. It also ushered in a situation where matters of orthodoxy assumed greater importance, and where theological bickering loomed large.

Howel Harris was the first victim of this new state of affairs. Both he and Daniel Rowland were men of imperious nature who worked better in separation than in unison. Harris' indifferent theology made him suspect of patripassianism (an ancient heresy which confuses the persons of the Father and the Son, and gives the impression that God the Father suffered on the cross). His undoubted arrogance and his consorting with Madam Griffith of Cefn Amlwch made matters worse and ended with the separation between him and his friends at the meeting of the Llanidloes Association in 1750. Harris retired to Trefeca to found his quasi-moravian (and agricultural) settlement. It was later to be the site of Lady Huntingdon's college where not a few of the clergy of the established Church received their training alongside their methodist brethren. Harris was reconciled with his old friends in 1762 but during the remaining eleven years of his life he never regained his old position of leadership and he concentrated his energies upon the settlement at Trefeca.

The second phase of Welsh methodism is marked with the ascendancy of Daniel Rowland. A revival at Llangeitho in 1762, stirred by the preaching of the Welsh 'Boanerges' and fanned by the hymns of Pantycelyn, produced some unedifying scenes. Complaints were made to the bishop of St. David's who deprived Rowland of his licence. Daniel Rowland now administered the sacrament in the meeting house which had been built at Llangeitho 1756-7. Howel Davies had been the first to do this. He administered the holy communion in his 'New Room' at Woodstock near Haverfordwest in 1754, and Howel Harris was highly critical of his action. The example of Davies and Rowland was to be followed by David Jones, vicar of Llangan 1768-1810, though he spent the last sixteen years of his life in Pembrokeshire. In 1775 he built a meeting house some three miles from his parish church and this became a centre of methodism second only to Llangeitho.

The concluding period of the methodist movement in Wales and its penetration into the north of the principality is associated with the work of Thomas Charles. A native of Carmarthenshire and a pupil at Carmarthen Grammar School, Thomas Charles graduated at Jesus College, Oxford and took a curacy in Somersetshire in 1778. On his marriage in 1783 he settled at Bala. In the following year he joined the Methodists. Previously north Wales had been little more than a mission field for itinerants from the south. Now the zeal and organising ability of Thomas Charles made Bala the centre of methodism in north Wales. He revived the idea of circulating schools in 1785 and four years later he organised his Sunday schools which were much more successful. He had a hand in the founding of the British and Foreign Bible Society. He provided Wales with large quantities of religious literature, including an important journal *Y Drysorfa*. He was also called upon to make the final decision, though he made it with great reluctance, by which the Methodists in Wales became a separate denomination.

The later stages of the methodist movement leading to secession in 1811 belong more to the annals of Calvinistic methodism than to the Church. The war with revolutionary France in 1793 created a situation which encouraged the Methodists, at the advice of Thomas Charles, to avoid the imputation of subversive activity by licensing their buildings and preachers as dissenting chapels and ministers. The lay preachers (or exhorters) were pressing for 'ordination' though Charles himself was opposed to the idea. The influence of men like Thomas Jones of Denbigh was considerable. Meant by his parents for the ministry of the Church, Thomas Jones deliberately chose to be a methodist preacher and took the lead in claiming that the call to preach the gospel involved also the authority to administer the sacraments. There is also some evidence that the Methodists were tiring of the discipline which bound them to receive the holy communion in the parish church. At the Watford Association in 1753 mention was made of 'brethren who had scruples about receiving the Sacrament in the Church on account of the ungodliness of the ministers and receivers'; but it was decided that they should continue to receive in the parish churches 'till the Lord should open a plain door for leaving her communion'. By the end of the century it was said that 'the objection to communicate at the parish churches only troubled the northern Methodists when the clergy became unkind as well as unclean'.[6] The references to ungodly and unclean ministers are significant. The sectarian is ever tempted to look for a 'perfect church' and is thus led into schism. The first methodist ordinations to 'the call of the Church' took place in 1811. The methodist clergy now had to make their choice. The un-beneficed clergy, three in north Wales and three in the south, threw in their lot with the Methodists. The beneficed clergy, about ten in number held to the Church, or at least to the establishment.

English tourists who passed through Wales in the eighteenth century usually remarked that the churches were poor and in need of repair. Their strictures should not be taken too seriously. Welsh churches were generally poor. The Welsh scale of things was very much smaller and humbler compared with what obtained in England. Wales had evolved a peasant architecture which blended into the landscape as did the scattered farms and cottages which they served, nor were the houses of the squirearchy, designated by the title Llys or Plas very grand at this period. All but a few of these churches have been ruthlessly improved by the church builders of the nineteenth century who spoke of them as 'rude barn-like structures' and had no understanding of their development. Many of them were in need of repair, but a considerable number of them were restored in the course of the century. Much of this rebuilding of churches—and also the building of chapels—has been forgotten because the gothic revivalists of the following century swept it almost all away.

One source of information is provided by the royal briefs which were granted at this time. These were warrants which allowed the petitioners to solicit help for charitable purposes throughout the parishes of the kingdom. The briefs were read in the churches and collections made. In the case of the walking brief, house to house collections were authorised. We know of fifty briefs which were granted for the restoration or rebuilding of churches in Wales. These include such notable restorations as Llandaff cathedral (1735), and St. Mary's, Monmouth (1732), and lesser rebuildings from Neath and Aberavon in the south to Builth and Knighton in mid-Wales and Dolgellau and Clynnog Fawr in the north. Nor were these fifty the only ones. St. Mary's, Swansea had been rebuilt in 1735, St. Mary's, Ruabon in 1770. The Queen Anne Bounty, as well as augmenting the value of many poor parishes, provided the means for church restoration. The correspondence, for example, between Isaac Williams of Llanrhystud, rural dean of Ultra-Aeron, and a succession of bishops of St. David's reveals that an extensive programme of restoration was taking place in that area, among them Llanddewibrefi (1781), Llanbadarn Odwyn (1778), Yspytty Cynfin (1782), and Tregaron (1805).[7] The county histories which were being written at the beginning of the nineteenth century refer to many churches as lately rebuilt or lately restored. The complete picture still eludes us but there is sufficient indication of much activity.

A church is designed as a setting for the liturgy, and changes in design reflect the changes in the understanding of that liturgy from age to age. The Prayer Book services and the usually long sermon were meant to be heard, and so the men of the seventeenth and eighteenth centuries designed or adapted their churches accordingly. Sir Christopher Wren spoke for them when he said, 'It is enough if they (the Romanists) hear the murmer of the Mass and see the Elevation of the Host, but ours are fitted as auditories'. The nave was therefore filled with pews, large box-type but often elegant structures, which gave some protection from the elements in churches which were generally unheated. The pews were dominated by the two or three-decker pulpits placed at the side but in some cases in the centre of the east end of the nave. It was not then considered a crime to have the view to the altar blocked by the pulpit. The chancel, where there was one, and architectural chancels were not common in Wales, was used as a communion aisle to which the faithful were bidden to draw near with faith on the infrequent occasions when the holy communion was administered. If extra accommodation was required, a gallery was built. The altar table was generally small and always undecorated. It was well into the nineteenth century before the more daring spirits would begin to adorn the altar with crosses, candlesticks and flower vases. The nonconformist chapels built at this time were furnished in a similar manner and were to continue, to the present day, the eighteenth-century ideal of plastered walls and massive brown woodwork, the lines of the pews leading the eye forward to the very prominent pulpit and back again along the contours of the gallery. The church, however, would have the royal arms set up in a prominent place, and also large plaques bearing the words of the Creed, the Lord's Prayer and the Ten Commandments. In the course of the century the walls of these churches were often adorned with sepulchral monuments characterized by classical motifs such as urns, pillars and cherubs. In the course of nineteenth-century restorations these were despised and reset in inaccessible parts of the building. Now they are coming to be appreciated for their artistic qualities. They were often the work of local sculptors and craftsmen whose work is their only memorial.

The clergymen who served these churches have often been severely criticised; but the clergy generally were unpopular in the eighteenth century, the rich ones despised as ambitious hypocrites and the poor ones as ignorant peasants. Rowland Williams remarked that 'any clerical student who preferred black letter in his parsonage to good company at an inn rarely escaped the reputation of conjuring (i.e. witchcraft), an art which was supposed to constitute one of the principal studies of the University of Oxford'. But he went on to reject allegations respecting scandalous ministers: 'Undoubtedly many accounts of the older Welsh clergy came through hostile channels . . . yet many families have traditions of clerical ancestors which do not accord with insinuations sometimes made of general irreligion'.[8] It had been intended that all the clergy should be graduates of the two universities, but this was not practicable as far as Wales was concerned. Bishop Lloyd of St. Asaph told the archbishop of Canterbury in 1686: 'We have a great many more cures of souls than we have graduates in this country; and as most of the people understand nothing but Welsh, we cannot supply the cures with any but Welshmen'; and the number of Welshmen able to proceed to the universities were very few. A large number of non-graduates were ordained in the eighteenth century in all the Welsh dioceses, with the exception of the diocese of Bangor where all the clergy were graduates. The non-graduates received their education at the grammar schools and at other places including the dissenting academies. They include such names as Griffith Jones of Llanddowror, William Williams, Pantycelyn, and the other methodist leaders; they include Isaac Williams of Llanrhystud, Thomas Beynon, Edward (Celtic) Davies and others whose record suggests that Bishop Lloyd was right when he said that, of those he had ordained, the graduates were not always the best scholars: 'I have more than once seen them shamefully outdone by men that never saw the university'. These men served the poor Welsh cures whose stipends did not come up to the expectations of those who had been to the university. They served as unbeneficed curates at stipends which varied between £5 and £10 per annum. So there emerged the race of pluralist curates referred to by Erasmus Saunders; and it was not until the last quarter of the eighteenth century that their lot was improved, notably, in the diocese of St. David's by Bishop Horsley in 1788.[9]

In the kingdom as a whole, this period saw a change in the status of the clergy. This has been well described by Dr. Kitson Clark:

At the beginning of the eighteenth century many of the clergy seemed to have formed a class, rustic in manners, primitive in outlook, which did not rank higher than the neighbouring farmers and tradesmen or the upper servants of the great houses of the nobility. As the century went forward many of them gradually assumed the status of gentry. Their style of life changed, their standing in the county was enhanced . . . and they developed a culture which was a good deal more civilised, not only than that of their rustic predecessors but than anything that could have been understood by the more boorish country gentlemen of the past.[10]

Conditions varied in different parts of the country, but this was a change which pointed forward to the nineteenth century. There are instances in Wales of clergy who 'became discontented with life in a cottage in a village street and either insisted on more elaborate parsonages probably a little way away from the other houses, or made the fact that there was no suitable house in the parish an excuse for not residing there at all'. For example, Edward Phillips, rector of Maesmynis, 1740-77, the methodist sympathizer and friend of the Wesleys, spurned his rustic parsonage and took a house in Builth, a mere two miles away. His parish registers show that he was a diligent parish priest, but, technically, he was a non-resident. Isaac Williams, vicar of Llanrhystud, 1762-1811, was more fortunate. He was able to rent a small manor house in his parish, Ystrad Teilo by name, where he was able to entertain bishops and other dignitaries, lay as well as clerical, in a manner more suited to his new status. These men were, admittedly, part of the upper crust of the clergy who were doing reasonably well because they were beneficed or pluralist. There were many others who were less fortunately placed. But they indicate the first signs that even in Wales a new society was coming into existence in which it was clear that the old-style rustic parson could hardly find a suitable place.

Whether they were graduate or non-graduate, the theological reading of these clergymen was generally the same. They were nurtured on the theology of the divines of the Reformation period; Grotius' *De Veritate Religionis Christianae*, Burnet's *De Fide et Officiis* and Pearson's *On the Creed* were books which both Samuel Horsley and Thomas Burgess required the candidates in the divinity classes of the grammar schools to read. Horsley favoured 'Wheatley on the Common Prayer' and 'Secker on the Catechism', while Burgess advocated 'Jewell's Apologia, Hooker's Ecclesiastical Polity and Mosheim's Ecclesiastical History'. These books were used well into the nineteenth century until some new and disturbing influences began to be felt. Natural theology figured largely in the thinking of the men of the eighteenth century and the works of William Paley exercised a profound influence upon them. They studied the heathen moralists, that is the classical authors who were thought to 'excite in the mind a disgust and abhorrence of some current vices'. The concept of religion as a system of morals lay heavily on them and they appear weak on the doctrine of the Church, but again that is to judge them by later standards.

The bishops of the period performed their office according to the ideas of the day, though many of them stayed but briefly in their Welsh dioceses. They were required to attend the House of Lords and therefore could only visit their dioceses in the recess. Even in the summer months travel was difficult. It took Samuel Horsley, for example, five and a half hours to travel from Cardigan to Aberaeron in July 1789, the 'abominable state of the roads' throwing him so much out in his reckoning that he had to excuse himself from calling at Llanrhystud where Isaac Williams was expecting him to dinner: 'My horses cannot proceed without rest, and were I to stop again at your house I should be in danger of being in the dark before I reach Aberystwyth, which would be very inconvenient as my drivers are unacquainted with the roads. In these circumstances I beg you to excuse my not waiting upon you'.[11] Yet these bishops held their ordinations, generally once a year, and the bishops of St. Asaph and St. David's have a good record for ordinations held in their own dioceses. They administered the rite of confirmation at various centres, often confirming very large numbers. They held their triennial visitations which were important means of administration in days when communications were slow; and when absent from their dioceses, they appointed commissaries to act for them. No bishop was more notorious for non-residence than Richard Watson, Bishop of Llandaff, 1782-1816. Yet the diocesan records show that he did not spend all his time on the shores of Lake Windermere. He performed his episcopal duties with a diligence with which he has not been credited. These bishops were remote from their flocks and there was a barrier of language between them and their people. It is likely that not a few of their confirmees thought that their reiteration of the words 'more and more' was a cryptic reference to the sea (môr). But this kind of criticism dates from the nineteenth century rather than from the eighteenth. Then a new concept of the bishop's office was beginning to emerge. It is generally held that Samuel Wilberforce was the founder of this new idea of episcopacy; but he did not become bishop of Oxford till 1846. It has sometimes been suggested that the success of the methodist movement in Wales was due to a lack of understanding and sympathy on the part of the *Esgyb Eingl*, the non-Welsh bishops of the period. This is to forget that a similar movement was taking place in England where, presumably, there was no such barrier of language between the bishop and his people.

By the end of this period the movements which reached their full development in the nineteenth century were taking shape. The Methodists were heading towards secession; the older Dissenters were awakening; and the way was paved for that development of nonconformity in Wales which took place particularly in the first half of the nineteenth century. The Church itself was showing some stirring towards the reforms which were to be completed later. The Queen Anne Bounty had begun the augmentation of the poorer livings; some care was being shown in the care of the fabric of the churches and in the training of the clergy; but the dead hand of the past still weighed heavily upon it. The French Revolution had a two-fold reaction. On the one hand it produced a suspicion of change which accounts for much of the opposition to the new ideas produced in the next century; on the other hand it helped to encourage the first stirrings of that liberal nationalism and the political radicalism which were to become prominent in the future. The revival of *eisteddfodau* in which some of the Welsh clergy, the *personiaid llengar*, played a prominent part, is a sign of an incipient romanticism. The Gorsedd ceremony which Edward Williams (Iolo Morgannwg) grafted on to the eisteddfod has been described as 'romanticism run wild'. The growth of population which was a marked feature of the nineteenth century had already begun, for the 400,000 inhabitants of Wales had become 587,000 by 1801. Migration to the towns was already taking place, and Merthyr Tydfil which in 1760 was a small hamlet had a population of 7,000 by 1801. In short, the first signs were appearing of rapid industrial expansion.

---

[1] R. Tudur Jones, 'The Older Dissent of Swansea and Brecon', *Links with the Past*, 126–7. It was for this reason that both churchmen and Dissenters gave a cool reception to the new-fangled evening services introduced by the Methodists.

120 A HISTORY OF THE CHURCH IN WALES

² *Wales Through the Ages*, edited by A. J. Roderick, II (Llandybie, 1960), 91. See also M. Clement, *S.P.C.K. and Wales* (1954) and her essay on Griffith Jones in *Hanes Methodistiaeth Galfinaidd Cymru* (Caernarfon, 1973), a book which provides a complete bibliography of the Welsh Calvinistic methodist movement.

³ The literature of this period has been studied in detail by Geraint H. Jenkins in his 'Welsh Books and Religion' (Ph.D. thesis, Wales, 1974). A summary of his findings has been made by Glanmor Williams who concludes: 'No recent research has shown more clearly that, far from being an age of torpor, this was an age of gestation'. (*J.H.S.C.W.*, XXV (1976), 26).

⁴ Quotations above from A. H. Williams, *John Wesley in Wales* (Cardiff, 1971), xix.

⁵ G. F. Nuttall, *Howel Harris* (Cardiff, 1965), 13, 43.

⁶ D. E. Jenkins, *Calvinistic Methodist Holy Orders* (Caernarfon, 1911), 156.

⁷ NLW 6203 E.

⁸ 'Methodism in Wales', *Quarterly Review*, 1850.

⁹ See Owain Jones, 'The Mountain Clergyman: His Education and Training', *Links with the Past*, 165–84.

¹⁰ G. Kitson Clark, *Churchmen and the Condition of England* (1973), 31.

¹¹ Horsley to I. Williams, NLW 6203E.

CHAPTER 6

THE CHURCH IN THE INDUSTRIAL REVOLUTION

by

E. T. Davies

THE eighteenth-century church, although not as moribund as it has been represented in the past, was nevertheless ill-prepared to meet the challenge of the Industrial Revolution. This was true of all those parts of Wales which were soon to be industrialised. It could be demonstrated, for example, from the history of the Swansea valley, then in the diocese of St. David's. It was especially the case in the old diocese of Llandaff. Its roots went deep into a rural community which accepted certain social values which were to be challenged in the nineteenth century, while its organization had been adapted to an earlier age; and it took the better part of the first half of the nineteenth century for the church to organize itself to meet the needs of what was, in a sense, a new society.

Basically, the fundamental weakness of what was, until 1919, the established church, was that, until the reforms of the 1830s, it was not a corporate body with control over its property and administration. Rather, it was a loose collection of small corporate bodies such as parishes, cathedral chapters, episcopal manors, and innumerable local trusts which had accumulated throughout the ages. Neither the church as a whole nor the diocese held any property; and administration was dispersed among two hundred or so parishes with an oversight on the part of the diocesan chancellor, who did the work of an archdeacon in the old diocese of Llandaff throughout the eighteenth century and into the 1840s. Neither the deanery nor the archidiaconal structure had been changed since the Middle Ages; there were no such bodies as diocesan boards of finance, diocesan trusts, parochial church councils or diocesan conferences. In practice, although not in theory, parishes were virtually ecclesiastical republics.

It was within this state of affairs that the bishops of Llandaff functioned. Throughout the eighteenth century they had performed their canonical duties of ordination and confirmation, even though ordinands had occasionally to travel beyond the diocese, and confirmation was administered at certain centres in conjunction with the triennial visitation, while institution to parishes was done either by proxy or wherever the bishop might be living at the time. After Bishop Beaw finally abandoned Mathern palace in 1705 no bishop of Llandaff had a residence in his diocese until Bishop Van Mildert was appointed in 1819 and came to live in Coldbrook, near Abergavenny. His successor, Sumner, lived in Llansanffraid, near the same country town (staying at the 'Cardiff Arms' for his ordinations in what remained of Llandaff cathedral), while his successor, Edward Copleston, ultimately settled in Hardwick Court, Chepstow, until his death in 1849.

But residence meant little more than a stay of four or five months in the diocese during the summer to carry out the episcopal functions, while it was becoming customary to spend the winter months in St. Paul's deanery, London, and in the House of Lords. The former office was necessary because of the poverty of the see. Llandaff was the poorest see in the church up to 1850 when Alfred Ollivant was appointed and provided with an adequate stipend and an episcopal residence, Llandaff Court. Moreover the patronage of the bishops of this diocese was severely restricted: not one living in Glamorgan lay in their gift, while Bassaleg (with its chapelries of Risca and Henllys), and Bedwellty were the only livings in Monmouthshire of which the bishop was patron.

The first reforming bishop of Llandaff was the much maligned Richard Watson who was bishop from 1782 to 1816. He spent as much time in his diocese as any bishop before him, i.e., the summer months, and the rest of the year 'on the banks of the Winandermere', but he neglected his parliamentary duties. He visited the diocese annually and attended the meeting of the Llandaff Chapter at Petertide as treasurer, and following this, an ordination was held, usually on the first Sunday in July. His triennial visitations were held regularly until his health began to fail in 1813, and he died before the next visitation was due. He made an extensive tour of his diocese in 1809, when he was over seventy years of age, and it was on that occasion that he held the first confirmation ever in Merthyr Tydfil, to which reference will be made later. It should be added that he wrote a manual for confirmation candidates: *An Address to Young Persons after Confirmation*. It has a distinctly eighteenth-century flavour, and it suffers from two defects: it is too long, and it was written in English when most of his confirmands would be monoglot Welsh speaking.

Although Watson left the state of the diocese very much as he found it,

he is the first bishop of Llandaff who is known to have sketched a programme of church reform. This he did in a letter to William Pitt, dated
April 16th, 1800, in which he proposed that:

> a law abolishing *in future* all pluralities ought to be accompanied with
> another making a decent provision for every resident minister. An
> hundred pounds a-year ought to be the very least stipend annexed to
> any benefice, and, such sum being assured, service twice every Sunday
> should be required in all. Houses of residence for the clergy should
> be bought or built at the public expense, or by the Governors of
> Queen Anne's Bounty, for livings under a hundred pounds a-year.
> The number of livings under an hundred a-year, their respective
> values, and the state of their parsonage houses, should be accurately
> ascertained, and laid before Parliament, in order that the additional
> public burden attending the giving a decent maintenance to the clergy
> might be known. Livings held *in commendam* or annexed without
> *commendam* to bishoprics, to headships and professorships in the
> universities, to public schools, etc., should be exempted from the
> operation of this law, as the residence of their possessors cannot be
> expected.[1] The greater part of the benefices under an hundred pounds
> a-year, are in the patronage of Lay Impropriators. Many of these
> Impropriators would, I doubt not, be moved by a sense of piety, and a
> regard for public safety, to contribute largely toward rendering the
> income of each place of worship in their patronage not less than the
> sum I have mentioned.

Time was to show that this scheme of reform was not sufficiently drastic to
meet the rapidly changing conditions in the diocese during Watson's
episcopate, for by the time he died in 1816 the Industrial Revolution had
reached every valley in the *blaenau* of the old diocese of Llandaff. When
Bishop Watson visited Merthyr Tydfil for a confirmation service in 1809
the iron industry had been established there for exactly fifty years, two
years after the iron industry had been established in Hirwaun, at the head
of the Cynon Valley. The growth of Merthyr Tydfil was rapid. B. H.
Malkin visited the township in 1803 and reported on the scanty provision
of the clergy and the neglected state of the churches. The parish church
was well attended, but there were about ten dissenting and methodist
meeting-houses in the place, and the Dissenters outnumbered the members
of the established Church by eight or ten to one. This was probably too
optimistic an assessment, for the visitation of Bishop Marsh in 1817 was to
reveal that Merthyr Tydfil could claim only forty communicants out of a
population of 11,104. Across the mountain, in the large parish of Aberdare,

there was only one church the condition of which was described by Malkin: 'The church itself is a most lame and impotent conclusion to the funereal magnificence . . . The natives of the Welsh mountains worship their Maker where an Englishman would not litter the most ignoble quadruped about his house'.

Industrialism, in the shape of the iron industry, had been established at the heads of the Cynon and Taff Valleys and at the head of every valley in north Monmouthshire: Rhymney, Sirhowy, Ebbw Fawr, Ebbw Fach, Afon Lwyd, and the Clydach valley in Breconshire, and all before Watson's visit to Merthyr Tydfil in 1809.[2] The scene was well set for the growth of an entirely new society, and the old iron industry communities were already in existence: Hirwaun, Merthyr, Dowlais, Rhymney, Tredegar, Nantyglo, Ebbw Vale, Blaina, Blaenafon, soon to be followed by an iron industry in the Llynfi Valley in the ancient parish of Llangynwyd; together with the growth, gradual at first, but rapid later, of an urban population in Newport and Cardiff. The established church was ill-equipped to deal with this development.

The essence of the problem which confronted the established church was the growth and concentration of population in north Glamorgan and north Monmouthshire in the first half of the nineteenth century. Between 1801 and 1851 the population of the former county grew from 70,879 to 231,849, and that of the latter county from 45,568 to 157,418, a smaller aggregate number, but the largest percentage increase in the United Kingdom with the exception of London; and of this Monmouthshire population only 15,764 were classed as agricultural and general labourers in 1851. Clearly, the concentration of population up to 1851 was in the *blaenau* of each county. Merthyr Tydfil was the largest town in Wales in that year and its phenomenal growth can be seen when it is recalled that in 1710 there had been only seven baptisms and seventeen burials in the parish, and that in 1750 these figures were still only 27 and 16 respectively.

This great increase in population was the result of migration from the agricultural areas of both counties and immigration from other counties. It would be inappropriate to overload this chapter with statistics, and, in any case, the general picture is clear: Glamorgan, throughout the last century had a more homogeneous population than Monmouthshire although changes were evident by the end of the century. A greater percentage of immigrants into the iron-districts and the later coal-mining districts came from the other Welsh counties than was the case in Monmouthshire. But, although every county in England and Wales was represented in the census of 1851 in Monmouthshire, yet the highest percentage of immigrants was from other Welsh counties, together with a stronger admixture from the neighbouring English border counties than was the case in Glamorgan. The industrial areas of Glamorgan were largely Welsh in stock and, in some cases overwhelmingly Welsh in speech, well into the fourth quarter of the last century, while Monmouthshire had an increasingly diluted stock and a resultant greater decline in the use of the Welsh language than was the case in Glamorgan.

The general conclusion is clear: the iron and coal industries brought into being a society in the old diocese of Llandaff which was largely of Welsh stock, predominantly Welsh in speech, and even when the language declined, Welsh in sentiment. It was also clear that these communities were largely Welsh nonconformist in their religious observances: chapels greatly outnumbered churches, to an extent we shall see later.

When Bishop Watson wrote his letter to William Pitt he had in mind a general reform of the established church with no particular reference to his own diocese. It was his three successors, Herbert Marsh (1816-19), William Van Mildert (1819-27) and Charles Richard Sumner (1826-27)[3] who began to pay attention to local, diocesan needs. Bishop Marsh held his primary visitation in 1817 by proxy, by his commissary, Benjamin Hall, father of the industrialist and grandfather of the first Lord Llanover ('Big Ben'). It was at this visitation that the state of the parish of Merthyr Tydfil, already mentioned, was announced. But apart from a temporary galvanizing into life of the office of rural dean, little else was done during Marsh's episcopate.

The first visitation charge given by the first bishop to reside in his diocese after a matter of one hundred and forty years was that given by Bishop Van Mildert in August, 1821. He claimed that the state of the diocese had improved under his predecessor, particularly in the repair of churches and chancels. But there was great need for places of worship in the populous areas, for 'while Meeting-Houses for Dissenters spring up on every side, many of our own flocks are almost driven from Communion with the Established Church by this lamentable deficiency' (of places of worship). In two places in the diocese, Caerphilly and Pontypool, steps had been taken to meet the need, but at Merthyr Tydfil there was church accommodation for only one-fortieth of the population; and although the erection of galleries had nearly doubled the seating accommodation in the parish church, still only 900 people could be accommodated out of a population of 18,000. Nor was the problem confined to the industrial areas: more than two-thirds of the livings in the diocese had no glebe-houses, and of those which possessed a residence for the parson, a large proportion were so mean as to offer but too good a plea for non-residence.

But it was the first charge of Bishop Sumner in 1827, who it will be remembered, spent only six months at most in the diocese, which gave the most comprehensive view of the old diocese of Llandaff in those days; and it was very probably the work of the chancellor, William Bruce Knight, who was to become virtually the most influential figure in the diocese during the second quarter of the nineteenth century.

The bishop began by saying that the improvement in the condition of the churches, announced by his predecessor, had continued, but new churches were badly needed in the industrial parishes. The new industrialists were not alone to blame for this 'desertion', although it was incumbent on them to make provision for the better instruction of those families which had been brought together by them. To aggravate this state of affairs he explained that the old parish endowments were no longer adequate for the needs of new areas, with the result that dissent had increased 'as we have been lately told . . . even to the half of the population of the kingdom'. This was a gross underestimate as far as his own diocese was concerned; and he might have added that many landowners, colleges and cathedral chapters had creamed off parish endowments through impropriations and appropriations. The lack and quality of parsonage houses, pluralities and non-residence (of which there were some bad cases in the diocese), the small number of Sunday services performed in the parishes (and, in some parishes, only once a fortnight in the language preferred by the parishioners), all contributed to the low condition of the church. And the bishop went on to say: 'In three parishes, whose united population amounted, at the census of 1821, to 936 souls, there are in all only 22 communicants, and 50 attendants at church, or about 1 in 20 of the whole population. In two other parishes, containing 1,646 souls, there are only 14 communicants, and 60 attendants at church, being 1 in 27 of the population. In five parishes of larger size, containing together above ten thousand individuals, the deficiency is more deplorable; the united number of communicants averaging only 82, and attendants at church 280; or about 1 in 38 of the population. Throughout the whole diocese, the gross number of communicants is stated to amount to 4,134, and of attendants at church to 19,169, of a population exceeding, in 1821, 150,000 of all ages.'

Clearly, although the voice was that of Bishop Sumner, the hand in this charge was that of William Bruce Knight who would have made an admirable bishop of the diocese. Although a native of Devon, he had learned Welsh and had attained a considerable knowledge of the language, and, moreover, he was a man of independent means who could probably have dispensed with an English deanery to eke out the very low stipend of the see of Llandaff. In 1843 he became archdeacon of Llandaff and when the office of dean was revived in the same year it was Bruce Knight who was appointed.

The man appointed bishop of Llandaff at the beginning of 1828 was Edward Copleston, provost of Oriel College, Oxford, and dean of Chester, and after his appointment to Llandaff, dean of St. Paul's. He remained in Llandaff for a generation (1828-49) at a time when the industrial areas of his diocese continued to grow rapidly and for this period the eighteenth-century tradition of a non-Welsh-speaking bishop, resident only in the summer, was perpetuated. It is not difficult to be just, indeed generous, to Copleston as a man: he was an eminent figure in church, university, and state and, moreover, was a good and generous man. But he ought never to have been appointed to a diocese undergoing such radical social and economic changes which he possibly did not understand and with which he certainly could not sympathise. His contacts were with Bruce Knight and John Montgomery Traherne, the former being the real administrator of the diocese and the latter sharing the scholarly and antiquarian interests of the new bishop. But with the iron masters, the Crawshays, Harfords, Baileys, Homfrays and Halls of his diocese he had no real contact and thought little of some of them; while a distinct animosity developed between him and Benjamin Hall III and his wife, Augusta Hall, because Copleston knew no Welsh and did not trouble to learn the language.

But two developments took place during the first ten years of Copleston's episcopate which were ultimately to help solve the problems of the diocese and particularly those of the industrial areas: the one was the establishment of the Ecclesiastical Commissioners for England (1836) and the other was the formation of the Committee of the Privy Council for Education (1839). The former body, set up under an Act of Parliament, administered the property of the established church and by a series of Orders in Council brought about the long needed administrative reform; while the latter gave annual grants for the building of schools, and these school-rooms became in many places the precursors of permanent church buildings and so alleviated the problem in populous areas. It is significant that in that same year the Llandaff Diocesan Committee for Education was formed, and by 1851 by far the greater part of primary education in Glamorgan and Monmouthshire was given in church schools or in the Works' schools set up by the ironmasters.[4]

But the process of church building was much slower, for it must not be forgotten that the Ecclesiastical Commissioners were not yet empowered to give grants for the purpose. Consequently, the record of new permanent buildings during this second quarter (and for that matter, the first half) of the nineteenth century is not impressive. The episcopal registers for this period refer to new churches in Caerphilly, Pontypool, Pontnewynydd, Cwmdu (Llangynwyd), where the proprietors of the Maesteg Iron Works purchased a building known as 'The Maesteg Old English Baptist Chapel', Abersychan, Whitebrook (Llandogo), Newport (St. Paul's), Dowlais, Tredegar, Pontypridd, Beaufort, Cwmgelly (Bedwas), Llanfair Grange (Llantilio Crossenny), Rhymney, and a reference in 1843 to a 'new church' in Cardiff. A year before Copleston died a Calvinistic-methodist chapel in East Aberthaw, in the parish of Penmark, a 'certain room situate at the Basin' in the parish of Llanfabon, and lastly, in 1849, a chapel at Glascoed, near Usk, were licensed for services in accordance with the rites of the established church.

It is significant that most of these developments, both the licensing of school rooms and the building of churches, took place at the end of the 1830s and throughout the 1840s. Of course, there were still the ancient mountain-top churches such as Trefethin, Aberystruth, Bedwellty, Mynyddislwyn, Gelligaer, Llanwynno, Merthyr Tydfil, Aberdare, Llangynwyd and others which had served a pastoral population for centuries. But the new industrial communities were settling in the bottom of the valleys where, naturally, the Nonconformists were building their chapels at a cost which must have entailed much sacrifice to what were then working-class congregations.

The mid-1840s saw a development in the administrative system of the diocese, made possible by the work of the Ecclesiastical Commissioners. They provided an adequate stipend of £4,200 for a bishop of Llandaff and an official residence which would give the diocese a full-time bishop, but this arrangement would not come into force until the next vacancy in the see. Next came the turn of the archdeacons (or rather the virtual revival of that office, for throughout the eighteenth century archidiaconal functions had been exercised by clerical chancellors of the diocese). Two archdeacons were appointed: for Llandaff, Bruce Knight who, in 1843, became the first dean of Llandaff since the Middle Ages, to be succeeded as archdeacon by Thomas Williams who also succeeded Knight as dean. The second archdeaconry was that of Monmouth formed in 1844, and whose first incumbent was William Crawley, rector of Bryngwyn. In 1857 the commissioners were able to annex a residentiary canonry in Llandaff cathedral to each archdeaconry. Thus the diocese was given the prospect of two full-time archdeacons and a resident bishop.

A further step was taken after 1844 which would facilitate the the reorganization of the large, upland, industrial parishes of the two archdeaconries, namely the creation of 'district chapelries' or 'perpetual curacies' whose income would be paid by the Ecclesiastical Commissioners. This pointed the way to the solution of two problems: the poor endowment of these large parishes, and their subdivision into smaller units. Not only were the original endowments of the industrial parishes very small, but much of it went either to lay or ecclesiastical impropriators (many of the latter outside the diocese). Thus, in 1866, the tithe commutation income for the whole diocese was £59,518 1s 4½d, of which only £34,050 19s 2d was available to the parochial clergy. With such small endowments large parishes could not be subdivided without outside aid, and this is what the commissioners provided. Up to 1850 the following 'district chapelries' (i.e. new ecclesiastical districts) were formed: Dowlais, Rhymney, Tredegar, Pen-maen, Cyfarthfa, Nantyglo, Beaufort, Abersychan, Pontnewynydd, Glyn Taff, Caerphilly, Skewen, Whitchurch and Newport (St. Paul's). This was the first step toward constituting these districts as ecclesiastical parishes.

Lastly, the commissioners provided parsonage houses both for the ancient rural parishes and the new industrial areas. The lack of glebe-houses was the usual excuse given for non-residence, but now the authority of the bishops to grant licences for non-residence was greatly curtailed. Copleston dealt with the question of clergy residence in his charges of 1845 and 1848, and at the time of his death in 1849 there still remained 53 benefices in the archdeaconry of Monmouth without a residence for the clergy, while there were others in a state of disrepair. But gradually there were built those Victorian parsonage houses which are still a feature of many of our parishes.[5] Again, a residence in the parish was bound up with the regularity and frequency of Sunday services. At the beginning of Copleston's episcopate the performance of one service per Sunday was general, but from the beginning he expected those clergy in charge of one parish only to do double duty in those parishes where the population demanded it. Here, again, there was an improvement by the middle of the century, for whereas in 1827 there had been only eleven churches in Glamorgan and fifteen in Monmouthshire with two services per Sunday, by 1849 this had increased to forty and sixty respectively. But this left the majority of parishes still with only one Sunday service.

Although the Industrial Revolution brought into being a largely

Welsh nonconformist society in the *blaenau* of the old diocese of Llandaff, the question of language was by no means confined to the industrial parishes; in fact, the language issue had been raised in Monmouthshire in the 1730s; and there exists correspondence between Bishop Barrington and Sir Charles Morgan, of Tredegar, in which the latter claimed to appoint an incumbent to the living of Bassaleg. Barrington made it clear that the living was in his gift and he objected to Morgan's nominee on the ground that he was not Welsh speaking. A compromise was reached: Thomas Leyshon would be instituted by the bishop provided he undertook to learn to speak the Welsh language. Whether he ever did so is not known.

Copleston had similar clashes with patrons: with the Jenner family, of Wenvoe, and with the dean and chapter of Gloucester cathedral over Llantwit Major. He was well aware of the problem (and, in any case, Benjamin and Augusta Hall were not likely to allow him to forget it), and he claimed that, with his limited patronage, he had done his best. He believed (probably rightly) that there was no purely Welsh parish in his diocese, but he deplored the practice of appointing a monoglot Englishman to a bilingual parish on condition that he would employ a curate able to minister in the native tongue: 'The patron is in fault who makes such a nomination; the clergyman is in fault who accepts it; the diocesan is in fault who knowingly permits the abuse'. A bishop in Wales had the legal right to refuse to institute a monoglot Englishman into a 'mixed' parish, but a government could appoint a bishop with no knowledge of Welsh to a diocese where the majority were bilingual and, possibly, a minority, monoglot Welsh. But Copleston saw no inconsistency in this, for he believed that a knowledge of Welsh was not necessary for a bishop in Wales, for the peculiar duties of a bishop did not require the use of that language, said Copleston. 'As well might the natives of Yorkshire claim the see of York, or those of Kent the see of Canterbury.'!

During Copleston's episcopate the population of Monmouthshire increased by 36.9% during the decade 1831-41 but dropped to an increase of 17.1% in the following ten years, and thereafter declined until there was a resurgence in 1881-91, whereas Glamorgan overtook Monmouthshire in the rate of population growth from 1841 to 1891. But the bishop's contacts with the areas of greatest growth continued to be few, as is shown by his confirmation centres in 1836.[6] They were mainly in the agricultural areas of the two counties, and the industrial areas are conspicuously absent. Certainly travel in these parts was very difficult: it was the pre-railway age; roads were poor; the usual routes up the valleys were along the tram-roads, or via the Abergavenny-Merthyr turnpike road which gave access to the iron works communities from the north rather than from the south; while there was no means of crossing from one valley to another except by going up to the top or down to the bottom of the valley and entering the parallel valley. But one wonders how different the church picture would have been if these outlandish places had had more episcopal oversight: a year after Rhymney church was opened Copleston went there for a confirmation when 473 candidates were presented to him by the vicar, Lodowick Edwards, who had been in the parish for only a year. It showed what could be done in a parish with an energetic Welsh speaking cleric and a permanent church.

During his latter years Copleston's health was failing, and he died on October 14th, 1849, at Hardwick Court, Chepstow. It is difficult not to come to the conclusion that a different kind of bishop would have made a greater impact on the new society which grew so rapidly from 1830 to 1850. Edward Copleston was a great man, but it is regrettable that he ever left academic circles, or that he was not content to be dean of St. Paul's; but the prime minister who appointed him to Llandaff in 1827 probably wanted him in the House of Lords. Hence, a bishopric was necessary.

The Ecclesiastical Commissioners of England had already made provision that Copleston's successor would be provided with an adequate stipend and an official residence in the diocese so that there would be no need to look around for an English deanery. But there were other demands, from the Association of Welsh Clergy in the West Riding of Yorkshire and, nearer home, from Benjamin and Augusta Hall, that the new bishop should be Welsh speaking as well as resident. And before Copleston was dead names were being canvassed.

On September 27th, 1849, John Williams, warden of Llandovery College and archdeacon of Cardigan, wrote to the Reverend David James, of Kirkdale, Liverpool: 'I believe that the Bishop of Llandaff is dying, and that there will soon be a vacancy there—if we are to make a rally *now* is the time. Lord John Russels' (*sic*) promise that the resolution of the House of Commons would be regarded by him and his party as binding upon them ought to be made public'. In a further letter, dated October 18th following, Williams wrote to James to say that a group in the University of Edinburgh was pressing his claims to what was now the vacant bishopric; and he went on to say: 'I think if the appointment could be stopped for eight days the chance of a Welshman Bishop would be much increased',[7] and of the Resolution of the House of Commons, John Williams wrote: 'Get up this point well and press it—it may not make me a Bishop, but may well make some other Welshman if well managed.' Later in the same month

Williams again wrote to David James to say that he had the support of the evangelical clergy, but 'There is no man whom the Aristocracy dislike more than they do myself as a probable Bishop'.

Williams was not the only correspondent to write to David James on this matter, for on October 24th, David Parry, vicar of Trecastle, wrote pledging his support for Archdeacon Williams. 'It is a sad pity', said he, 'if this opportunity be lost, by our not having a Welshman appointed—a man acquainted with the Language, the habits, and the peculiar character of the people. The Church will never thrive in Wales until this object be attained.'

There were other forces working to the same end. W. H. Owen, Rhyllon, St. Asaph, in a letter dated October 26th, 1849 (recipient not named), indicated that the *Liverpool Standard* and the Bath Lay Association were equally interested in the choice: 'it is a bright augury that the press, both provincial and metropolitan, has universally declared itself in our favour.' On the same day *The Times* had referred to the vacancy in Llandaff in an article in which it was said that 'a considerable feeling was shown in favour of conferring the mitre on a Welshman', and with this the newspaper agreed, for if it was impossible to appoint a non-Welsh speaking cleric to a Welsh parish, it was unwise to appoint a non-Welsh speaking bishop to a Welsh diocese, although 'the same objection does not apply so strongly to a bishop as a preacher'.

But there was an uneasy feeling locally that all was not well. On October 27th, 1849, the *Monmouth Beacon* announced that the new bishop would be Lord Auckland, Bishop of Sodor and Man; and on the same day, Sir Thomas Phillips, the Monmouthshire industrialist and very faithful layman,[8] wrote to William Addams-Williams (Jr.) of Llangybi, to inform him that a meeting of influential people interested in the appointment had been held in London at the Freemason's Tavern to prepare a Memorial to the Prime Minister, and that Sir Benjamin Hall had written independently to urge the appointment of a Welshman to the office. Phillips hinted in his letter that Lord Auckland would be the next bishop; there were certain handicaps: he had ten children but no Welsh, but he had been an energetic pastor in Battersea and he was without tractarian sympathies. Phillips concluded: 'I wish he could resolutely master sufficient of the Welsh language to administer the rite of confirmation in that tongue.'

The prophets, however, were confounded, for on the same day as Phillips wrote to Addams-Williams, John Williams wrote once more to David James: 'Dr. Ollivant is Bishop of Llandaff—he owes his preferment to the Lampeter men and those of your party in the Church, Hughes of

Cardiganshire[9] leading them there. It is not a bad nomination if you overlook the hypocrisy which requires us to accept him as a real Welshman.' The local reaction was not at first unfavourable, even from the Llanover family. On December 31st, 1849, Sir Benjamin Hall wrote to S. R. Bosanquet, of Dingestow: 'We have lately had a new Bishop appointed who once lived in a neighbouring Welsh diocese; and I trust that his lordship will minister to the spiritual requirements of the Welsh inhabitants of his diocese, and avoid the errors of his predecessor'. But these sentiments did not last long, or perhaps they had never been shared by the Bee of Gwent[10] (Lady Hall), for on March 31st, 1850, she wrote to David James that as Dr. Thirlwall, bishop of St. David's, 'was so caressed and flattered by the Welsh clergy for his *supposed* acquaintance with the (Welsh) language, that when Llandaff was vacant the Ministry had discovered they *cd try* another humbug with impunity.' Lady Hall's objection to Ollivant was based not only on the question of language but also because of his association with St. David's College, Lampeter, for which institution she had no good word to say, since she accused the authorities there of having neglected the chair of Welsh; and John Williams, of Llandovery, went so far as to say, in a letter to David James on November 10th, 1851, that the appointment of Ollivant had been engineered by Colonel Harford, 'the wet and dry nurse of Lampeter', whose nephew and heir had married the daughter of Chevalier Bunsen who, in turn, had influence with the Prince Consort.

Alfred Ollivant, a native of Manchester, was fifty-two years of age when he was appointed bishop of Llandaff. At the time of his appointment he was professor of Divinity and fellow of Trinity College, Cambridge, and had previously served as vice-principal of St. David's College, Lampeter, where he had learned Welsh and had preached in that language; and, in addition, he was vicar of Llangeler, where his curate was John Griffith. No bishop of Llandaff has ever been confronted with so formidable a task as faced Ollivant in 1850, but he faced it with a high sense of duty and was temperamentally fitted to meet the challenge. He was essentially a man of action, and although his visitation charges are still worth reading for their theology and learning, he kept close to the well-known paths in his thought, having no originality of mind and probably being suspicious of theological speculation. No better insight into Ollivant himself can be obtained than in the concluding sentences of his first visitation charge, given in September, 1851: 'If in the remarks which I have thought it my duty to address to you, I have abstained from matters of doubtful disputation and confined myself to questions of practical interest, the reason for my doing so will readily have suggested itself to your own reflections. The condition of the diocese is such as peculiarly to call for practical exertion. The difficulties with which we have to contend are not speculations, but realities; not nice distinctions of doctrine, but deficiencies in the resources and agency of the Church. Around us and in the midst of us are thousands entirely without, or inadequately provided with, the means of grace.' When Ollivant spoke those words he probably knew the worst, for on the preceding March 30th the only religious census of the century had taken place, when everyone who attended a church or chapel on that day had been enumerated.

Different interpretations can doubtless be given of the figures which emerged from this census as far as the old diocese of Llandaff was concerned, but the following conclusions are not likely to be challenged:

(i) It was abundantly clear that nonconformity, and particularly Welsh nonconformity, had made tremendous strides in the old diocese of Llandaff in the first half of the nineteenth century, and that by the middle of that century an industrial society in which nonconformity predominated had become well established. In the industrial belt, taken as a whole, Nonconformists outnumbered Anglicans by six or seven to one, and in such areas as Aberdare and Merthyr Tydfil, by an even greater proportion.

(ii) In the rural areas—the old, historic, agricultural parts of Glamorgan and Monmouthshire—the balance was more even, but nonconformity tipped the scales here because of its growth in such country towns as Abergavenny and the growing urban areas of Cardiff and Newport. It is probable that the Anglicans were in a majority in most of the *purely* rural parishes.

(iii) Similarly, in church accommodation the Nonconformists greatly surpassed the Anglicans. Chapel building had gone on on a large scale in the fifty years previous to the census of 1851, and by this latter date the Nonconformists had many more chapels than there were churches and consequently a far larger seating capacity.

(iv) Taking the diocese as a whole, Nonconformists outnumbered the Anglicans by 4 or 5:1.

(v) But there was a concealed factor which the census did not directly reveal but which was of the greatest importance: that nonconformity flourished where the incidence of Welsh speaking was highest. It was clear that the Welsh language and nonconformity were the cultural and religious counterparts of the same pattern. It is impossible to tell how many Welsh immigrants had become Nonconformists because of the paucity of places of worship in the new industrial communities, but it is clear that when a churchman began to go to chapel he usually stayed there, and so nonconformity became a family tradition, and was to remain so throughout the remainder of the century and the first generation of the present century. The corollary is equally important: although it cannot be statistically proved, it is highly probable that the established church ministered largely to the English immigrants in the iron and coal-mining areas.

Statistics and their implications were sufficiently discouraging in themselves, but the magnitude of Bishop Ollivant's task can only be estimated by revealing the causes of nonconformity's success up to 1850 and beyond; for the obvious cause, namely, the inability of the established church to act except in accordance with an Act of Parliament and an Order in Council does not go deep enough; the truth is that nonconformity had certain in-built characteristics in those days which enabled it to capture this new industrial society.

The basic reason for its success was that in those days it was a working-class movement in a working-class area. Dr. Thomas Rees, of Beaufort, a prominent nonconformist historian, wrote to the *Nonconformist* on December 26th, 1866: 'We readily recognise the distinction of classes in our daily intercourse and secular transactions, but the moment we cross the threshold of the sanctuary, or meet to hold a religious service anywhere, our social distinctions are entirely forgotten'; and he went on to accuse the clergy of the established church of pandering to a social élite in their parishes and of perpetuating social distinctions by means of pew-rents. In addition to this, Rees attributed the success of nonconformity to vigorous preaching, the organisation of Sunday schools, and to the periodic religious revivals which broke out in these areas which added hundreds to the membership of chapels. In a letter to *The Christian Witness* on May 7th, 1850, Thomas Rees claimed that the recent revival of 1849 (which coincided with one of the periodical cholera epidemics of those days) had added 1,200 to 1,500 members to the nine congregational churches in Merthyr Tydfil, and that thousands had joined the baptist churches in Glamorgan and Monmouthshire.

No doubt these factors contributed to the success of nonconformity, but there were others which were at least equally important. The first was the prominent place given to laymen in the chapels. While it might be an exaggeration to describe nonconformity as a lay movement, there is a large element of truth in the statement. Thus, in any given chapel, the influence of the laity was very strong, and there were many tasks and offices which they were called upon to fill. The origin of many non-conformist 'causes' was due to lay initiative, when a group of co-religionists would come together, begin holding services in a cottage or any other convenient place, ultimately build a chapel and 'call' a minister; and in many cases the minister, unless he were an outstanding personality (and some of them were), would be just a *primus inter pares* in relation to his deacons. The established church, in contrast, had little to offer its laity except to attend divine service; authority was concentrated in the incumbent and church wardens (one of whom could well be a Nonconformist). There was no means of training church laity for office and responsibility.

Above all, the success of nonconformity in those days was probably due to the relationship of the chapels to the community. These industrial areas were, for a long time, drab and colourless from a social standpoint. Social institutions were few in most of them: the chapels and the public-houses were the most prominent and popular, and consequently there was little alternative between being a chapel-man or a regular attendant at a public-house. The chapels filled a social need in these districts, and their success cannot be understood unless it is remembered that they were social centres of great importance as well as places of worship. Up to the end of the nineteenth century and beyond, chapel vestries were the venue of some function or other, religious or social, for four or five nights a week. There grew up in the industrial areas what can be described as a 'chapel-vestry culture', which was the popular culture of those parts: *eisteddfodau*, competitive meetings, etc. Nonconformist families found their cultural activities as well as their means of grace in their chapels, and the debt of the industrial areas to this aspect of nonconformity was very great. Non-conformity was probably the most powerful formative influence in the society created by the Industrial Revolution in South Wales; and when, after the middle of the last century, nonconformity became increasingly political in its interests, its hold on these districts was temporarily strengthened. Thomas Rees was able to inform the bishop of Llandaff in a letter to the *Star of Gwent* on September 5th, 1857, what the bishop no doubt already knew, that the parish of Aberystruth had 4 churches and 17 chapels, that of Bedwellty 5 churches and 42 chapels, Merthyr Tydfil parish contained 6 churches and 44 chapels, and Aberdare had 6 churches and 34 chapels.[11]

Thus the task that confronted the new bishop of Llandaff in 1850 was not one of bricks and mortar only, even though church buildings had to be given priority. As Bruce Knight had briefed Bishop Sumner in 1826 so now Thomas Williams, dean of Llandaff, briefed Bishop Ollivant in preparation for two public meetings called at Bridgend and Newport respectively on October 29th and 30th, 1850, as a result of which the Llandaff Church Extension Society was established. This was the first time that a bishop of Llandaff appealed to the diocese as a whole for money to build churches, and those responsible for the organization of this Society were the leading laymen in the old diocese: H. A. Bruce (later Lord Aberdare), Sir Thomas Phillips, Bruce Pryce, John Nicholl, Richard Blakemore, and others,[12] with the first named as secretary. The building of churches was not the only task undertaken by the society; it also gave grants toward the maintenance of clergy in new districts and parishes, and, in this respect the Ecclesiastical Commissioners were able to give more aid after 1863, especially for additional curates. Nor was the building of churches for the period 1850 to about 1890 due solely to the activity of the Llandaff Diocesan Church Extension Society, for its income was much too small for the purpose. The Church Pastoral Aid Society, the Church Building Society, local efforts, and many munificent gifts by landowners and industrialists made possible the extension of church work by means of buildings and clergy. When Ollivant became bishop it can be said that the immediate problem lay in the old iron-works districts in the *blaenau*, but after 1860 or so deep-coal-mining created new communities further down the valleys. Thus after 1860 the old parish of Ystradyfodwg or Ystrad Rhondda, comprising the two Rhondda Valleys was transformed, and a little later, in the 1880s, the mid-Glamorgan valleys, the Llynfi, Ogmore, and Garw, with the old parishes of Llangynwyd and Llangeinor became industrialized, and later still, the anthracite areas further west. The deep-coal-mining period saw a tremendous growth too in urban areas such as Cardiff and Newport, and these had to be provided with buildings and clergy. The progress of church building and the provision of clergy cannot be dealt with in detail in this chapter, but it can be claimed that it did not lag behind industrial development in the second half of the century as it had during the preceding fifty or sixty years, and consequently the old diocese of Llandaff saw the greatest expansion in the number of parishes and buildings that it had seen in its history. By the beginning of the present century most of the industrial and urban areas had been covered. The Report of the Llandaff Diocesan Church Extension Society was able to say, a few months after the death of Ollivant in 1882: 'In short a vast amelioration of the condition of ecclesiastical affairs in this diocese has undoubtedly been accomplished during the late Episcopate. The ruined cathedral has been restored to more than its ancient splendour; the number of the Clergy has been largely increased; about 170 churches have been built, re-built, or restored; there are comparatively few churches which are not in a good condition; about £360,000 has been spent in the work of church building or restoration since 1849; a vast increase has taken place in the number of Incumbents resident in their parishes; 42 Lay Readers have been appointed; the number of Celebrations is immensely increased; and the observance of the greater Festivals of the Church has undergone much improvement during the period under review.'

Ollivant was succeeded as bishop by Richard Lewis (1883-1905), archdeacon of St. David's, of Welsh stock but not particularly fluent in the language. But he proved to be an energetic bishop: e.g., he was the bishop of Llandaff who began the practice of instituting a new incumbent in the church of the parish to which he had been appointed. (It was the railway age which made this possible.) He was succeeded by Joshua Pritchard Hughes, vicar of Llantrisant and son of a former bishop of St. Asaph, an appointment that must have been a surprise, if not a bit of a shock, to the diocese, for he had played little part in diocesan affairs.[13] He remained bishop until 1928.

The period from the death of Ollivant to the beginning of the First World War saw a steady development in the administrative organs of the diocese. The establishment of the Diocesan Conference was achieved in 1884 and on May 11th, 1895, Bishop Lewis signed and sealed the scheme for the reorganization of the deaneries, a scheme which was promulgated by Order in Council on June 29th, 1895.[14] At the same time the number of church societies increased very considerably: during the first half of the century they were limited to a Society for the Improvement of Church Music, and the Llandaff Diocesan Council for Education. But they proliferated after 1883: some are still with us but others have been made redundant by disestablishment. Diocesan funds were established for various purposes, and in 1913 the Diocesan Board of Finance was set up and in the following year began to make financial demands on the parishes. The Quota had arrived, and the modern diocese of Llandaff had evolved.

But beneath these outward changes other and more important changes were taking place. When Alfred Ollivant became bishop in 1850 there were two distinct societies in the diocese, distinct socially and, to a large extent linguistically. The parishes of the Caldicot moors, the Gwynllŵg moors and the vale of Glamorgan were then, and for a few generations to come, substantially eighteenth-century in their outlook. The construction of the South Wales Railway in 1850 and the Vale of Glamorgan Railway a generation or so later had little effect on the majority of these rural parishes, apart from the continued growth of Cardiff and Newport, and the rise of Penarth and Barry. But country towns such as Bridgend, Cowbridge, Chepstow, Abergavenny, and Monmouth saw no radical changes until the end of the First World War; while the agricultural depression which began in the 1880s and went on until 1914 drained these parishes of their prosperity and encouraged the migration from the agricultural areas to the coalfields. And it was these rural parishes which attracted clergy of the 'squarson' type: monied men, many of them, who enjoyed more than one living, and were necessarily non-resident in one of their parishes. These were the Hardings, Lisles, Leyshons, Biedermanns, Casberds, Mabers, and Staceys of the diocese, men to whom Copleston too readily granted certificates of non-residence, but expressed his opinion of some of them quite freely in his correspondence with Bruce Knight: 'It is not very generous to keep a man in a laborious and important and ill-paid office, because he does the duty well, when others live at their ease and enjoy the greater part of the pay', wrote Copleston on February 26th, 1836; and on November 20th, 1838, he wrote (again to Bruce Knight): 'I hope you will not think me too brusque, but to say the truth I have no patience with your Gaisfords, your Janes, your Watsons, *et hoc genus omne.* They present one of the greatest abuses in the English church.'

Such men as these (and, indeed, many of the curates they employed), would have been singularly ill-equipped to minister in the new industrial parishes, for they accepted certain social values which did not apply in the iron districts and coalfields. A new breed of cleric was called for, and, fortunately, it was forthcoming: the success of Lodowick Edwards in Rhymney will be recalled. But the cleric who became most involved in the social as well as the religious life of an industrial parish was undoubtedly John Griffith, who went as vicar to Aberdare in 1847, to a parish fifty or sixty square miles in extent, a population of 13,000 and with only one church. As far as his own upbringing and personal propensities were concerned, Griffith would probably have been more at home in 1847 in the vale of Glamorgan than in Aberdare; and it took him some time to become settled in an industrial parish. He was appointed rector of Merthyr Tydfil in 1859 and by this time had had experience of the wretched conditions in which industrial workers were forced to live in those days. At first he was at loggerheads with the Nonconformists of Aberdare, but such was his social conversion in the two large industrial parishes of which he was incumbent that he came to have more in common with the Nonconformists than with the church establishment as represented by Llandaff. He was a very vigorous preacher in the evangelical tradition and an inveterate writer to the press, and by word and writing he expressed convictions not likely to endear him to those in authority in church or state. Thus, he deplored the spending of money on the restoration of Llandaff cathedral and St. Woolos church, Newport, when so much was needed in industrial parishes. He declared himself in favour of the disestablishment of the church in Wales, and so when he died in 1885 he had not received any diocesan or cathedral preferment.[15] But it was he who began a strong church tradition in the old parish of Aberdare where he virtually had to begin from scratch; but in Merthyr Tydfil some progress had been made during the incumbency of J. C. Campbell, who was appointed bishop of Bangor in 1859.[16]

No doubt the secret of John Griffith's ultimate impact on a large industrial parish and of his growing understanding of, and with, Non-conformists, was his strong evangelical zeal, and in this he was characteristic of many of the prominent clergy who served in the new parishes of the coalfield. He shared, as did many of his clerical brethren, the strength and the narrowness of the evangelical theology of those days. But the general tone of the diocese, both rural and industrial, was evangelical and 'low-church', except in those areas such as Caldicot, Llanfrechfa, certain Cardiff parishes, Margam and, before the end of the century, Aberdare itself, where the tractarian movement took root. The tractarian movement in the old diocese of Llandaff must be treated in summary fashion: Bishop Ollivant in the 1860s and 1870s maintained a recognizably anglican position between the warring factions, and, as a theologian, he was more concerned with doctrinal than with ritualistic issues. When Richard Lewis came to the diocese as bishop in 1883 there were other things to think about, for the disestablishment campaign was gathering strength.

Slowly the problem of staffing the new parishes with bilingual clergy was being solved, partly because of the number of ordinands who came to the diocese from rural, Welsh Wales; and at the same time the position of the laity in the church was being changed. Since 1850 the prominent laymen in the church had played an active part in connection with the Llandaff Diocesan Church Extension Society, but these were almost exclusively landowners and industrialists, and their activity was confined to the raising of money. Unless they happened to be churchwardens in their respective parishes they had no administrative functions; and the great mass of the laity had no voice in the affairs of their parishes. But Bishop Ollivant took the first step when he licensed the first lay-readers in his private chapel in Llandaff on April 27th, 1870.[17] Ollivant clearly had some misgivings about this innovation lest it should be regarded as a preliminary step to ordination, and he rightly stressed that they were licensed to serve the church as laymen. Ollivant was not the only person to have doubts about the wisdom of commissioning lay-readers, for a conference of rural deans in 1867 had decided that it would be undesirable in a Welsh diocese to give a lay-reader's commission to a class of men who, in point of education and social condition, would be indistinguishable from dissenting ministers. As most rural deans in those days represented country parishes this social bias throws an interesting light on the cleavage which then existed in the diocese between the rural and industrial societies. A further step to bring the laity into the picture was taken in 1881 when Ollivant made it clear in his visitation charge of that year that he would allow the setting up of church councils, comprising of clergy and laity, in the parishes. There was no constitutional authority for this, but it was allowed to take place in those parishes which wanted to take advantage of the bishop's advice.[18]

By this time Ollivant had been in the diocese for over thirty years and was now over eighty years of age. He might not have felt equal to taking the step of setting up a consultative council for the diocese, and it is certain that he had misgivings on this matter: he feared that such a body would discuss doctrinal matters. Thus, this step was left to the new bishop, Richard Lewis, who in 1884 inaugurated the Llandaff Diocesan Conference, and thus gave the diocese, clergy and laity, a forum in which matters affecting church and society could be voiced. An examination of the annual reports of the Llandaff Diocesan Conference shows the extent to which its members took advantage of this new opportunity, and the reader is struck with the variety of subjects discussed in the diocesan conferences in those days: 'Intermediate Education for Wales' (1886); 'How best to meet the bilingual problem' (1887); 'Housing needs' (1893); 'Divorce and remarriage', 'Biblical criticism', 'Sunday observance' (1896),[19] 'Art and the Church' (1899); 'That in view of the Welsh National Awakening it is the duty of the Church to adapt her policy to the present needs of the Principality' (1904); 'That this Diocesan Conference desires to express its sincere sympathy with the objects of the National Insurance Bill now before Parliament' (1911); 'The Church and Socialism' (1912).

By the beginning of the First World War the expansionist programme begun in 1850 was spent. There were still areas which called for attention, but, generally speaking, the diocese, and particularly the industrial parishes, was well served with clergy and buildings; in fact, more so than today because of the large number of mission rooms and national schools which were used for divine worship and have since disappeared. Since 1850 the diocese had been reshaped, not only administratively and structurally, but, more important, in the more prominent place given to the

142   A HISTORY OF THE CHURCH IN WALES

laity and in the new type of cleric that ministered in it. This changed the image of the church in those areas created by the Industrial Revolution; and, when all credit is given to Bishop Richard Lewis and, to a lesser extent, Bishop Hughes, it is Alfred Ollivant who transformed the diocese to which he was appointed in 1849.

But in spite of the great advances the established Church made in these industrial parishes, it failed to capture them from nonconformity. As long as outward religious practices were observed in the south Wales coalfield, and even though the established Church in Wales was a very different church in 1914 as compared with what it had been in 1850, the tone and temper of this industrial society remained nonconformist. But the historian of the future may well see the end of the First World War as the religious watershed in these areas: hitherto they had been 'religious' communities as far as attendance at public worship was concerned, but thereafter there has been a decline in both church and chapel attendance. This has been accompanied by a reduction in the number of those who speak the Welsh language and the political change from liberalism to socialism during this same period. The fortunes of politics, religion and language were interlinked, for the triple foundations of the establishment in the coalfield for over half a century had been the Welsh language, the liberal party, and nonconformity. They declined together.

---

[1] Watson was, of course, a notorious pluralist; and so was his son who held livings and offices in the diocese of Llandaff.
[2] The location of the old iron industry was due to the local supply of coal, iron ore, limestone and water.
[3] Six months of his episcopate were spent in St. Paul's deanery, London.
[4] The following school rooms were used temporarily as places of worship: Nantyglo, Devauden, Nantgarw, Cyfarthfa, Hirwaun, Pontypool, Ebbw Vale, Cilybebyll, Skewen, The Hayes (Cardiff)—these all appear in Copleston's Register, now in the National Library of Wales.
[5] It will interest the present generation to know what the Ecclesiastical Commissioners considered a fit residence for a parson in those days: 'Two sitting rooms, study, kitchen, and scullery, each about sixteen feet by fourteen, the study and scullery somewhat less, according as may suit the general arrangement of the plan, and not less than five bedrooms. There should also be a pantry, or china-closet, larder, water-closet, linen-chest, wine and beer-cellar, coal house, dust-bin &c.'
[6] Merthyr Tydfil, Neath, Bridgend, Llantrisant, Cowbridge, Cardiff, Newport, Caerleon, Chepstow, Usk, Pontypool, Llangattock Vibion Avel, Raglan, Skenfrith, Trellech, Magor, Llantilio Crossenny, Abergavenny, and, after 1844, Monmouth, Caerphilly, and 'Waun near Merthyr'.
[7] John Williams had been rector of Edinburgh Academy, and it was he whom Walter Scott had described as the finest schoolmaster in Europe. Whether the diocese of Llandaff needed the finest schoolmaster in Europe as bishop in 1850 is doubtful!
[8] Phillips was mayor of Newport when the Chartists marched on the town on November 4th, 1839.
[9] Hughes was vicar of Llanbadarn.

[10] Lady Hall's bardic name was Gwenynen Gwent.

[11] At the same time it must not be supposed that the progress of nonconformity was uniform. There were 'dry' periods in the history of many chapels, and after 1880 or so its growth was checked, the first indication of this being the decline in the number of 'hearers', a class which inflated nonconformist statistics considerably in the nineteenth century.

[12] One notable absentee was Benjamin Hall. His contribution to the effort was to send emissaries around certain areas to check on the case made by the bishop for a diocesan effort. The Hall family of Llanover was to be as great a thorn in Ollivant's flesh as it had been in that of Copleston.

[13] It was known that the vacancy had been offered to Frederic William Edmondes, archdeacon of Llandaff. He refused the offer and suggested that John Owen should be translated from St. David's.

[14] The deaneries in the archdeaconry of Llandaff: Aberdare, Barry, Caerphilly, Groneath Lower (Eastern Division), Groneath Lower (Western Division), Groneath Upper (Eastern Division), Groneath Upper (Western Division), Llandaff, Merthyr Tydfil, Penarth.
    Archdeaconry of Monmouth: Abergavenny, Bedwellty, Blaenau Gwent, Caerleon, Chepstow, Monmouth, Netherwent, Newport, Raglan, Usk. Thus was fixed the administrative structure of the diocese until disestablishment.

[15] A son of his, C. E. T. Griffith, became dean of Llandaff.

[16] It would be invidious to attempt to make a list of the clergy who laboured faithfully, and not without success, in the industrial and urban parishes of the old diocese. John Griffith has been chosen because he is the prototype of the new kind of parson; there were others who worked more quietly and were equally effective.

[17] Their names deserve to be recorded here: Edward Brogden, James Bunter Coulthurst, George Walden, Benjamin Jones, Henry Harries, and David Richards. One of these was licensed to the parish of Dowlais and the others to the parish of Gelligaer.

[18] The first two parishes to do so were Penarth and Caerleon.

[19] Lest it be thought that these important issues could only be dealt with cursorily, it should be remembered that a diocesan conference lasted two days.

CHAPTER 7

THE WELSH CHURCH IN THE NINETEENTH CENTURY

by

Owain W. Jones

R URAL Wales, no less than the industrial areas, had its problems. The 'land question' became acute in the course of the nineteenth century, just as across Offa's Dyke the 'condition of England question', as Carlyle called it, exercised men's minds. During the first half of the century there was a rapid and continuous increase in population. This was the result of natural increase; the days of immigration into Wales were not yet; and the reasons for this natural increase have yet to be explained. The social problems of the day arose from the strain imposed upon a backward economy by the larger population. One effect was the continued cultivation of the Welsh uplands. During the Napoleonic Wars it had been economic to farm these marginal lands. The decades after Waterloo were times of depression, but the Welsh upland farmer had to stay where he was because there was no alternative. Later, some of the bolder spirits escaped by emigrating to the New World. In the second half of the century the industrial towns offered another avenue of escape. Even now the remains of many abandoned cottages can be seen high on the barren hillsides of mid-Wales; for after 1851 the rural population of Wales began to decline, and this process has persisted to the present day.

Equally dramatic was the transformation of the religious scene. The Calvinistic Methodists (the present Presbyterian Church of Wales) left the anglican Church in 1811. They grew steadily in numbers in the decades that followed until the Religious Census of 1851 revealed that they constituted the largest single denomination in the principality. The older dissent also developed rapidly. It has been calculated that by the end of the eighteenth century there were about 100 congregationalist chapels in Wales. By 1851 the number increased to 684. In 1800 there were 46 congregationalist ministers. In 1851 there were 319. The Baptists also increased in numbers; in the counties of Breconshire and Radnorshire

Y BEIBL CYS-SEGR-LAN. SEF YR HEN DESTA-MENT, A'R NEWYDD.

2. *Timoth.* 3. 14, 15.

Eithr aros di yn y pethau a ddyfcaift, ac a ymddyried-
wyd i ti, gan wybod gan bwy y dyfcaift.
Ac i ti er yn fachgen wybod yr fcrythur lân, yr hon
fydd abl i'th wneuthur yn ddoeth i iechydwria-
eth, trwy'r ffydd yr hon fydd yng-Hrift Iefu.

Imprinted at London *by the Deputies of*
CHRISTOPHER BARKER,
Printer to the Queenes moft excel-
lent Maieftie.

1588.

PLATE 5. Title-page of William Morgan's Bible, 1588

PLATE 6.   William Bruce Knight, dean of Llandaff
(*Friends of Llandaff Cathedral*)

they outstripped the Calvinistic Methodists. The tiny Roman Catholic population increased tenfold during these fifty years, being reinforced by an influx from catholic Ireland into the industrial areas of south and north Wales. They numbered a little over five and a half thousand in 1851. The Religious Census of that year, the first and the last ever attempted, revealed that the Nonconformists accounted for nearly 80% of the worshipping population (not the total population as has sometimes been suggested). Over half of the total population remained unaccounted for on the Sunday of the Census, and this became a matter of concern for both churchman and nonconformist.

To some extent the rapid increase in nonconformity resulted from the failure of the Church to make provision for a growing and shifting population. The ecclesiastical parishes had been carved out in the Middle Ages, according to the needs and social patterns of the time. The creation of new parishes was a tedious process involving parliamentary procedure. The reform of the administrative system of the Church, unchanged since medieval times, was urgently needed. It was taken in hand after 1835, but still the reforms proceeded slowly.

The training of the clergy continued to be a problem. Thomas Burgess, bishop of St. David's 1804-25, still used the divinity classes already established at the grammar schools, but he extended the course of training to seven years. He saw that there was an urgent need for a college in Wales to cater for those who could not afford to proceed to the existing universities. He tithed his own income, and he urged his clergy and others to do the same, to raise funds for the new institution. Burgess had already been translated to Salisbury when St. David's College, Lampeter, opened its doors to the first students on March 1st, 1827, but the importance of his foundation is beyond dispute. Yet the college had many difficulties to face in the early days. It was said at the time of the opening that very few of the natives of the diocese would be able to afford to send their sons there. The cost of residence and the poverty of the Welsh countryside created this problem. Also there was a tendency to regard it as a diocesan college, despite the fact that a number of English bishops had ordained men who had been trained there. In the diocese of Llandaff there were divinity classes in the grammar schools at Cowbridge and Usk, the latter being replaced in 1830 by Abergavenny. These classes continued in existence until Bishop Ollivant closed them, on the resignation of the headmaster of Cowbridge in 1850, and on the death of the headmaster of Abergavenny in 1856. In the diocese of St. Asaph some use was made of Ruthin school and some men were ordained from the St. David's grammar schools. Later the college at St. Bees in Cumberland (founded 1817) provided a number of clergy for the diocese. One notable product of St. Bees was Robert Roberts, the *Sgolor Mawr*, who stated that the bishop of Bangor would not accept men from St. Bees. At Bangor the vast majority of ordinands still were graduates. The first candidate from Lampeter was ordained there in 1851, and from St. Bees in 1862.

Contemporary observers noted that the opening of St. David's College coincided with a decline in the numbers attending the grammar schools and in their standards. The college was blamed for this decline, but it would seem rather that these institutions, which might have been sufficient for the needs of the eighteenth century, were hardly adequate for the nineteenth and needed to be reorganised. Primary education also left much to be desired, despite the efforts of the National Society (1811) and the undenominational British and Foreign School Society (1808) whose work was hampered by the fact that Nonconformists could not agree among themselves. The lamentable state of education in Wales was clearly demonstrated in the report of a Commission of Inquiry published in 1847. Unfortunately the Commissioners overreached themselves and included provocative statements about the social and moral condition of the principality. They equated ignorance with the use of Welsh and immorality with the prevalence of nonconformity. Hence the report has passed into history as *Brad Y Llyfrau Gleision* (The Treachery of the Blue Books), and it provided new weapons for political nonconformity. But the factual parts of the report cannot be disputed and it reveals the inadequacy of much that passed for education in Wales at this time.

The problem of language was also becoming acute. Rowland Williams, vice-principal of St. David's College 1850-62, was one of the earliest advocates of bilingual education, yet he wrote these words to Bishop Carey of St. Asaph in 1851:

> In fact, our pupils know *no* language, but are engaged in acquiring the rudiments of several. Welsh they cannot write and English they cannot speak. The real remedy would, in the natural state of things, be to lecture in Welsh, but this course would be prevented partly by difficulties and partly by prejudices.[1]

St. David's College was being criticised at the time for neglecting Welsh. The most vociferous critics were Sir Benjamin Hall (later Lord Llanover) and John Williams, archdeacon of Cardigan and warden of the new Llandovery College. But English had long been the only medium of instruction in all Welsh educational establishments, both church and dissenting. Difficulties and prejudices affected the use of Welsh in the parishes. The difficulties arose from an anglicised gentry and from English immigration, so that the Church had to minister to a bilingual society. There was also much prejudice against the language itself. Rowland Williams (senior), vicar of Ysgeifiog in the diocese of St. Asaph, wrote in the preface to a printed sermon (1847) which had a wide circulation at the time:

> As a Welshman and a clergyman, I must also strongly protest against frequent practice of introducing the English language into places where it is not understanded of the people. Many of our Welsh prelates have most unwisely sanctioned this custom because they consider it as a means of great advantage, by accelerating the general introduction of English into the Principality. Even in this view the spiritual welfare of the present generation must be compromised. But I would respectfully ask how it happens that, while the English language is almost universally used in Radnorshire, this, of all the Welsh counties, presents the least signs of improvement.

Williams was also concerned about the failure of the Church to make use of the printed word at a time when, he said, 'the Welsh are becoming a nation of readers . . . and the mighty influence of the press, so powerful for good or evil, is with a few, and these very honourable exceptions, employed in Wales for the dissemination of sectarian tenets'. He himself had been an active member of the Bangor Tract Society and a contributor to the *Gwyliedydd* and the *Cambro-Briton*. He was also one of those who produced the 1841 edition of the Welsh Prayer Book, the others being Archdeacon John Jones of Bangor, Rice Rees, Chancellor Bruce Knight of Llandaff, and Morris Williams (Nicander) who acted as secretary. Williams was also one of the early church builders of the nineteenth century, rebuilding his parish church at Ysgeifiog in 1842.

The long-overdue reform of the Church's administration got under way with the appointment of the Ecclesiastical Commission in 1835. It was intended to recommend measures for 'the more equal distribution of episcopal duties', the greater efficiency of cathedral and collegiate churches, and the 'best method of providing for the cure of souls'. A large number of Acts of Parliament incorporated the reforms suggested by the commission. Two proposals relating to the Welsh dioceses aroused alarm. There was a need for new bishoprics in England, but there was also a determination not to have any more bishops in the House of Lords. It was, therefore, thought necessary to combine some of the existing dioceses. The proposal to unite Llandaff and Bristol fell through as impracticable. The next plan was to unite Bangor and St. Asaph, and this was only prevented by an Act steered through Parliament by Lord Powys in 1846. His countrymen expressed their gratitude to Lord Powys by founding the scholarships which bear his name and which are still awarded to ordination candidates of the Church in Wales. The Powys scholarships were then worth £60 per annum and could be held at any college or hall in Oxford or Cambridge. It was hoped that they would assist in providing a supply of competent clergy for the principality. The examiners appointed to make the first awards were Archdeacon John Williams and Rowland Williams (junior), fellow of King's College, Cambridge.

The last surviving collegiate church in Wales was a victim of the commissioners' reforms. The College of Christ in Brecon had been moved there from Abergwili in 1542. Its prebendaries drew their income from sinecure rectories, and, as they died, their incomes passed into the hands of the commissioners. The old institution was finally abolished in 1853 and the present school rose upon its site. Thus the benefits of the ecclesiastical Acts did not operate immediately. It was often many years before the passing of vested interests made it possible for the various provisions to take effect. Nevertheless the work of the Ecclesiastical Commission was of considerable importance. Bishop Blomfield of London claimed that it saved the Church of England; but Dr. Chadwick writes: 'Blomfield was complacent: the Church was carried by currents deeper than the pools and eddies of the Commissioners' Board'.[2] These were the movements for reform within the Church itself, represented by the evangelicals, the tractarians, the broad churchmen, perhaps we should also include the ecclesiologists. But the party tags should not be allowed to disguise the variety of thought among those who, for convenience, have been grouped together under those names. To think of them in rigid party terms can lead to serious misconceptions about the religious history of the first half of the nineteenth century.

The origins of the evangelical movement go back to the eighteenth century. It was a reaction against the theology and attitudes of the Age of Enlightenment. Evangelicals stressed the experience of conversion, the doctrine of the atonement and the primacy of scripture. It moved into the nineteenth century through three avenues, the Methodists, the Dissenters and the anglican evangelicals. In England they got together in groups, like the Clapham Sect, and they transformed the life of their parishes. There is no parallel evidence from Wales, but the primary doctrines of evangelicalism figure largely in the minds of many Welsh clergy, especially in their response to the introduction of broad church principles into the country. Nor was the movement without its dangers. A group of students at Lampeter in the 1830s carried evangelical doctrine to its extreme; and the 'Lampeter Brethren' became the leaders of a perfectionist sect called the 'Princites'—after their leader H. J. Prince. They eventually established themselves in their *Agapenone* or 'Abode of Love' in Spaxton in Somersetshire.[3] Indeed, the growth of denominations of all kind at this period— including sects of the lunatic fringe—suggests that the doctrine of *laissez faire* applied as much to religion as to politics or economics.

The Oxford or tractarian movement also has its roots in the previous century, among the old high churchmen of which there were not a few in Wales. The movement began with the activities of a group of friends at Oxford, all of whom had been influenced to a greater or lesser degree by John Keble. The assize sermon preached by Keble in Oxford in 1833 is usually held to mark the beginning of the movement. But this is an oversimplification for the advocating of 'church principles', as they called them, had started some years before. The early leaders at Oxford were John Henry Newman, Hurrell Froude, Isaac Williams (from Aberystwyth), John Copeland, William Palmer (of Worcester College), and others. They were joined by E. B. Pusey and so prominent was his name that they were often called 'Puseyites'. They had friends in the country, John Keble, Thomas Keble, Sir George Prevost and a host of others who shared their aspirations. They published the *Tracts for the Times*; they wrote poems and sermons; they translated the early fathers. They influenced their students and their friends who went back to their parishes to practise their church principles and to recall their contemporaries to the consciousness of their heritage as members of the catholic and apostolic Church in this land.

They aroused a good deal of opposition because they were thought to be high church—even suspected of being secret agents of the pope. By modern standards their churchmanship was very mediocre. They insisted on the daily service, that is the public recitation of morning and evening prayer in church. They aimed at a weekly celebration of the holy communion, but they were content with 'once a month' if the time was not ripe. Most of them celebrated the eucharist standing at the north end of the altar (in the twentieth century the hallmark of a low churchman). They were keen on the sacraments and began to revive the use of the sacrament of penance. They established monastic orders, but the monastic vows proper were not taken until the end of the century.

In the 1850s some of the younger and more daring adherents were seen to wear stoles embroidered with gold and silver crosses. Their elders, on the other hand, wished that the crosses were engraved in the heart rather than on the vestment. These young men were the precursors of the ritualists, the leaders of the anglo-catholic movement, a natural development perhaps, but a definite advance from the aims and methods of the first tractarians.

The new church and parish of Llangorwen near Aberystwyth, opened in 1841, were the first in Wales where the ideals of the Oxford Movement were put into practice. The moving spirit behind it was a layman, Matthew Davies Williams, the elder brother of Isaac Williams. A number of prominent tractarians emerged from this area in north Cardiganshire, two cousins of Isaac Williams—Lewis Evans of Llanfihangel Y Creuddyn, Lewis Gilbertson, the first incumbent of Llangorwen—and the brothers Evan and David Lewis. The second of the two brothers followed Newman to Rome in 1846. Evan Lewis became dean of Bangor in 1884. Basil Jones, later bishop of St. David's, was another of them, but he became suspicious of the tendencies of the movement and he withdrew his support. At the other end of the diocese the church and parish of Llangasty Tal-y-llyn were transformed from 1847 onwards by another layman, Robert Raikes (the great-grand-nephew of the founder of Sunday schools) who had been at Oxford in the days of the *Tracts*. Bishop Thirlwall of St. David's was rather mystified by these developments and he confided to Samuel Wilberforce, 'Williams at Aberystwyth and a Mr. Raikes in Brecknockshire have tried the High Church way, and it has failed'.[4] But this was, surely, a premature judgement.

The only Welsh bishop who had any sympathy for the tractarians was Christopher Bethell, bishop of Bangor 1830-59. He brought to the diocese a number of young clerics who had been influenced by the Oxford Movement, among them Philip Constable Ellis, Morris Williams (Nicander) and Evan Lewis. It was reckoned, a few years after Bethell's death, that about a third of the clergy of the diocese were tractarian sympathisers. The new church at Glanogwen (1862) was built to further their ideals. The position in the diocese of St. Asaph is more obscure, but a number of clerical bards, in particular R. W. Morgan of Tregynon (Mor Meirion) and John Williams (Ab Ithel), who later moved to the Bangor diocese, were no strangers to tractarian teaching.

Many of the early tractarians have been lost to sight. More interested in doctrine than in ceremonial, they were not always outwardly distinguishable from their neighbours. Yet they brought dignity and order into the worship of the Church, seeking to remedy a situation described by W. J. Conybeare in the *Edinburgh Review* in 1852:

A choir, consisting frequently of the most drunken reprobates in the parish, bawled out the 'Hanthem' which they sang in parts, that is in a complicated kind of discord. No other music varied the service except the singing of a metrical psalm from which the poetry had previously been extracted by Tate and Brady.

All this, Conybeare continued, is now changing. Hymns were coming into use and the psalms were being chanted. This was done in tractarian parishes to Gregorian modes.

In 1857 Bishop Ollivant of Llandaff congratulated his clergy, as he had already done on his two previous visitations, because they had not become involved with controversies over sacraments and rubrics. In other words, the influence of the Oxford Movement was negligible in his diocese. In 1872 Arthur Jones became vicar of St. Mary's, Cardiff, and the former calm was disturbed. At the same time F. W. Puller (later Fr. Puller S.S.J.E.) went to Roath and the 'Roath System', begun by him and continued by his successors, was gravely debated in English theological colleges and thought to be too severe for the human frame. These men were ritualists or anglo-catholics and they and their fellows were quite distinct from their low church neighbours. They were interested not only in doctrine but also in eucharistic vestments, incense and the ceremonial of the western rite. The anglo-catholics were most prominent in the towns of the north and south coastal plains, but they were not restricted to these areas. Aberdare, for example, had a strong tractarian tradition, having Evan Lewis as its incumbent from 1859, and later C. A. H. Green was successively curate and vicar. It was the first home of the Theological College of St. Michael and All Angels founded in 1892, the first warden being *Y Tad* H. R. Johnson, then a curate in Aberdare. All the theological colleges of the nineteenth century were founded as a result of tractarian influences. In 1911 St. Michael's College moved to the elegant gothic revival buildings, designed by John Prichard, which had been prepared for it at Llandaff.

In 1863 Connop Thirlwall delivered his triennial charge to the clergy of St. David's. Looking back over an episcopate which had already lasted twenty-three years, he said:

> During the whole of this period the Church has been more or less threatened from without and agitated from within. I need hardly remind you of the controversies which arose in the last generation, and have been carried on uninterruptedly to the present day, with regard to Sacraments and the whole range of theological questions concerned with them . . . Now, within the circle in which the earlier controversies were waged, the contending parties have suspended

their old conflict to unite their forces against a movement which seems to threaten all that they hold most dear.

And indeed, evangelicals and tractarians were united for the first time in opposition to a group of men who were as much concerned with the reform of the Church as they were. These were the broad churchmen.

Biblical criticism had developed in Germany. Little was known about it in this country in the early decades of the century, and it was the poet, Samuel Taylor Coleridge, who was chiefly instrumental in introducing the new ideas into this country. A few translations came to be made. Connop Thirlwall translated one of Schleirmacher's works in 1825. Strauss' *Life of Jesus*, published in 1835, appeared in English some eight years later. But it did not help matters when it was noted that subsequent translations came from a free-thinking circle centred on George Eliot. By the end of the 1820s a new word came into currency, neology, to denote lax ideas about the Bible, and in particular, laxity of the German variety. The suspicion of neology lessened the authority of many leading divines, and Thirlwall himself took some time to live down his early dalliance with the German critics.

At this time the historical (even the scientific) accuracy of the Bible was still taken for granted. The theory of the plenary inspiration of the scriptures was generally held. This preserved the scriptures from all mistakes except for some minor contradictions or a few errors which were patently the mistakes of copyists. The study of geology, however, was beginning to show that Archbishop Ussher's date for the creation of the world 4004 B.C., could hardly be sustained; and the biblical critics were threatening to undermine many of the accepted ideas. Men's minds were still dominated by the old evidential apologetic. Miracles and prophecy were still regarded as the evidences for Christianity. By prophecy was meant the God-given power of foreseeing the future. What better proof was there of inspiration than that the prophecies were subsequently and accurately fulfilled? How else, asked a learned bishop as late as 1862, could Christianity be defended? He was Harold Browne, bishop of Ely and formerly vice-principal of St. David's College. The biblical critics seemed to be undermining these two pillars of the faith, questioning the miracles (at least of the Old Testament), rationalizing the prophecy, and thereby destroying the authority of scripture.

Rowland Williams, the son of the vicar of Ysgeifiog, came from Cambridge to Lampeter in 1850 as vice-principal. This was a time when it could be said of Lampeter, as was later said of a famous English college, that its vices were more important than its principals. He was one of the leading Hebraists in this country, at a time when that language was not a popular field of study. He was one of the pioneers in the comparative study of religion. He was a keen amateur scientist and an enquiring historian. He was, therefore, well aware of the new studies and the new ideas of his time. He was concerned about what seemed to be a widening breach between religion and science. He had read Coleridge and he became convinced that the widening horizons of knowledge called for a restatement of what was then the accepted orthodoxy. He found the answer to these problems in the new science of biblical criticism and he devoted himself singlemindedly to its furtherance.

While at Lampeter Williams made his views known in two books, *Rational Godliness* (1855) and *Christianity and Hinduism* (1856). Today his ideas seem very unexciting. But to suggest in 1855 that the statement in the Book of Joshua about the sun standing still was poetry, not fact; to deny that Isaiah the son of Amoz foretold the conquests of Cyrus by claiming that chapter XL and the following section was the work of a different author; to refer to the Book of Jonah as an allegory; to argue for the Maccabaean date for the Book of Daniel; and to call the Bible 'the voice of the Church', all these were explosive in the extreme. The date of Daniel was a particularly sensitive matter. Pusey, in his *Lectures on the Prophet Daniel* (1865), argued for the traditional date and attacked Rowland Williams in particular. The point was that if it was allowed that the book dated from the second century B.C., as Williams asserted, then the miracles recorded in the book lost their force; and the prophecies became not prognostications but a summary of events that had already taken place. If that was so, then the evidences of Christianity were completely undermined.

The reaction in Wales was sharp and immediate. The opposition of the lower clergy was led by John Powell Jones, then the evangelical vicar of Loughor and later of Llantrisant. Jones was an upholder almost of the literal inspiration of scripture. He held meetings of the clergy, wrote booklets and pursued Williams in the columns of *Yr Haul* where he stated, 'Rhieni, nid diogel i chwi osod eich plant yn efydwyr yng Ngholeg Lanbedr tra byddo egwyddorion Germaniaidd *Rational Godliness* yn cael eu hau yno' ('Parents, it is not safe for you to place your sons as students in Lampeter College while the German principles of *Rational Godliness* hold sway there'). The bishop of Llandaff, Alfred Ollivant, formerly vice-principal of St. David's College and regius professor of Divinity in the University of Cambridge, revealed in his charge of 1857 that he too held to the plenary inspiration of scripture and would have none of

Williams' ideas: 'If there is a charm in certain parts of the work which are not controversial, it may sweeten but cannot neutralize the poison thus presented to our lips'. Williams expected support from Connop Thirlwall who, unlike many of his contemporaries, knew all about these matters. Thirlwall, however, refused to commit himself; indeed the evidence suggests that he had repented himself of his earlier support of the German critics.[5]

When *Rational Godliness* first appeared, it was given a brief but enthusiastic welcome in the *Traethodydd*, the journal of the Calvinistic Methodists. In May 1856 a long review appeared, in which the same writer trod more warily and parted with Williams on the subject of the inspiration of scripture. Ollivant noticed this, for he, like Thirlwall, had acquired a good working knowledge of Welsh, and he wrote in the notes to his published charge: 'Was the volume (R.G.) then praised after a mere glance at its contents; or has a reclamation from the older members of the body, in this case against a spirit of Rationalism possibly beginning to develop amongst the younger, produced this second and sounder article?' Perhaps Ollivant was right. The reviewer reveals that he was familiar with the works of the English broad churchmen and with at least some of the German writers. But he was not prepared to become the kind of martyr to the cause that Rowland Williams did not hesitate to be.

Williams was one of the contributors to *Essays and Reviews* which in 1860 presented the results of biblical criticism to a totally unprepared public. His was the most explosive article in that controversial work. He was now vicar of Broad Chalke in Wiltshire, and he was prosecuted for heresy by the tractarian bishop of Salisbury, Walter Kerr Hamilton, one whom Williams described as 'a man of little learning and of medieval leaning'. Condemned on three charges in the Court of Arches, Williams won his appeal to the Privy Council and established the right of freedom of enquiry for the clergy of the Church of England.

So great was the uproar over *Essays and Reviews* that, for a while, Darwin's *Origin of Species* (1859) passed almost unnoticed. Then the theory of evolution added to the complexities of the conservative defenders of the authority of the Bible. Gradually the Church came to terms with Darwin and with biblical criticism. The change in the climate of opinion in Wales may be illustrated by the words of two prominent Nonconformists. Thomas Parry reviewed *The Life and Letters of Rowland Williams* in the *Traethodydd* in 1874 and stated that he was not sound in the faith ('nad oedd yn iach yn y Ffydd'). In 1903 Thomas Witton Davies, professor of Hebrew at Bangor, delivered a public lecture on the German scholar,

Heinrich Ewald. He spoke also of Rowland Williams and said: 'Dr. Williams was one of whom Wales had good reason to be proud, but he was one of whom neither England nor Wales showed itself worthy.'

The rapidly increasing population brought with it a problem of pastoral superintendance and church accommodation. This became particularly acute in the diocese of Llandaff. In December 1850 the new bishop, Alfred Ollivant, issued a statement which was designed to call the attention of the members of the Church to the desperate situation in the diocese. The population of the counties of Glamorgan and Monmouth was 117,107 in 1801. By 1841 it was 305,542 and still increasing. In particular parishes, Merthyr Tydfil, Aberdare, Bedwellty, Aberystruth are among those mentioned, the increase had been still more remarkable. Extensive immigration was taking place: 'At the Census of 1841 only 62% of the inhabitants of Monmouth and 74% in Glamorgan were natives of the diocese. There is, therefore a need for both Welsh and English clergy'. The table giving the 'present amount of church accommodation and number of pastors actually employed' in the most populous parishes shows how far the Church had slipped behind the growth of population. In Merthyr and Dowlais, where the population was about 50,000, there were six pastors and church accommodation for 2,500 (and this included the large church of St. David's built in 1847). Aberdare had 13,000 people with church accommodation for 176 and 2 pastors (hence it was that three new churches were started there in the 1850s). The growth of Cardiff had not really begun. The figures given are population 3,000 and pastors 3. The Church in Llandaff, the bishop declared, 'despoiled of its property, was unable to supply more pastors or church accommodation of its own resources'. In 253 parishes, for example, out of a total gross rent charge of £59,000, only £34,000 was annexed to the diocese; in a further 53 parishes the tithe was wholly abstracted. Ollivant called meetings at Newport and Bridgend and formed a Society for Providing Additional Pastoral Superintendance and Church Accommodation in the Diocese of Llandaff. During his episcopate, 1849-82, about 170 churches were built, rebuilt or restored at a total cost of some £360,000.

The needs of the other dioceses were urgent, if not so acute as those in Llandaff. Thirlwall noted in 1851 that 15 new churches had been built and over 40 restored in St. David's in the previous ten years. By 1857 the pace had accelerated. In St. Asaph it has been calculated that, during the episcopate of Vowler Short (1846-70), new churches were built and others restored at the rate of five a year. St. Asaph also has a fine record for the building of National schools so that by 1870 the diocese was the best provided in the whole kingdom. In Bangor about £160,000 was spent in church building during this same period. The four Welsh cathedrals were also being restored, Llandaff 1845-69, St. Asaph 1859-75, St. David's 1864-73, and Bangor 1869-84.

Thus the second half of the nineteenth century was a time of great activity in church building, both in building the new and in restoring or rebuilding the old. Given the will and the means to build, the next question that had to be faced was that of style. The churches built in the south Wales valleys in the earlier part of the century provide a number of examples where the classical style was continued. The medieval parish church at Merthyr Tydfil was rebuilt in this style in 1829 (to be redesigned by Pearson in 1895). St. George's, Tredegar (1836), St. David's, Rhymney (1839), and St. Mary's, Cardiff (1842 but altered later) had round headed windows and galleries which made them visually not dissimilar to nonconformist chapels. High churchmen disliked the classical tradition of the eighteenth century and churches which looked suspiciously like meeting houses. So they began to build in the newly revived gothic style, Llangorwen (1841) and Llangasty (1847) setting a fashion which was soon to be followed by others.

A new word had appeared in the English language—ecclesiology—defined in the *Century Dictionary* as treating 'of all the details of church furniture, ornaments etc. and is cultivated especially by the High Church party of the Church of England'. High churchmen did not keep the monopoly of it. Evangelicals were not long in following suit, and many Nonconformists succumbed to its influence. There were many chapels rebuilt at this time with ostentatious classical façades. There were also not a few which were built in the correct 'middle pointed' gothic style so beloved of the ecclesiologists.

The Cambridge Camden Society was founded in 1839 as an antiquarian society for a few undergraduates. It grew very rapidly and was refounded in London as the Ecclesiological Society in 1845.[6] Through its journal, *The Ecclesiologist*, which was issued 1841-68, the society exercised an enormous influence on matters of style and taste. Evangelicals were suspicious at first of Camdenian symbolism but in the end they either capitulated or imitated. The result was the triumph of the Camdenian version of the gothic revival, producing that state of mind which has persisted to the present day, which thinks that buildings which have pointed arches, quatrefoils or lancet windows are 'religious', while those that do not have them are not.

The interiors of these new or restored churches show that a change had taken place in the understanding of the liturgy, largely as a result of tractarian influences. The ecclesiologists waged war on box-pews and galleries. By the end of the century almost all of them had disappeared, the former being replaced by the now familiar 'low open stalls', the latter, which often contained woodwork from medieval screens, being thrown out or otherwise disposed of. The three-decker pulpits were replaced by reading desks and lecterns. In 1841 the eagle at Llangorwen had given great offence—almost a breach of the second commandment—but by the end of the century the eagle had captivated all and sundry by its beauty and its symbolism, and it stood resplendent in brass in almost every church. Now spacious chancels were required for a more elaborate ritual, and to be filled for the first time with surpliced choirs. Altars were being used more frequently, so the neat little altar-tables of earlier times were replaced with more elaborate structures, now considered to be the focal point of a church and requiring an uninterrupted view. They came to be decorated with crosses, candlesticks—even with flower vases. In the middle of the century such histrionic practices would have caused riots.

The mistakes made by the ecclesiologists and their followers in Wales were many, especially in the country areas where the local church patterns were completely missed. Their faults were aptly described by Dr. Glyn Simon in his presidential address to the Cambrian Archaeological Association in 1965.

There is our special heritage in Wales of hundreds and hundreds of little ancient churches. They are for the most part unknown, and come as a revelation to architects and lovers of the past who see them for the first time. They are quite different from any in England. They are small and simple and very much home-made. They fit the land-scape and the climate; they are the offerings of a poor people, harrassed over the centuries by war, and living on land very different from the rich rolling counties of England . . . Because our idiom is so different it is apt to be despised. Ecclesiologists last century described our churches as 'rude, barn-like structures' and ruthlessly improved them by the insertion of arches and windows in the second pointed style,[7] for them the last word in 'correct' church architecture . . . The Welsh scale of things, the traditions, the achievements, should all be judged from a quite different level from England, for everything is on a smaller scale, and the very poverty, small size, and simplicity of many of our churches is part and parcel of our heritage.

These words can be applied to many little meeting houses, dating from the eighteenth century and unimproved in the nineteenth, which can still be found in the remoter parts of Wales. Set in our hills and valleys, built out of their stones and timber, these little churches and chapels are an integral part of our history.

When Thirlwall noted in 1863 that the Church had not only been agitated from within but also threatened from without, he had good reason for that statement. Though disestablishment still lay in the distant future, most of the arguments for it had already been ventilated.

As early as 1830 the columns of the *Seren Gomer* sparked off a controversy about the nature of the Church and the validity of its connection with the State. The argument was continued in the journals of the Welsh Independents, notably *Y Dysgedydd* and *Y Diwygiwr*, for the Independents represented the radical element in Welsh nonconformity. The Calvinistic Methodists held aloof from political matters, wishing only, in the words of John Elias, 'to lead a peaceful and quiet life in all godliness and honesty'. However, a number of factors tended to draw the Methodists closer to the more politically-minded Dissenters. The campaign against slavery and the temperance movement quietly undermined 'the pietistic prejudices of many people in both camps against participation in politics'.[8]

The controversy about church rates was another factor. The old vestry was still a part of the civil as well as the ecclesiastical administration of the parish. Every parishioner had the right to attend and to elect churchwardens who retained some vestiges of their former duties as civil officers. One of their functions was to levy a church rate for the repair of the church or the maintenance of the churchyard. The church rate could not be enforced, and in most of the towns in the United Kingdom it had fallen into abeyance. It continued in use in many country parishes until Parliament finally, and somewhat tardily, abolished it in 1868. In the meanwhile Nonconformists had discovered that they could pack the vestry and carry a motion that the church rate be deferred for a twelvemonth. This ruse was successful in many places, and it was sometimes accompanied by the election of Nonconformists as wardens. This happened in Llanelli and Llannon in 1836 when John James (a member of Capel Als) was elected warden of the one parish, and David Jones, a Unitarian, in the other. Both men carried out surveys of their respective churches and summoned meetings of the vestries to levy the rate. In both cases motions were carried that the matter be deferred. The incumbent of these parishes, Ebenezer Morris, decided to take action against his nonconformist wardens. Cited before the consistory court at Carmarthen for neglecting their duties, they were admonished and ordered to pay the costs of the proceedings. They refused to pay, were deemed contumacious, and they were lodged in Carmarthen gaol. John James had friends who paid the costs and so he was released; but it is significant that he apologised to his supporters for his inability to stay longer in prison. David Jones lodged an appeal and he was released on a fortunate technicality. When a second writ was prepared against him, he took to flight. His death, as a result of an accident, brought the matter to a tragic end.

These incidents received great publicity and aroused deep passions. Ebenezer Morris might have been unwise to force a confrontation of this kind. On the other hand, John James and David Jones need not have accepted the office of warden. They had the legal right to refuse. They both consented and swore a solemn oath to serve the church. They were, in short, the willing victims of the radical faction which elected them.

Two other factors helped to draw the Methodists and the Dissenters together at this time. One was the Oxford Movement. The *Tracts for the Times* proclaimed a doctrine of the Church which alarmed those Nonconformists who were still well disposed to the Church, and looked to it as a barrier against Roman catholicism. Also the reawakening of the Church, of which the Oxford Movement was one of the outward signs, added to the tension between church and chapel. Another factor was the controversy over the Blue Books of 1847. A number of churchmen were loud in criticism of the report, notably Sir Thomas Phillips, Rowland Williams, Dean Cotton of Bangor, and H. T. Edwards, but the controversy assumed an increasingly nonconformist character, and gave a new impetus to their journals; and it came at a time when Welsh Nonconformists were evolving an efficient means of influencing opinion. The Liberation Society, founded in 1844, originated in England, but it spread into Wales and became almost a national organisation, with disestablishment as its goal. Cells were formed throughout the country and by 1868, 'Welsh nonconformists possessed the nucleus of coherent political organisation, well financed, with a constant stream of speakers and of political literature. Without this organizational basis, Welsh radicalism would have remained subdued and ineffective'.[9]

The election of 1868 is a landmark in the history of Wales, though it was not the 'national awakening' that it was later claimed to be. Of the thirty-three members returned to Parliament, twenty-three were liberals; but thirty of the total were Anglicans; and only three, Henry Richard at Merthyr Tydfil, E. M. Richards in Cardiganshire, and Richard Davies in Anglesey, represented direct nonconformist majorities. Yet for the first time the old dominance of the landed families was threatened. Some of the landowners in Cardiganshire and Carmarthenshire reacted to the defection of their tenants at the polls by evicting them from their holdings. The liberal cause was thus provided with a roll of martyrs whose sufferings were retailed, with suitable embellishments, from electoral platforms for many years to come. The election of 1868 was a victory for liberalism rather than for nationalism. But the period 1868-86 marks a transition from radicalism to nationalism, and the cry for disestablishment alters its tone. The desire for the removal of the religious inequalities of the Nonconformists becomes replaced by the demand for abolishing the privileges of what now came to be called the 'alien' church, *Yr Eglwys Loegr*, or 'The Church of England in Wales'.

One of the more obvious targets for criticism was the long line of *Esgyb Eingl*, the English bishops who had held sway in Wales since the days of Queen Anne. Many of them had been able and devoted men, and, in particular, Campbell of Bangor (1859-90), Vowler Short of St. Asaph (1846-70), Thirlwall of St. David's (1840-74) and Ollivant of Llandaff (1849-83) were exemplars of the new model of episcopacy which emerged in the nineteenth century, living in their dioceses and administering them efficiently. Thirlwall, accounted the most learned man of his age, had added Welsh to his stock of learning, and often preached in that language. Ollivant also acquired a good knowledge of literary Welsh. But these two bishops were exceptions. A demand for Welsh-speaking bishops had come from the Church itself. A group of Welsh clergy in the West Riding of Yorkshire appealed to Sir Robert Peel in 1835. The evils resulting from English-speaking bishops were expounded by clerical pamphleteers in the course of the century. In 1870 H. T. Edwards, dean of Bangor presented a memorial to Gladstone, and in that same year Joshua Hughes, then vicar of Llandovery, was appointed to succeed Vowler Short at St. Asaph. Hughes was not particularly distinguished, but the appointment of a Welsh-speaking bishop, the first for over one hundred and fifty years gave great satisfaction. Four years later, Basil Jones became bishop of St. David's; but it is unfortunate that this very able man should be chiefly remembered for voicing an opinion (shared by many others) that Wales was no more than 'a geographical expression'.

Dr. K. O. Morgan has pointed out that a number of external factors contributed towards the development of Welsh radicalism in a nationalist direction. The example of Ireland, where the Church was disestablished in 1870, is significant. Again, the growth of democracy is not peculiar to Wales; but the extension of the franchise and the protection of the ballot box resulted in the return of a solid body of liberal Members of Parliament

PLATE 7.   A. G. Edwards, bishop of St. Asaph, first archbishop of Wales

PLATE 8.
Gwilym Owen Williams,
bishop of Bangor,
seventh archbishop of Wales

from Wales. Nonconformists became more involved with local government when in 1889 the new county councils took over what had been the preserve of tory magistrates; and the prominent Methodist, Thomas Gee, became the first chairman of Denbighshire County Council. Above all, the great land depression after 1878, the result of international factors, led to a tithe war in Wales which complicated and embittered the question of disestablishment.

The tithe had long been a mixed blessing to the clergy. Rarely able to collect it all, they often had to be content with a part of it. Since the dissolution of the monasteries a good deal of the tithe was owned by lay impropriators, and this seems to have been another matter. The farmer who grumbled about paying the parson usually paid his tithes to the squire as a matter of course. The Commutation Act of 1836 altered the old system and substituted a money payment, a tithe rent-charge, fixed on the average price over seven years of wheat, barley and oats. The actual value of the rent-charge fluctuated a good deal in the course of the century. After 1878, because of the fall in world cereal prices, the value went into decline. By 1889 a tithe rent-charge of £100 was worth £89. By 1901 it had dropped to £66. In the kingdom generally, the agricultural community was severely shaken by the disastrous fall in staple prices, and the rancours of the tithe disputes of earlier times returned in the new disputes over the tithe rent-charge. In Wales the great recession added to the burden of an already depressed rural community, and Welsh farmers became particularly responsive to liberationist arguments against the established Church. Anti-tithe leagues were formed in most of the Welsh counties and these became amalgamated with Thomas Gee's Welsh Land League. Refusals to pay the tithe rent-charge were followed by attempts on the part of the authorities to distrain the non-payer's goods. Then demonstrations of solidarity were made in the victim's support. At first these demonstrations were peaceful enough, but later on they erupted into violence, particularly in the Vale of Clwyd, in Gee's native county. At Llangwn, in May 1887, there was a scuffle between the crowd and the police, and the troops were called in. The Riot Act was read at Mochdre in June in the same year after disturbances in which fifty people, not counting thirty-four policemen, were injured. A government commission was appointed to enquire into these disturbances; and finally the Tithe Act of 1891 eased the situation by making the tithe payable by the landlord and not by the tenant. The bill was initiated by the new bishop of St. Asaph, A. G. Edwards, who was very concerned about the hardships suffered by his clergy, many of whom were obliged to take a fraction of what was due to them for fear of getting nothing at all, and 'to keep on good terms with the parishioners'. The tithe continued to be a source of trouble and intermittent tithe wars flared up in various parts of the kingdom until Parliament finally abolished it in 1936.

During the last quarter of the century it was becoming clear that the Church was gaining ground. Some churchmen called for a religious census, but Nonconformists were opposed to the idea. They were hostile to the principle of state interference. They also feared that those who were uncommitted to any denomination, nearly half the total population, would be put down as 'church'. In 1887 Thomas Gee attempted to make a census of attendance at all the churches and chapels of Wales; but his efforts were said to have done 'untold damage in encouraging the parsons'. The Church was still outnumbered by nonconformity, but there were indications that it was 'apparently advancing at a faster rate, and the realization that it might soon be the largest single religious body in Wales added urgency to the activity of the nonconformist leaders.'[10] Yet, at the same time, Welsh voters continued to return Members of Parliament who belonged to the party (the liberals) which was now committed to the disestablishment of the Church in Wales.

[1] *The Life and Letters of Rowland Williams*, by his wife (1874), I, 200.
[2] O. Chadwick, *The Victorian Church* (1966), I, 126. For the work of the Ecclesiastical Commission see also G. F. A. Best, *Temporal Pillars* (Cambridge, 1964), and O. Brose, *Church and Parliament* (Oxford, 1959).
[3] See Owain Jones, 'Prince and the Lampeter Brethren', *Trivium* (1970), 10–20. See also R. Knox, *Enthusiasm* (Oxford, 1950), 568–75.
[4] Quoted in Owain Jones, *Isaac Williams and his Circle* (1971), 92 and note. For tractarianism in Wales see also Eifion Evans, 'Mudiad Rhydychen yng nglogledd sir Aberteifi' and the sequence of related articles in *J.H.S.C.W.*, IV (1954), 45–75, VI (1956), 92–104, VIII (1958), 82–92, and X (1960), 66–82.
[5] For this paragraph see 'Rational Godliness, A Welsh Controversy', *Theology*, February, 1958, 51–7, M. A. Crowther, *Church Embattled* (Newton Abbot, 1970), chapter 4, and Owain Jones, 'Bunsen's Reviewer', *J.H.S.C.W.*, X (1960), 43–51.
[6] B. F. L. Clarke, *Church Builders of the Nineteenth Century* (London, 1938; reprint, Newton Abbot, 1969), B. F. Anson, *Fashions in Church Furnishing* (1960 and 1965). See also Owain Jones and R. W. D. Fenn, 'Church-builders in the Nineteenth Century', *Links with the Past*, 215–240, J. B. Hilling, *Cardiff and the Valleys* (1973), 113–26.
[7] The ecclesiologists used the terminology, first, second (or middle) and third pointed to describe the three main phases in gothic architecture, early English, decorated, and perpendicular. They came to the arbitrary decision that the decorated period was the best, hence the predominance of that style in the gothic revival. A good deal of use was made of early English, especially in smaller churches; but after 1850 there are a number of examples of early French gothic. The latter, I am informed by Canon Basil Clarke, was the thirteenth-century style of the more progressive architects, the style used, for example, by Charles Buckeridge for his Welsh village churches, e.g. Llanllywenfel and Llyswen. In comparison with early English, the lancets were

shorter and wider: if there was anything above them it would be a large, plain, uncusped circle; and shafts, if there were any, were fat and stubby. John Prichard was another who used this style in Wales.

8 R. Tudur Jones, 'Origins of the Nonconformist Disestablishment Campaign', *J.H.S.C.W.*, XX (1970), 55.
9 K. O. Morgan, *Wales in British Politics* 1868–1922, 17; see also I. G. Jones, 'The Liberation Society and Welsh Politics', *W.H.R.*, I (1960–1), 193–200.
10 For this paragraph see K. O. Morgan, *Wales in British Politics*, 83–4.

CHAPTER 8

DISESTABLISHMENT AND INDEPENDENCE

by

David Walker

THE Welsh Church had lived under the shadow of disestablishment and disendowment for many decades before they were finally imposed on it in 1914. As Owain Jones has shown in the last chapter, radical nonconformity had seen in disestablishment and disendowment the twin methods of attacking the Church, and had appealed to these remedies at intervals since the 1840s. Dr. K. O. Morgan sees this as 'a supreme national cause' which gave unity and purpose to the radicalism of the middle decades of the nineteenth century. 'Into this single theme,' he wrote, 'all the various grievances, real and imaginary, felt by nonconformists everywhere were absorbed.' The foundation of the National Liberation Society in 1844 provided the machinery through which many of their aims could be pursued. Dr. Morgan quoted with approval John Morley's remark that 'home rule is not more essentially the Irish national question than disestablishment and disendowment are the Welsh national question.'[1] In the local politics of Wales the attack on the anglican Church in Wales was sustained over long periods of time, but in terms of the national parties and of Parliament the issue came to the forefront only sporadically. 'Enemies', as Dr. Bell has written, 'are of prime importance to any nationalist movement', and in Wales the enemies were identified as 'the landlords and the established church'. In 1880 conditions in British politics began to change to the advantage of the opponents of the Welsh Church and the idea of disestablishment could then become a serious political issue. The sweeping liberal victories of 1880, with twenty-nine of the thirty-three Welsh parliamentary seats falling to the liberals, produced a strong body of opinion in the Commons which could not easily be ignored. The balance changed slightly as the years passed, but the Welsh liberal members remained a considerable pressure group. Within a few years the claim that special legislation could apply to Wales as a separate unit within the United Kingdom was given real meaning, with the Welsh

Sunday Closing Act of 1881, separate financial grants for the Welsh university colleges in 1883 and 1885, and the Welsh Intermediate Education Act in 1889. Through each enactment the same message was proclaimed, that Wales need not be regarded as a mere appendage of England for parliamentary purposes. In a different way the Local Government Act of 1888 was a landmark, for it made possible the extensive defeat and limitation of the aristocracy and the squirearchy in local administration. If squire and parson were allies, the serious undermining of one partner brought increased danger to the other. At the same time there were changes of considerable import among the men in power in the liberal party. Joseph Chamberlain had included the disestablishment of the Church in Wales as part of his unofficial programme, but Gladstone was not to be rushed, even though he recognised the pressure now effectively being brought to bear by Welsh liberals. By 1891 he was changing his mind, and before the end of the year he had included Welsh disestablishment as a major element in the Newcastle programme, the manifesto on which he proposed to fight the forthcoming election.

Bills for disestablishment and disendowment were introduced in 1894 and 1895 but they made little progress. A decade later Campbell Bannerman was anxious to institute an enquiry into the state of the anglican Church and other religious bodies in Wales, and in response to careful prompting from the archbishop of Canterbury, Randall Davidson, he set up a royal commission. It moved slowly, and the way was not clear for another bill to be introduced until 1909. This time the liberals were too much occupied with their constitutional struggle over Lloyd George's 'people's budget' and the Parliament Act, and while the fate of the House of Lords was under active debate the Welsh Church was relegated to the background. Finally, in 1912, a disestablishment bill was passed by the Commons, and when the Lords rejected it, the Act was slowly forced upon them through the provisions of the Parliament Act in 1913 and 1914. It was accepted belatedly in the autumn of 1914 in circumstances which produced great bitterness. With the Irish Home Rule Act it was to be held in suspension for twelve months, or for the duration of the first world war. Randall Davidson and the Welsh bishops understood that both Acts would be treated in precisely the same way, but the Asquith administration took a different view. As far as the Irish Home Rule Act was concerned they decided that 'no steps shall be taken to put that Act into operation', but for the Welsh Church Act they determined that 'the date of disestablishment shall be postponed.' This allowed some of the preparatory measures for disestablishment to be implemented at once. Randall

Davidson was deeply disturbed and could not disguise his agitation, but in Wales a much harder view prevailed and Asquith's policy was regarded as a clear betrayal. Alfred Edwards, bishop of St. Asaph, and later to be first archbishop of Wales, was bitter and angry at the treacherous way in which the government had dealt with the Welsh Church, and he could not shake off the conviction of bad faith by Asquith and his colleagues. He wrote in his *Memories* of the 'craft and subtility' by which the two Acts were treated so differently, and he endorsed the common charge of 'a deliberate and disgraceful subterfuge.'

In this mood of bitter recrimination Welsh churchmen were slow to accept the finality of the decision of 1914. They persisted in the belief that the Act would be repealed, and certainly there were indications that repeal would be likely if and when the conservatives returned to office. From 1915 onwards the liberals showed some desire to obtain from the opposition an undertaking that they would not repeal the Welsh Church Act. It is easy to understand why the Welsh bishops believed that repeal was both necessary and probable. Before the end of the war there was a substantial hope that the whole question of disestablishment might be reconsidered. At the same time, as even Lloyd George acknowledged, there were grave difficulties in seeking to plan for the future of the Welsh Church when so many of the clergy and prominent laymen were away at the war. Altogether, conditions did not encourage swift acceptance and early planning for a future which was neither desirable nor welcome.[2]

As far as the principle of disestablishment was concerned, churchmen were anxious to defend the idea that the province of Canterbury should not be broken up. Those who stood for church defence argued that the Welsh dioceses were an integral part of the province and the defence of the Welsh Church was a defence of the whole province. While their opponents were concentrating on the contrast between Welsh and English, leading spokesmen for the defence emphasised the links and similarities between the Welsh bishoprics and the English Church. Randall Davidson and Cosmo Lang, then archbishop of York, made a number of telling speeches in this sense, and Bishop John Owen of St. David's travelled the length and breadth of England arguing the case against disestablishment. Bishop Edwards found some difficulty in reconciling with these tactics his profound conviction that the Church in Wales—the British Church as he called it— was 'older by centuries than the Throne or Parliament of England', institutions which ought not to tamper with the structure of so ancient a Church.

Disendowment threatened economic hardship which contemporaries saw as penury. Randall Davidson could speak of 'the catastrophe of impoverishment' which hung over the Welsh Church. The County Councils of Wales had been promised the spoils of the Church's endowments, and expropriation was viewed with chagrin by Welsh churchmen and with unconcealed delight by liberal and nonconformist councillors. The four boroughs of Cardiff, Merthyr Tydfil, Newport and Swansea, together with the University of Wales were to share in the forthcoming handout. It was not easy to set precise figures to the Church's assets, but in 1912 it was estimated that the Church had property and income amounting to £260,000 a year, and the Bill made provision for the Church to retain £102,000 of this. There was an additional sum of £31,000 which the Ecclesiastical Commissioners and Queen Anne's Bounty paid to the Welsh dioceses and which might be continued if they chose to do so. Income estimated at £158,000 was to be sequestered.[3]

The delay of more than four years in implementing the Welsh Church Act worked to the ultimate advantage of the new province. Temporary financial expedients and the prospect that administrative changes could not be completed by the end of 1919 made some amendment of the Act essential. There was widespread concern, not shared by Welsh Nonconformists, that the financial implications of the Act would be crippling and should be ameliorated. There was also a feeling, tacitly accepted by Bishop Edwards and Bishop Owen though not by all Welsh churchmen, that a review of the financial terms of the Act might be more practicable than a sustained campaign for repeal. This review was achieved in the Welsh Church Amending Act of 1919. To say that this Act created vast confusion for the future is an understatement. It was ill-considered and badly designed, though this was hardly surprising in the circumstances in which it was produced. In the early months of 1919 Bishop Edwards was in close touch with Bonar Law who spoke of the prospect of an amending bill, but by some unexplained omission no attempt was made to draft a provisional measure. Lloyd George, deeply involved in the peace negotiations at Paris, could play no part in these final stages. Then, early in June, Edwards had a long interview with Lloyd George which left him 'puzzled if not discouraged', and Law, too, seems to have been less forthcoming than had hitherto been the case. Suddenly, and without warning, on Thursday, July 24th, Law confronted the bishop with the demand, 'Get a Bill drafted of your proposals ready to put in the Prime Minister's hand on Saturday.' Despite the urgency of the occasion drafting could not begin until Friday afternoon when Frank Morgan, future secretary of the Representative Body, joined forces with an experienced parliamentary draftsman. By

4.30 on the Saturday morning the work was finished, and by 11 o'clock it had been printed and delivered to Lloyd George who was later to be credited with its imperfections.

The financial provisions of the Amending Act depended upon a number of variable factors which made the task of accurate accounting difficult almost to the point of impossibility. A group of Commissioners of Church Temporalities in Wales, set up to handle the involved financial clauses of disendowment, found that they could not do their work effectively without government aid, and they were given a grant of £1,000,000 from which the new province would benefit, and which has been called 'a sort of re-endowment.' In 1914 the general fear was that the Welsh Church would lose £158,000 a year. After the full effect of the Amending Act had been made apparent, Bishop Owen estimated that the Church had lost £48,000 a year. The importance of this estimate is not that it was accurate but that it was accepted by his colleagues as the figure they had to make good if the effects of disendowment were to be cancelled out. To set crude figures of this kind one against the other may not produce accurate results, but the comparison is a useful indication of the scale of the problem faced by the Welsh Church, and also of the extent to which the terms of disendowment were modified between 1914 and 1920. Alfred Edwards, John Owen, and Frank Morgan were justified in believing that they had salvaged much more for their province than the most ardent of optimists might have expected. Some of the bitterness of seeing church property pass into secular hands was removed by the fact that the Welsh Church Commissioners, saddled with heavy interest charges, could not release the money for many years. Then, in two stages, in 1942 and 1947, they transferred large sums of capital amounting altogether to £3,455,813 10s. 8d. to the beneficiaries, and since that time Welsh Church Funds have been used for a variety of purposes. Many cultural activities, in particular, have been given financial support from this source and the people of Wales have derived considerable benefit from the disendowment of the Welsh Church.

During the last years of the first world war Welsh churchmen had been brought reluctantly to the point of creating a machinery for governing the new province. The hope that disestablishment might be staved off encouraged the view that detailed plans for independence would be inappropriate but by 1917 the most prominent advocate of this policy of delay, Bishop Watkin Williams of Bangor, had been won over. As early as 1914, a joint meeting of the diocesan conferences of the four Welsh dioceses met and established a committee to examine the problems of independence in detail. Their deliberations owed much to the work of two judges, John Sankey and John Bankes, and to the critical acumen of a third judge, J. R. Atkin. Sankey was to acknowledge later that he had underestimated the grasp of their proposals by Charles Green, then archdeacon of Monmouth, later to be bishop of Monmouth, then of Bangor, and finally archbishop of Wales. The first essential was a body which might receive and administer the possessions and revenues of the Welsh Church, and there was little opposition to the creation of the Representative Body for this purpose. Policy was to be in the hands of a Governing Body, the establishment of which was not so easily achieved. At first it was assumed that dioceses would be represented in proportion to the number of their clergy and communicants, but this would have weighted both the Representative Body and the Governing Body heavily in favour of Llandaff and St. David's. Not until the principle of equal representation had been asserted and the bishop of Bangor had been won over could plans for the present system of government in the Welsh Church be brought to the point of finality. A convention held in Cardiff in 1917 gave legal force to these arrangements, and from its first meeting on January 18th, 1918, the Governing Body assumed its responsibilities.

There remained the delicate question of the exact relationship between the Welsh bishops and Canterbury. In May, 1919, Bishop Edwards wrote to Randall Davidson to seek advice 'as to the possibility and the wisdom of attempting to retain our place in the Convocation of Canterbury, on, of course, the same terms of equality as heretofore?' He went on to pose the alternative as a direct question: 'Or would your Grace advise the Church in Wales to accept the new conditions and to form its own Welsh province?' In a long, characteristic, graceful letter, Davidson argued the case. He assured Edwards that he wished to do only what the Welsh bishops desired, and he deplored the loss which must come to his own province if they withdrew. But he invoked the support of the great majority of the English bishops and he declared that 'it will conduce to the happy and orderly working of the whole Church in England and Wales if by our own joint action a separate Province be formed for Wales.'[4] So, by formal enactments, he released the Welsh bishops from their obedience to Canterbury and he announced that the four Welsh sees would, after March 31st, 1920, form a separate and independent province of the anglican Church. The long process of revival and adjustment to the radically changing conditions of the principality ended in the separation of the Welsh and English Churches. Davidson's final contribution to the new province was to preside at the enthronement of Edwards as first archbishop of Wales. The new primate took his oath to observe the constitution and laws and approved customs of the Church in Wales, and took personal pleasure in using for the purpose the original 1567 edition of William Salesbury's Welsh New Testament. The bishops professed obedience to their new metropolitan and Wales was free of the ties which had bound it to Canterbury for some seven hundred years. It was freedom gained by surgery, a freedom imposed upon the Welsh Church by its enemies.

During the earliest years of its existence financial problems seemed all-important. An appeal for £1,000,000 to make good lost revenues realised the considerable capital sum of £700,000, and a provincial levy of £45,000 augured well, but the leaders of the new Church could not easily shake off the fears and apprehensions of the long struggle over dis-establishment. John Owen favoured a bold investment policy which would commit large sums of money to long-term developments. There were many who were quick to argue that the Church's lost endowments were essentially parochial endowments and that the immediate priority was to maintain the level of stipends. The level of investment and of stipends rose steadily over the years. In 1924, for example, the archdeaconry of Brecon was expected to find £4,660 and the archdeaconry of Gower £8,735 for the Quota which was the first charge on the resources of the Church. In 1971, the archdeaconry of Brecon contributed £16,700 to the Quota and the archdeaconry of Gower £28,405. The central financial resources of the Church were carefully husbanded, and immediately after the second world war an appeal for new capital was launched with a target of £500,000. By 1953, more than £600,000 had been contributed. It was, however, the use of capital which proved the greatest problem in the 1950s. In February, 1955, as a result of advice given by Hugh Dalton, chancellor of the exchequer, the Governing Body increased the freedom of action of the Representative Body to invest in non-trustee securities. For the first time, the financial advisers of the Church in Wales were free to make the Representative Body's portfolio of investments more fluid and more profitable. The primary responsibility for this operation lay with David Vaughan, chairman of the finance committee, and under his expert guidance the Church's income has increased quite remarkably. The im-mediate and most spectacular move was the purchase of Bush House, a large office-block in central London, in February, 1955. Without the income from this property the Church could not have kept pace with post-war inflation. Then, in February, 1972, the Representative Body sold Bush House, and found itself with a massive capital of some £20,000,000 to reinvest. Three years of sharp inflation have made inroads into the income which the Church enjoys in the 1970s. In April, 1975, the arch-bishop of Wales, G. O. Williams, warned the Church of the dangers inherent in the 'Bush House syndrone': a complacent sense that the financiers would deal successfully with any financial difficulties, and a failure to assume the responsibility for maintaining the work of the Church adequately out of current giving.

Such security was beyond the wildest dreams of Welsh churchmen in 1920, but in one respect the new province was adventurous. Within four years of disestablishment two new bishoprics had been created, Monmouth and Swansea and Brecon. There had already been much debate about the need to reduce the size of Llandaff with its massive concentration of population in the industrial valleys of south-east Wales. This was brought to a head in 1921, and in the September of that year the Governing Body approved the creation of a new diocese 'for the territory comprised within the archdeaconry of Monmouth.' There were attempts to have the new diocese called either Gwent or Newport, but Monmouth was preferred. Various places were suggested as the centre of the new see; Usk, the county town, Chepstow, gateway to Gwent, and Monmouth and Aber-gavenny with their fine priory churches. In the event, Newport was chosen. The original intention was to build a new cathedral and close, complete with deanery, chapter house, and houses for the archdeacons and canons. Lord Tredegar, a generous benefactor of the two new dioceses, provided the land for this scheme, but the money could not be raised. The new bishop, C. A. H. Green, had to use the Norman parish church of St. Woolos as a pro-cathedral. A cathedral chapter was not formally constituted until 1930, and it was not until 1949 that St. Woolos became the cathedral church of the diocese. From the earliest days of the existence of the new diocese, diocesan administration was expanded by the creation of a new archdeaconry of Newport, a diocesan conference, and other indispensable bodies.[5]

Swansea and Brecon was founded in 1923 to ease the burden on the bishop of St. David's whose diocese was the largest in England and Wales.[6] It covered 2,238,000 acres and its population of 496,000, many of them living in scattered farms and hamlets, was served by 456 clergy. Since at least the 1880s there had been some discussion of the possibility of splitting this vast diocese. Bishop Basil Jones set up a committee of the diocesan conference to examine the prospect but a decision was still to be made when John Owen became bishop in 1897. Few advocates were more insistent than Wilfrid Seymour de Winton, who argued for many years that there should be seven or eight bishoprics in Wales, with a new diocese created for Monmouthshire, another to be based on Swansea, a third based at Aberystwyth, and a fourth diocese, particularly dear to de Winton's heart, with its centre at Brecon. However vigorous his pleading, there were not the resources to be found for so many new bishoprics, either before or after disestablishment. Throughout 1921 the plans for Monmouth were being brought to fruition, but further west there could only be one new diocese, and gradually it was determined that this should be called Swansea and Brecon and have its cathedral church at Brecon. De Winton had been born in the Priory House at Brecon (now the Deanery), and for many years he had been building up a fund to provide for the time when the priory church of St. John the Evangelist should become a cathedral. The archdeaconry of Brecon and the two deaneries of East and West Gower were combined to form an elongated diocese extending, as its first bishop was fond of saying, from Beguildy to Rhosili. Brecon priory was one of the greater monastic churches of Wales, while Brecon itself was within comfortable travelling distance of the furthermost parts of the new diocese. The great draw-back of using Brecon as a cathedral centre was that the bishop would live forty miles away from the heavily populated, wealthy industrial area of Swansea, and there were many who thought that the bishop should be on the spot, in constant touch with the leaders of industrial and civic life. By 1922 the debate was over and the necessary steps could be taken to set up the new diocese. In April, 1923, a motion for the creation of the diocese of Swansea and Brecon was passed by the Governing Body. Edward Latham Bevan became the first bishop and proved to be a generous and far-sighted diocesan. He loved Brecon, and he used every opportunity to make the priory church a worthy cathedral, buying up property around the cathedral, renovating buildings, and, in the end, providing a substantial endowment for the fabric.

To trace the trends which have become apparent in the fifty years or so for which the Church in Wales has been an independent province is not easy. It would be a mistake to underestimate the sense of near-disaster with which the first generation of Welsh churchmen faced disestablishment. It was a traumatic experience from which they had emerged bruised and lacerated. In these circumstances it is not surprising that leadership and personality should play a dominant role in the unfolding story of the Church in Wales in the twentieth century. At the same time, the Church tended to put its trust in experience, and its archbishops were consistently chosen on the grounds of seniority. One useful method of exploring the course of events is to concentrate on the leading figures.

In the earliest days, when bold and reassuring leadership was essential, two bishops were the men who provided it. One was Alfred Edwards, bishop of St. Asaph since 1889, and the other was his protégé and adjutant, John Owen, bishop of St. David's.[7] They had borne the brunt of the fighting during the long-drawn-out campaign over disestablishment, and in 1920 they took the lead in steering their Church through the first years of independence. In 1920 there was no danger that the two men would be rivals. When the bishops met at Llandrindod Wells to elect the first archbishop of Wales, Owen proposed the name of Alfred Edwards and he was elected by a unanimous vote. In those days there was no retiring age for bishops. Edwards was already seventy-three and he continued as archbishop until he was eighty-seven. He was still archbishop when John Owen died in 1927. Edwards was a man of granite who faced personal bereavement and national crisis with equal courage. His grandfather and father had been parish priests in rural Wales and he was steeped in the traditions of the Welsh country-side and the Welsh Church. He lacked Owen's subtlety of mind, but the strength of his character was what the Church in Wales much needed in the 1920s. As a young man he had become warden of Llandovery after only one year's experience as a schoolmaster, and he then had to face all the problems of reviving the fortunes of a decayed school which was, to all outward appearances, on the verge of extinction. Ten years saw great changes in the College, and in 1885 he went to Carmarthen as vicar and rural-dean. Then in 1889, as part of the deliberate policy of appointing Welsh bishops inaugurated by Gladstone, Lord Salisbury invited him, in terms which were less than generous, to be bishop of St. Asaph. He was to be bishop for forty-five years, and archbishop for fourteen. During his time the Church in Wales came to realise that disestablishment, far from being a disaster, was a challenge and an opportunity, and the mood of dark depression so characteristic of the years between 1914 and 1920 gave way to a mood of optimism.

John Owen followed Edwards as warden of Llandovery in 1885, and, at his invitation, went to St. Asaph as dean in 1889. Then for five years he enjoyed a measure of greater independence as principal of Lampeter before he became bishop of St. David's in 1897. As bishop, Owen was in the forefront of contemporary battles, maintaining the Church's place in education and fighting vigorously and persistently in the great controversy over the Swansea Church Schools between 1907 and 1911. Throughout the disestablishment campaigns he had been deeply involved in the politics of the struggle. He and Edwards believed themselves to be capable of handling Lloyd George, Edwards because of their personal friendship and

Owen because of his agile and fertile mind. In fact, neither of them was in the same class as Lloyd George when it came to political manoeuvring. After disestablishment, Owen's great contribution to the Church in Wales came through his defence, unexpected in a man of his caution, of adventurous ways of facing the immediate problems of reorganisation.

The other two bishops at the time of disestablishment were men of different stamp. Watkin Williams, bishop of Bangor, had laid the foundations of his reputation with twenty years as vicar of Bodelwyddan, followed by a shorter spell as archdeacon of St. Asaph (1889-92) and then dean (1892-98). He acquired an unexpected fame after his retirement in 1924, for he lived for another twenty years to the great age of ninety-nine, and when he died in 1944 he was believed to be the oldest bishop in the world. Joshua Hughes, bishop of Llandaff, had a name famous in Wales for his father and namesake had been the vicar of Llandovery who, in 1870 became the first Welshman after an interval of more than a century and a half to hold a Welsh bishopric. The younger Joshua spent thirty-four years as curate and vicar of parishes in Glamorgan, at Neath, Newcastle, and Llantrisant. He was completely absorbed in his work as a parish priest, and his appointment as bishop in 1905 was something of a surprise for he had made no effort to establish any influence outside his own parish. In a long episcopate of thirty-one years he endeared himself to his diocese, but as a national figure he had little contribution to make.

Dioceses tend to take the stamp of their bishops; much less frequently does the province take its tone from the archbishop. Here, Edwards set a difficult example for others to follow, with his firm, strong character tempered as it was by kindliness. His successor was a man of very different quality, Charles Alfred Howell Green. He, too, was the product of a clerical household and he early showed himself to be a man of scholarly cast of mind. His life-long interest in liturgy, ecclesiastical law and technical problems of administration made him admirably equipped to be not only an exponent of the new constitution of the Church in Wales but also an authoritative commentator. The parish with which he was particularly associated was Aberdare where he was appointed as curate in 1889 and vicar in 1894. Twenty-six years there set the tone of the parish and proclaimed the outlook of the man. Green was a high churchman and somewhat aggressively a party man. His advancement was welcomed by his friends as successes for their own brand of churchmanship. Despite the great division of outlook between himself and his bishop, Joshua Hughes, he was appointed archdeacon of Monmouth in 1914, and his expert gifts as a scholar were at the disposal of the Welsh Church during the critical years of planning for the government of the new province. In September, 1921, when the new diocese of Monmouth was founded, Green was elected as its first bishop, and when Archbishop Edwards died in 1934, Green, by that time bishop of Bangor, was elected to succeed him. His greatest contribution to the life of the Church had already been made and the ten years of his primacy were not marked by any major new departures.

David Prosser, the third archbishop of Wales, had little chance to show his mettle as primate, for he came to the office late in life when he had neither the inclination nor perhaps the power to change his life-style. He was above all a parish priest. It is an indication of the impression he made on people that the thirteen years he spent as curate of Christ Church, Swansea, at the beginning of his ministry should still be remembered as an important period for him and for his parish when he was made archbishop half a century later. It was said that in his Sunday School he would oblige young men of eighteen to stand and repeat the basic material of his lessons until they had mastered it. If it was tough discipline it was rewarding, and they came back regularly for more. His experiences during the first world war made him a softer and more understanding man. He followed this seminal period in Swansea with a spell as vicar of Pembroke Dock before he became archdeacon of St. David's in 1920 and bishop of that diocese in 1927. His predecessor, John Owen, had lived in the full glare of publicity, but by 1927 the big battles were over and Prosser could devote himself to ruling his diocese with quiet and unobtrusive authority. He brought to the task the qualities which had made him a firm but kindly parish priest. He was already an old man when he succeeded Green in 1944 and he was denied the health and strength essential for his new task. With memory fading and with a fondness for making formal arrangements in private conversation, he was said to have caused some confusion in his diocese; a number of stories, probably apocryphal, accentuated this trait. His life-long combination of simplicity and sincerity and firm piety survived to the end. His last years were dogged by illness and he died in 1950.

John Morgan, archbishop from 1950 to 1957, left an indelible impression of kindliness and geniality on those who knew him closely, but his public image was that of a stern disciplinarian. His father had been rector of Llandudno and archdeacon of Bangor, and he grew up in north Wales. There, too, he served as parish priest at Llanbeblig with Caernarfon for fourteen years before returning briefly to his father's old parish as rector of Llandudno. He was destined to spend the rest of his life in the south for he was elected bishop of Swansea and Brecon in 1934 and was translated to Llandaff in 1939. He was a sensitive man, easily hurt. He enjoyed music and was an accomplished organist. In his prime he was considered one of the great preachers of the Welsh Church, and even in old age, with a well-balanced and musical voice, he could hold a large congregation with ease. His primary task was to guide the Church in Wales through the difficult days of the war and the years of reconstruction which followed. He was a firm, not to say peremptory, chairman, and in his work as archbishop, as in his visitations, he had a grasp of detail which enabled him to give firm directives. He has been described as 'one who wanted things done decently and in order, and he believed in law and obedience.' He was not an advocate of change.

When Morgan died, the succession produced a marked change, for Alfred Morris, the new archbishop, broke a long tradition. He was an Englishman and he spoke no Welsh. In 1924 he became professor of theology at St. David's College, Lampeter, where he lived through the lean years of uncertainty in the history of that foundation. Then, in 1945 he was appointed bishop of Monmouth, where he quickly gained the reputation of being a firm disciplinarian whose injunctions were clear and concise and meant to be obeyed. It was the first time in his life that he could call himself a member of the full-time ministry of the Church in Wales, and it gave him pleasure and amusement that a bishopric was the first post for which the Church paid him a stipend. As bishop and archbishop his public statements were prepared with meticulous care, usually written out in longhand. He invariably read his speeches in order to avoid infelicity and inaccuracy. On occasions, especially at meetings of the Governing Body, he could command an emotional response though as a matter of habit he disliked such reactions and eschewed any attempt to win over his audience. He was a man of great courage, not always wise in the timing or the phrasing of his public utterances, and perhaps lacking an ingredient of humour which might have saved him from some pitfalls. Like John Owen, he considered himself to be charged with the duty of defending the Church's position in open controversy, a duty which he neither shirked nor compromised. A pamphlet on the God-given blessings of alcohol said many sensible things and presented both the dilemma and the hypocrisy of those who, in the debates about Sunday opening, approved of drinking during the week but would forbid it on Sunday. It did not, however, strike a sympathetic chord in nonconformist circles in Wales, and it left Morris open to a ridicule which he did not deserve. On another occasion a speech to the Governing Body dealt in trenchant terms with the problems of nuclear weapons. Morris had little sympathy for those who looked to nuclear disarmament as the way out of that particular moral issue. He was called upon to lead the Welsh Church in the difficult territory of the ecumenical movement and a cautious optimism inspired much of his work in this field. He also watched the financial experts transform the economic structure of the Church, and reflected the bewilderment of many churchpeople at the process. Like Edwards, he had the opportunity as archbishop to give positive leadership to the Church in Wales, and he enhanced his own reputation in doing so. He faced criticism because of his lack of Welsh, his lack of parochial experience, and his unyielding empirical approach to practical problems, but there is no doubt that he left his mark on the whole province. He has been somewhat underrated since his retirement and death, but he was a very considerable figure and a notable archbishop.

The election of his successor, Glyn Simon, was a turning point in the story of the Church in Wales in the twentieth century. Since 1920 the election had consistently gone to the senior bishop. In 1968 the senior diocesan was David Bartlett, formerly professor of theology at St. David's College, Lampeter, and since 1950 bishop of St. Asaph. He gave and received great affection, for people responded to him from the heart. On this occasion the electoral college decided to pass over the senior bishop and discarded him as deliberately as a modern political party might throw off an unwanted leader. With Glyn Simon, for the first time, the province elected an archbishop because of his potential powers as a leader. In doing so, a precedent was set for the future; archbishops are now chosen for what they will do once they are in office.

Glyn Simon was one of the outstanding personalities of his day, and a man full of contradictions. He was shy and retiring by nature, yet there was in him a streak of arrogance which drove him to make pronouncements on controversial issues and to invite publicity. Scholarly and judicious, he was often driven by emotion; capable of balanced appraisal, he embraced party causes. The consequence was that to hear him at his best it was necessary to hear him speak at length on liturgical problems which he could expound with supreme lucidity, and also to hear him speak in very different vein in support of nuclear disarmament or the Welsh language. Hard and unhappy schooldays at Christ College, Brecon, left an indelible mark on him, and may well account for many of his contradictions. He found deep contentment at Oxford, though he was never a brilliant scholar, and after a brief apprenticeship in an English curacy he served the Church in Wales in posts where his gifts could be used to full advantage. He was warden of Church Hostel, Bangor, warden of St. Michael's College, Llandaff, chancellor and eventually dean of Llandaff.

He was elected bishop of Swansea and Brecon in 1954 and was translated to Llandaff in 1957. His great strength was two-fold. Among many controversial utterances, he had the gift of saying important things. His judgment of occasion was sometimes fallible but his assessment was always to be taken seriously, and when he gave a lead it could never lightly be ignored. The second source of his strength lay in his gifts in debate. Again and again, speaking from the side of the platform, he could bring the Governing Body back to points of principle which mattered. He was at his peak as bishop of Llandaff between 1957 and 1968, for he was secure among friends, and he had freedom to intervene as and when he chose in the counsels of the Church. For that decade, by a mixture of astute timing and commanding speech, he was often the guiding influence in the Church. He was probably better known and more influential outside Wales than any Welsh bishop since Archbishop Edwards. It is easy to see why his supporters were anxious to secure his election as archbishop. His tragedy was that it was entirely the wrong move. As archbishop he no longer had the freedom to intervene in debate as he had done so effectively in the past. Now, when he did so, it seemed that he was issuing a ruling as chairman where he wished only to guide as a bishop. The archbishopric was a constraint within which his particular gifts could not be used to the full. There were occasionally signs that he found this situation irksome. They were soon overshadowed by signs of a greater constraint, for it became apparent that he was a very sick man. In 1971, only three years after his election, he resigned, and before he had had time to adjust to retirement he was dead.

Those who have served as bishops in Wales since disestablishment have been a varied and interesting cross-section of the Church. Daniel Davies, for example, spent a life-time in large parishes in the diocese of St. Asaph, as vicar of Brymbo, Denbigh and Wrexham. In 1923 he was a contender for the newly-established diocese of Swansea and Brecon, and in 1925 he was elected to Bangor, only to die at the comparatively early age of sixty-six after three years on the bench. The man who won the contest for Swansea and Brecon was Edward Latham Bevan, a younger son of a clerical dynasty of considerable standing in Breconshire. His grandfather had been high sheriff for the county, and his father was vicar of Hay-on-Wye for fifty-six years, and, in his last years, archdeacon of Brecon. He himself was set on a clerical career in the south of England when, in 1897, he was invited to be vicar of Brecon. He became archdeacon of Brecon in 1907 and suffragan bishop of Swansea in 1915, and finally bishop of Swansea and Brecon from 1923 until his death in 1934. Another Breconshire man who served as vicar of Swansea and who was to be bishop at St. Asaph and later of St. David's was William Havard. He earned a rugby blue at Oxford, and as a curate, played for Llanelli and was capped for Wales. Having earned his immortality in entirely the right way, he took up Association Football, and played for Swansea Town! It was a sign of liveliness in the Welsh Church that an energetic and popular man like Havard should be elected bishop of St. Asaph at the early age of forty-eight. When he died, still in his prime, the Church lost a forceful leader. Gilbert Cunningham Joyce, bishop of Monmouth from 1928 to 1940 was a scholar with a substantial reputation. Edward Williamson, bishop of Swansea and Brecon from 1939 until 1954, was a quiet and unassuming scholar of antiquarian tastes whose work was held in high regard by his fellow medievalists.

Over the years the Church has drawn on a wide range of experience in recruiting to the episcopate, but inevitably the emphasis has fallen on the large parishes where forceful incumbents may make their mark. The exceptional record of one parish, St. Mary's, Swansea, is a clear indication of the way in which the Welsh Church has made use of its resources. At the end of the nineteenth century the vicar of Swansea was Prebendary J. Allan Smith who moved on to become eventually dean of St. David's. His successor, the Hon. W. Talbot Rice, moved to a fashionable living in Onslow Square, London. Then five vicars in succession became bishops. Harrington Lees was made archbishop of Melbourne in 1921 and C. W. Wilson went to Middleton as suffragan bishop in 1928. The Church in Wales itself began to claim vicars of Swansea for the episcopal bench. W. T. Havard became bishop of St. Asaph in 1934 and later moved to St. David's. Edwardes Davies was elected bishop of Bangor in 1943 and J. J. A. Thomas became bishop of Swansea and Brecon in 1958. Few parishes in England and Wales have made so considerable a contribution to the higher echelons of the Church.[8]

There was a real danger that the Welsh Church might turn in on itself and become absorbed with its own problems to the exclusion of all others. This would scarcely have been surprising in view of the Church's internal difficulties and in view of the terrible economic plight of the people of south Wales in the sad years of the depression. The election of bishops whose experience lay outside Wales was a valuable corrective. Timothy Rees, bishop of Llandaff from 1931 to 1939, was a member of the Community of the Resurrection who could claim a wide experience in many parts of the world before he tackled the problems of Llandaff. An even more striking example was John Charles Jones, bishop of Bangor from 1949 to 1956. He had worked for many years in Uganda and had been asked to accept nomination as bishop in Uganda when he was elected to Bangor. He brought to the northern diocese a range of experience unusual in a Welsh bishop.[9] The appointment of men drawn from the provinces of Canterbury and York has been a delicate issue likely to arouse emotions and engender controversy. The fact that Welsh clerics found English livings, and occasionally appointments in English cathedral chapters, more desirable or more profitable than Welsh incumbencies has not always produced the most cordial of reactions among those who stayed in Wales. The long connection with Canterbury also raised the fear that to appoint a prominent English divine to a Welsh see might imply a lack of capable men in Wales or that it might be seen as a continuation of establishment conditions in the Welsh Church. The diocese of Monmouth made a bold but unsuccessful attempt to attract a leading English theologian, Leonard Hodgson, by electing him bishop in 1940, but he declined the invitation.

Perhaps it would be true to say that in a Welsh context bishops stand out more sharply than they might in England because there are not the opportunities in the ranks of the clergy to hold specialised ministries except on a very limited scale in the University of Wales, and in hospital or industry. Nor has the Church in Wales the endowments to provide for scholarly appointments. With rare exceptions, canonries are not residentiary; where, in the English Church, such an appointment may be used to provide for the scholar, the novelist, or the poet, in Wales such men must combine their creative activities with the normal routine of parish duties. Euros Bowen and R. S. Thomas have added lustre to modern Welsh literature, but the Church has not been able to provide them with opportunity or leisure—the two essential requirements—for their great talents to be developed. In recent decades liturgical work of a high order has been achieved in Wales, but all those who work on the Standing Liturgical Commission must add the tasks which it imposes to time-tables which are already very full. The few appointments which allow scope for specialist interests and academic pursuits are those connected with St. David's, Lampeter, and St. Michael's College, Llandaff, and there the demands of teaching take first priority. The deaneries of the Welsh cathedrals, which might be expected to attract scholars and specialists and in some instances have done so, are too often burdened with other duties. Gwynno James was one of the more considerable intellectuals in the Welsh Church, and like Professor Moelwyn Merchant, he had a feel for things artistic and musical which made him a noted patron. He did his best work as archdeacon of Llandaff, and when he moved to the deanery of Brecon, instead of leisure to think he found a busy parish to serve in addition to the normal duties of his cathedral church. On the other hand, the sense that all must labour in the vineyard has one advantage, for the clergy of the Church in Wales cannot be divided into those who work in parishes and those who enjoy easier and in some senses more productive conditions.

Two theological colleges have been primarily responsible for training Welsh clergy. St. David's College, Lampeter, has had a long record of educating men for the ministry in Wales.[10] In the inter-war years Lampeter was an important source of manpower and Lampeter men put their own stamp on the Welsh Church. The problem of the university status of St. David's and the relationship of the college to the University of Wales were much under discussion in the 1950s and 1960s and St. David's was first 'sponsored' by the University College of South Wales and Monmouthshire and finally made a constituent institution of the University of Wales. Part of this long process of discussion and definition involved the place of vocational training in theology, as opposed to academic work in the discipline, and Burgess Hall has been maintained from money other than that supplied by the University Grants Committee. The position of the Hall became uncertain, then precarious, and finally it was decided in the session 1974-5 that the Hall must be closed. St. Michael's College, now at Llandaff, was a tractarian foundation which owed much to the generosity of Olivia Talbot and to the patronage of Richard Lewis, bishop of Llandaff. From the first it was envisaged as a high church foundation, and in 1892 it found its first home at Aberdare and its first warden in H. R. Johnson of that parish. The College moved to Llandaff in 1907. Its buildings were destroyed by a land-mine in 1941, and the students found a temporary home in the bishop's house, Llys Esgob, until the college was rebuilt. Close links with the Community of the Resurrection at Roath, and later, with the sisters of St. Teilo's, have emphasised the continuing tradition of the college. The personality of the warden and, to some extent, his churchmanship, play a large part in the influence which the college has on the parishes of the Church in Wales. Much turns on the skill with which the warden combines the duty to provide for students drawn from the whole spectrum of churchmanship with the duty to maintain the intentions of those who founded the college. With the eclipse of Lampeter for vocational training, St. Michael's has something close to a monopoly of the training of ordinands in Wales, a monopoly broken only by the healthy practice of sending a number of Welsh ordinands to English theological colleges. In the last twenty years or so, St. Deiniol's Library, at Hawarden, has become a valuable centre for theological training which has been especially useful for training older recruits for the ministry.

Churchmanship, and the particular loyalty of which it is the outward expression, can cause many problems. Wales has been spared the unhappy conflicts between parties which have been so marked a feature of the English scene. The tension between evangelical and catholic is not characteristic of Wales, mostly because the Church in Wales has maintained a central tradition and the strength of two opposing wings has not been a factor of major importance in the counsels of the Church. Between the two world wars, Lampeter did much to contribute to this central tradition and it is no accident that one of its leading advocates has been Archbishop Morris, himself an influential theologian at Lampeter for some twenty years. The present condition of the Welsh Church is itself the product of a long process of change. So much of the constructive work of the Welsh Church in the nineteenth century was due to a virile and effective evangelical tradition,[11] but over a long period of time, between the 1870s and the 1930s, the evangelicals declined, even in the town parishes of the industrial south. The ritualism and the anglo-catholic loyalties of men like C. A. H. Green, which were once the cause of great concern for the future of the Welsh Church, did not become the force in Wales which similar movements became in England. Even so, that section of the Church which would call itself catholic has gained strength; since the second world war it has been under some strain. Changes have been the order of the day in many spheres of church life and a catholic voice has emerged as a defensive voice. In the 1970s there are signs of party conflict in the Governing Body which are more obvious than they have been in earlier decades. As elsewhere, the catholic movement tends to be introspective, and it cannot match the enterprise or the achievements which can properly be credited to the evangelicals in the nineteenth century. This lack of dynamic is a factor of anglican history, and not merely of the story of the Church in Wales.

When the Church in Wales was inaugurated there was little to suggest that the new province would exercise much influence outside the principality. In the 1920s there was, for example, intense debate about the revision of the Book of Common Prayer which culminated in the rejection of the new Prayer Book by Parliament in 1927 and again in 1928. It was an episode of critical importance for the Church of England, which had to wait another thirty years before, under Archbishop Michael Ramsey, any real advance could be made. But with that episode the Church in Wales was not concerned.[12] The Lambeth Conference was a well-established feature of the anglican scene and the conferences held in 1920 and 1930 were important occasions, if only because of the powerful personalities which dominated the debates. For the Welsh bishops the wounds of disestablishment were still smarting. Hensley Henson, an acute observer and meticulous diarist, noted that at the 1920 conference Archbishop Edwards was a curiously isolated figure, seeking sympathy in unexpected quarters. Ten years later, the Welsh bishops, as he reported, kept themselves as a separate group and hardly uttered a word.[13] In the post-war era things were very different, with all the Welsh bishops making their contributions, and with Glyn Simon, then bishop of Llandaff, as joint secretary of the committee which, in 1958, considered 'The Holy Bible: its Authority and Message.' The Welsh bishops regularly attend informal bishops' meetings at Lambeth, though how influential they are at such meetings and what effect their attendance has upon the life of the Welsh Church are questions which cannot be answered.

A similar change has taken place in terms of relations between the Church in Wales and other Churches. In 1920 the Nonconformists were still enemies who had at last triumphed over the established Church. Such an attitude was slow to die. It might perhaps be expected that chaplains returning from war fronts would introduce a more liberal approach. In the first world war the influence of chaplains to the forces coming home from active service had been a potent factor, but the generation of chaplains returning from the second world war exercised much less influence. Since the end of the war the Church in Wales has responded, first to patient leadership by Archbishop Morris and Bishop Bartlett, and more recently by G. O. Williams, bishop of Bangor and archbishop of Wales, and Bishop J. J. A. Thomas of Swansea and Brecon. The archbishop, working chiefly through international groups and big public occasions, and Bishop Thomas, working mainly through local groups and working parties, have increased the pace of change, and, more than any other, have persuaded the Governing Body to adopt and endorse bold lines of thinking. Welsh representatives have taken part in international gatherings, in the World Council of Churches and the British and Welsh Councils of Churches. They have joined in conversations with representatives of different denominations. The long debate about a scheme of unity between Anglicans and Methodists was seen initially as a domestic matter for the English Church and the Church in Wales was only involved in the discussions at a later stage. The English provinces had reached the point of decision and had failed to produce a requisite majority in favour of the scheme before the Church in Wales was called on to voice its opinion. In the circumstances it could only ratify what had already been determined elsewhere. Out of the long debate there emerged a conviction in Wales that joint action which involved more than two churches would be the next step to explore. As a result, the Church in Wales has moved into a formal covenanting relationship with the Methodists, the United Reform Church and the Presbyterian Church, and current thinking about closer unity between the Churches is now being formulated within the framework of the covenant.

There remains the great test: has the Church in Wales achieved integration in Welsh society? The idea of the anglican Church as an alien Church in Wales has long been fashionable, whether it be myth or fact. George Borrow quoted the landlord of a Welsh inn who 'seemed to think that the time was not far distant when the Anglican Church would be the popular as well as the established Church of Wales.'[14] In one sense, the primary task of the disestablished Church has been to achieve that popularity. It is true that the Church was never as alien an element in Welsh life as its opponents liked to maintain. Since the 1870s especially the identification of Church and country was increasingly close. It is also true that the chapel had a claim on men's loyalties which the Church could rarely match. The Church was identified with the ruling classes; the chapel provided for the workers, artisans, and tradesmen. So the case would be presented in its crudest terms. In a study of the Rhondda valleys the basic contrast where religion is concerned was the contrast between chapel and club, between those who found their focus in Christianity and those who found the solution to their problems in politics. The Church played little part in the local scene which was dominated by the chapel and its culture. On the other hand, when a deputation travelled from the Rhondda to see the Prime Minister, Ramsey Macdonald, three men spoke for them: the Rev. T. Alban Davies, minister of Bethesda Welsh Congregational Church, Ton Pentre, whose ministry in the Rhondda was to extend over forty-six years; the Rev. John Roberts of Cardiff; and Bishop Havard of St. David's.[15] In the same way, it was a bishop who saw the tragedy at Aberfan and who spoke for the conscience of Wales when disaster hit that village in 1966. One hundred and forty-four people were killed when a tip collapsed and poured down the mountainside on to the village below, one hundred and sixteen of them children. Glyn Simon was soon on the spot and he did not hesitate to condemn the greed and selfishness which had taken its toll in this industrial disaster. There was a major task of rehabilitation to be done before Aberfan could become a community in the aftermath of its tragedy. But when that constructive work was described and assessed by a trained social worker, representatives of other Christian bodies were singled out for special praise.[16]

In the case of the Rhondda and of Aberfan, it might well be that the anglican ministry could not identify easily with the close-knit mining community. A Church which recruits its ministry largely from the great urban centres cannot automatically provide men whose background and outlook enable them to work in, or to identify with, such communities. For a middle-class priest to come to terms with an industrial community dependent upon a single industry, is, at best, a slow business. One of the things which made the ministry of John Griffith at Aberdare and Merthyr Tydfil so rewarding in the nineteenth century was his ability to learn from experience. He came to identify himself closely with the people of his parishes, but he exercised little influence on the establishment.[17] Experiments in industrial chaplaincies in the twentieth century point to the same urgent need; to be successful, an industrial chaplain must be taken for granted by the men with whom he works. Too often he finds himself an object of suspicion as the management's man. It is very much open to question whether the Church in Wales has ever crossed that great divide.

In country parishes the distinction is less clear. Long-standing custom and the conservatism of the country community give the parish church and the parish priest a place, and the influence which a patient country parson may exercise is out of proportion to the number of Anglicans to whom he ministers in a formal sense. Somewhere between these limits must be placed the rôle of the Church in an urban society. Men and women may live in one place, work in another, and travel habitually to a third for leisure and pleasure. The problem in such circumstances is to provide a ministry flexible enough to deal with the family at home or at leisure, and the man and woman when they are away at work. The problem is acute in such areas as Swansea, where men may work in Llanelli or Port Talbot, and find relaxation in Gower. The same condition could be illustrated with the large steel plant at Newport or with the industrial complexes of Deeside.[18] In the nineteenth century the Welsh Church was slow to react to the challenge of industrial expansion. At least it must be said that in the twentieth century the nature of the problem has been identified, and the search for a practical solution is being pursued.

What of Welsh culture? How far has the Church in Wales bridged the gap between anglicanism and Welsh culture? The nineteenth century saw the growth of a close accord between nonconformity and Welshness which the anglican Church could not match. A revived interest in the National Eisteddfod was one means of redressing the balance. Bishop John Owen asked, a little plaintively, 'Why we had allowed the nonconformists to capture the Eisteddfod?'[19] He, and in a later generation, John Charles Jones of Bangor, were members of the Gorsedd, and the tradition of identifying with and through the Eisteddfod has been maintained by present members of the episcopal bench. Anglicans are no longer out of place in the Eisteddfod field. A ministry recruited from the traditional source of Welsh clerics might have helped, but it is a marked feature of the twentieth century that the steady flow of men from country parishes has gradually diminished. Instead, the chief source of supply for the ministry has become the town parishes and especially the parishes in those parts of Wales which have been most heavily anglicised. These factors help to explain why identification through language has become at once so significant and so controversial. The limitations of English in a bilingual society can be seen now to have been a cause of weakness during the nineteenth century. In the first half of the twentieth century, with the use of Welsh in secular society on the decline, the use of Welsh in the Church has become increasingly important. Among the younger generation and among the Welsh intelligentsia, the use of Welsh has developed steadily throughout the 1950s and 1960s. Parity of the language has been secured in law. There is a strong case to argue that Welsh is now essential within the Welsh Church. The constitution of the Church in Wales has been translated into Welsh. Agenda papers for the Governing Body are printed in both languages. For the first time in April, 1975, the Governing Body was able to use simultaneous translation facilities so that Welsh and English could be used indifferently in debate.

Unfortunately, in church affairs as in state affairs, language can be the subject of great controversy, and a divisive factor. From the earliest days of independence down to the mid-1970s the demands for the use of Welsh have produced bitter recriminations. In 1923, when Edward Latham Bevan was elected bishop of Swansea and Brecon, one of the critical issues in the election was the fact that Bevan had no Welsh. His great champion, Bishop John Owen, argued that although Welsh was one among many qualifications for high office it need not be an indispensable requirement. With the tide of nationalism rising, and with the issue of language so much tied up with national sentiment, it has become increasingly difficult to sustain Owen's arguments even though their basic soundness remains unaltered. When Glyn Simon was active, the pre-emptive demands of Welsh were proclaimed in clamant tones. One of the major contributions made by the present archbishop of Wales has been to give Welsh due prominence but to maintain in public and in private a bilingual policy. In the last analysis, integration in Wales is integration into both Welsh-speaking and English-speaking communities, and in the third quarter of the twentieth century that complex issue remains the most delicate and the most critical question for the Church in Wales to solve.

[1] K. O. Morgan, *Freedom or Sacrilege? a History of the campaign for Welsh Disestablishment* (Church in Wales, 1965), is a lucid and forceful account of the long process of disestablishment. I have quoted comments from pp. 3 and 6. Dr. Morgan's *Wales in British Politics 1868–1922* (Cardiff, 1963), is a valuable study of the political background. The most recent study is by P. M. H. Bell, *Disestablishment in Ireland and Wales* (1969). The account which follows is based on a paper which I wrote for the fiftieth anniversary of the creation of the Church in Wales as an independent province, 'The Welsh Church and Disestablishment', in *The Modern Churchman*, XIV (1971), 139–54.

[2] P. M. H. Bell, *Disestablishment*, 226–59; A. G. Edwards, *Memories* (1927), 226–87; G. K. A. Bell, *Randall Davidson*, 3rd. ed. (Oxford, 1952), 981–90.

[3] I have taken these estimates and figures from Bell, *Disestablishment*, 250–53.

[4] G. K. A. Bell, *Randall Davidson*, 987.

[5] E. T. Davies, 'From Archdeaconry to Diocese (1844–1921)', and A. E. Morris, 'The Jubilee of the Diocese of Monmouth', *The Diocese of Monmouth 1921–1971* (Newport, 1971).

[6] David and Margaret Walker, 'A View of the Past', *Swansea and Brecon 1923–1973*, ed. David Walker (Swansea, 1973).

[7] Archbishop Edwards is revealed most clearly in his autobiographical book, *Memories* (1927). Bishop Owen's daughter, Eluned E. Owen, produced a two-volume biography, *The Early Life of Bishop Owen*, and *The Later Life of Bishop Owen* (Gwasg Gomer, Llandyssul, 1958, 1961).

[8] I have set these events in their perspective in *A Short History of St. Mary's, Swansea*, 3rd. ed. (Swansea, 1967).

[9] E. Lewis, *John Bangor, the People's Bishop* (1962). The tradition of looking to the Church overseas for new bishops has been continued. John Poole-Hughes, elected bishop of Llandaff in 1975, had long experience as a bishop in Africa. B. N. Y. Vaughan, bishop of British Honduras until 1971, was dean of Bangor until his election to Swansea and Brecon in 1976.

[10] See above, pp. 145-147, and Owain Jones, 'The Mountain Clergyman: his Education and Training', *Links with the Past*, 165-84. The first volume of a history of St. David's College by William Price, is now in the press.

[11] This point is developed at length in chapter 6 by E. T. Davies and chapter 7 by Owain Jones. See also, Wilton D. Wills, 'The Clergy in Society in Mid-Victorian South Wales,' *J.H.S.C.W.*, XXIV (1974), 27–43.

[12] A. G. Corten has recently examined this crisis in an unpublished dissertation, 'The Prayer Book: our Hope and Meaning? A study of the Proposed Changes in the Prayer Book of the Church of England in 1927-8 and the effects on the Church during this period', U.C.W., Aberystwyth.

[13] *Retrospect of an Unimportant Life*, ii (Oxford, 1943), 16, 277.

[14] *Wild Wales*, chapter lxxii. Bell quoted this comment as an introduction to his chapter on 'The Welsh Church', *Randall Davidson*, 981.

[15] *Rhondda Past and Future*, ed. K. S. Hopkins (Rhondda, 1975), xi, 16, 120.

[16] The report was written by Joan Miller, *Aberfan: a Disaster and its Aftermath* (1974).

[17] See above, p. 139.

[18] C. C. Harris has examined the implications of this fluidity in an urban society in *The Church in a Mobile Society*, ed. V. Jones (Llandybie, 1969). He has considered the implications of a rural diocese in a detailed report on the diocese of Bangor.

[19] Eluned E. Owen, *The Later Life of Bishop Owen*, 559.

GAZETTEER OF PLACE-NAMES

Welsh place-names offer considerable problems for the modern writer. Many have been anglicised, some in form and many more in spelling. In recent years there has been an increasing tendency to restore Welsh spellings and to popularise Welsh forms. I have retained familiar names for well-known places: Swansea, for example, and not the Welsh alternative, Abertawe. I have tended to use the more familiar spellings of well-known places: Merthyr Tydfil, and not Merthyr Tudful. But it would be merely doctrinaire to retain all anglicised spellings, and at the risk of some inconsistency I have tried to use place-name forms which would make the text clear to the widest number of readers. Even with places which have very different English and Welsh names I have not sought consistency for its own sake. Holyhead and Caergybi are used easily and naturally as alternatives in conversation and both forms have been used as occasion might suggest in the text. Archenfield and Erging afford another example of interchangeable usage.

The following list indicates familiar forms with the Welsh forms and modern Welsh spellings which occur in this book.

Aberavon	Aberafan
Aberdare	Aberdâr
Aberffraw	Aberffro
Abergavenny	Y Fenni
Aberthaw	Aberddawan
Anglesey	Môn
Archenfield	Erging
Bardsey	Ynys Enlli
Barry	Y Barri
Bassaleg	Basaleg
Beaumaris	Biwmares
Beguildy	Begeildy
Berriew	Aberriew
Blaina	Blaenau
Brecon	Aberhonddu
Brecknock(shire)	Brycheiniog
Bridgend	Pen-y-bont ar Ogwr
Builth	Buellt
Builth Wells	Llanfair-ym-Muallt
Cardiff	Caerdydd
Cardigan	Aberteifi

Caerleon	Caerllion
Caerphilly	Caerffili
Carmarthen	Caerfyrddin
Carew	Caeriw
Chepstow	Cas-gwent
	Strigoil
Coedkerniew	Coedcernyw
Coldbrook	Colbrwg
Conway	Conwy
Cowbridge	Y Bont-faen
Denbigh	Dinbych
Dingestow	Llanddingad
Ebbw Vale	Glynebury
Flint	Y Fflint
Glamorgan	Morgannwg
Glasbury	Y Clas-ar-Wy
Glascoed	Glasgoed
Glascwm	Glasgwm
Gower	Guher
Hawarden	Penarlâg
Hay	Y Gelli
Holyhead	Caergybi
Kidwelly	Cydweli
Knighton	Trefyclo
Lampeter	Llanbedr Pont Steffan
Lamphey	Landyfai
Laugharne	Lacharn
Llandaff	Llandâf
Llandough	Llandochau
Llandovery	Llanymddyfri
Llangattock Vibion Avel	Llangatwg Feibion Afel
Llangeinor	Llangeinwr
Llangennith	Llangynydd
Llangunllo	Llangynllo
Llanover	Llanofer
Llanthony	Llanddewi Nant Hodni
Llantilio Crossenny	Llandeilo Gresynni
Llantwit Major	Llanilltud Fawr
Loughor	Llwchwr
Magor	Magwyr
Mathern	Matharn
Mathry	Mathri
Merioneth	Meirionnydd
Merthyr Tydfil	Merthyr Tudful
Monmouth	Trefynwy
Montgomery	Trefaldwyn
Nash	Yr As Fach
Neath	Castell Nedd
Newport	Casnewydd-ar-Wysg

Ogmore	Ogwr
Pembroke	Penfro
Pembrokeshire	Sir Benfro
Penmark	Penmarc
Picton Castle	Castell Pictwn
Pontypool	Pont-y-pôl
Pontypridd	Glyn-taf
Radnorshire	Maesyfed
Raglan	Rhaglan
Risca	Rhisga
Rhymney	Rhymni
Ruabon	Rhiwabon
Ruthin	Ruthun
St. Asaph	Llanelwy
St. Bride's	Saint-y-brid
St. David's	Tyddewi
St. Dogmael's	Llandudoch
Sirhowy	Sirhywi
Skenfrith	Ynysgynwraidd
Skewen	Sgiwen
Slebech	Slebets
Swansea	Abertawe
Talley	Talyllychau
Tintern	Tyndyrn
Trecastle	Trecastell
Tredegar	Tredegyr
Trefethin	Trefddyn
Trellech	Tryleg
Usk	Brynburga
Welshpool	Y Trallwng
Wenvoe	Gwenfô
Whitchurch	Yr Eglwys Newydd
Whitebrook	Llandogo
Whitland	Hendy-gwyn
Wrexham	Wrecsam

SUGGESTIONS FOR FURTHER READING

A full bibliography for the history of the Church in Wales would be very substantial. What follows is a selection of the works which are available. *A Bibliography of Welsh History* (Cardiff, 1962) with supplements published at intervals in the *Bulletin of the Board of Celtic Studies* provides the most detailed list of books and articles relating to ecclesiastical history in Wales. The *Y Bywgraffiadur Cymreig hyd 1940* (London, 1953) published in English as *The Dictionary of Welsh Biography down to 1940* (Oxford 1958) is a valuable compendium. Since 1947 the Historical Society of the Church in Wales has published 25 issues of its *Journal* and articles on Welsh ecclesiastical history have also appeared in the *Welsh History Review* and in the transactions of local antiquarian societies.

GENERAL

E. J. Newell, *A History of the Welsh Church to the Dissolution of the Monasteries* (London, 1895) was a careful survey of the period which it covered. J. W. James, *A Church History of Wales* (Ilfracombe, 1945) was a tour de force by a distinguished historian who has continued to write important articles for the past thirty years. The *Handbook of the Church Congress* containing the text of lectures delivered at the Congress at Llandrindod in 1953 is the most recent survey of the whole field in brief compass.

Diocesan histories, once a popular form of historical writing, vary in quality. W. Hughes's volume on *Bangor* in the S.P.C.K. Diocesan Histories appeared in 1911. An ambitious scheme to write the history of Bangor is now in hand, and a volume by M. L. Clarke on *Bangor Cathedral* (Cardiff, 1969) is the first of this series to be published. For St. David's, W. B. Jones and A. E. Freeman, *The History and Antiquities of St. David's* (London, 1856) is still valuable. W. L. Bevan wrote an attractive account of the diocese in the volume on *St. David's* which he produced for the S.P.C.K. Diocesan Histories in 1888. A new history of the diocese is planned. Meanwhile, W. T. Morgan has explored the records of the diocese and in particular has examined the working of the consistory courts and the condition of the diocese in a series of articles in the *Journal of the Historical Society of the Church in Wales*, VII (1957), 3-25, VIII (1958), 58-81, XII (1962), 28-54, XXI (1971), 5-49, and XXII (1972), 12-48. E. J. Newell wrote the S.P.C.K. Diocesan History for Llandaff in 1902, and W. de G. Birch produced a useful volume in *Memorials of the See and Cathedral of Llandaff* (Neath, 1912). In 1960 the diocese celebrated the 1400th anniversary of its foundation and *The Story of the Church in Glamorgan 560-1960*, edited by E. T. Davies (London, 1962), published to mark that occasion, deserves to be more widely known. D. R. Thomas, *The History of the Diocese of St. Asaph* (3 vols., Oswestry, 1908-13), and the same author's *St. Asaph* (S.P.C.K. Diocesan Histories, 1888) are useful studies.

For the two dioceses founded in the twentieth century there is a booklet issued to mark the jubilee of the diocese of Monmouth, *The Diocese of Monmouth, 1921-1971*, edited by E. T. Davies (Newport, 1971); and for Swansea and Brecon, two studies by David and Margaret Walker, 'Epilogue: A New Diocese, 1923' in *Links with the Past*, 241-51, and 'A View of the Past', in *Swansea and Brecon, 1923-1973*, edited by David Walker (Swansea, 1973). *Links with the Past: Swansea and Brecon Historical Essays*, edited by Owain W. Jones and David Walker (Llandybie, 1974) is a useful collection of essays which has been described as a *festschrift* to mark the jubilee of the diocese of Swansea and Brecon.

There are many studies of individual churches. Tenby, for example, has been described at length in two studies by W. G. Thomas, 'The Architectural History of St. Mary's Church, Tenby', *Arch. Camb.*, CXV (1966), 134-163, and *Tenby Parish Church* (Tenby, 1961), and its records have provided the material for *The Church Book of St. Mary the Virgin, Tenby* (Tenby, 1907). Gwynfryn Richards has written sympathetically on 'The Church of St. Mary and All Saints, Conway' in *J.H.S.C.W.*, XVI (1966), 28-60. The early registers of Conway are available in print, *Conway Parish Registers, 1541-1793*, edited by Alice Hadley (London, 1900). In *A Short History of St. Mary's, Swansea* (3rd. ed., Swansea, 1967) David Walker has examined the story of the parish and its church with particular reference to the architectural history of the church and the growth and division of the parish in the nineteenth century. In *The First Hundred Years: St. James's Church, Swansea, 1867-1967* (Swansea, 1967) he has traced the history of the chapel of ease in the parish of Swansea with special reference to the changing social structure of the area. These two studies may be set in context in David Walker, *Nerth yr Eglwys* (Swansea, 1964), a brief history of the archdeaconry of Gower and its churches.

THE CELTIC CHURCH

The Celtic Church has produced a large literature. The collections of essays published by Nora K. Chadwick in collaboration with a number of other scholars have a lasting value: see, for example, *Studies in Early British History* (Cambridge, 1954) and *Studies in the Early British Church* (Cambridge, 1958, reprint, Archon Press, Connecticut, U.S.A., 1973). P. A. Wilson has written on 'Romano-British and Welsh Christianity: continuity and discontinuity?' in *W. H.R.*, 3 (1966-7), 5-32, 103-120, and R. W. D. Fenn covers a similar theme for the Dark Ages in 'Isolation or Involvement?', *Links with the Past*, 21-36. The lives of the Celtic saints are available most conveniently in *Vitae Sanctorum Britanniae et Genealogiae* edited by A. W. Wade-Evans (Cardiff, 1944) and in the works of G. H. Doble, *St. Patern* (Lampeter, 1940), *St. Iltut* (Cardiff, 1944) and *St. Dubricius* (Guildford, 1943). *Rhigyfarch's Life of St. David* edited by J. W. James (Cardiff, 1967) is a crucial text; the influence of St. David has been examined by Glanmor Williams, 'The tradition of St. David' in *Links with the Past*, 1-20. The difficult question of the areas covered by Celtic churches is discussed by T. Thornley Jones, 'Districts of the Ancient Welsh Llanau', *J.H.S.C.W.*, XVIII (1968), 7-12. Francis Jones, *The Holy Wells of Wales* (Cardiff, 1954) is an important study.

THE MEDIEVAL CHURCH

The foundation of much recent work on the medieval Welsh Church is the collection of material in *Episcopal Acts and Cognate Documents relating to the Welsh Dioceses, 1066-1272*, edited by J. Conway Davies (Historical Society of the Church in Wales, 2 vols., 1946, 1948). These two volumes cover the dioceses of St. David's and Llandaff. A third volume dealing with Bangor and St. Asaph was left unpublished when J. Conway Davies died, but is now in preparation. The development of the Church under Norman influence can be examined in J. E. Lloyd's classic, *A History of Wales from the Earliest times to the Edwardian Conquest* (2 vols., 3rd. ed., London, 1939), or in briefer compass in David Walker, *The Norman Conquerors, A Students' History of Wales* (Llandybie, 1976). The Book of Llandaff and its textual problems can be assessed in *Liber Landavensis*, edited by J. G. Evans and J. Rhys (Oxford, 1893) and in papers by J. W. James, notably in 'The Book of Llan Dâv: The Church and See of Llan Dâv and their critics', *J.H.S.C.W.*, IX (1959), 5-22, 'The 'Concen Charters' and the Book of Llan Dâv', *Trans. Cymm.* (1963), 82-95, 'The Book of Llan Dâv and the Diocesan Boundaries Dispute, c. 960-1133', *N.L.W.J.*,

XVI (1969-70), 319-352, and 'The Book of Llan Dâv and Canon G. H. Doble', *N.L.W.J.*, XVIII (1973), 1-36. This source has been reassessed by Dr. Wendy Davies whose views are summarised conveniently in 'Liber Landavensis: its construction and credibility', *English Historical Review*, LXXXVIII (1973), 335-51. See also her paper, 'Saint Mary's Worcester and the Liber Landavensis', *Journal of the Society of Archivists*, 4 (1970-73), 459-85.

Much of the history of the Church in Wales in the twelfth and thirteenth centuries is dominated by Gerald of Wales, whose voluminous works were edited, with minor exceptions, for the Rolls Series in eight volumes by J. S. Brewer, James F. Dimock and George F. Warner (1861-91). The most recent edition of a work by Gerald is the *Speculum Duorum* edited by M. Richter, Y. Lefèvre, and R. B. C. Huygens, with a translation by Brian Dawson (Cardiff, 1974). There are many accounts of Gerald; for example, J. Conway Davies, 'Giraldus Cambrensis, 1146-1946', *Arch. Camb.*, XCIX (1947), 85-108, 256-280; M. Richter, *Giraldus Cambrensis: The Growth of the Welsh Nation* (Aberystwyth, 1972), is a reprint of papers originally published in the *N.L.W.J.*, XVI and XVII; David Walker, 'Gerald of Wales, Archdeacon of Brecon', *Links with the Past*, 67-88. For a survey of recent writing on this subject see David Walker, 'Gerald of Wales: a Review of Recent Work', *J.H.S.C.W.*, XXIV (1974), 13-26. R. W. Hays deals with a conflict at Bangor in 'Rotoland sub-prior of Aberconway and the controversy over the see of Bangor, 1199-1204', *J.H.S.C.W.*, XIII (1963), 9-19. For an analysis of the bishops who served a Welsh diocese see David Walker, 'The Medieval Bishops of Llandaff', *Morgannwg*, VI (1962), 5-32. The most recent study of a single medieval diocese is F. G. Cowley, 'The Church in Glamorgan from the Norman Conquest to the fourteenth century', and Glanmor Williams, 'The Church in Glamorgan from the fourteenth century to the Reformation', *Glamorgan County History*, III (Cardiff, 1971), 87-166. *The Welsh Church from Conquest to Reformation* by Glanmor Williams (Cardiff, 1962) is a fundamental work for the historian of the later Middle Ages. Decima Douie's *Archbishop Pecham* (Oxford, 1952) has much of value about Pecham's dealings with Wales. Papers by William Greenway published before his untimely death examined and illuminated a number of facets of the history of the Welsh Church in the later Middle Ages: 'The Papacy and the Diocese of St. David's, 1305-1417', *Church Quarterly Review*, clxi (1960), 436-448, clxii (1961) 33-49; 'The Election of John of Monmouth, Bishop of Llandaff', *Morgannwg*, V (1961), 3-22; 'The Medieval Diocese of Llandaff', *The Story of the Church in Glamorgan, 560-1960*, 29-48; 'The

Election of David Martin, Bishop of St. David's, 1293-6', *J.H.S.C.W.*, X (1960), 9-16; 'Archdeacons of Carmarthen in the Fourteenth Century', *Carm. Antiq.*, iii (1960), 63-71; 'Archbishop Pecham, Thomas Bek and St. David's', *Journ. Ecc. Hist.*, xi (1960), 152-163. *The Episcopal Registers of St. David's, 1397-1578* edited by R. F. Isaacson (3 vols., Cymm. Rec. Ser., 1917-20), and *The Black Book of St. David's* edited by J. W. Willis Bund (Cymm. Rec. Ser., 1902) provide material which is not available for other Welsh dioceses. *The Llyfr Ancr: The Elucidarium and other Tracts in Welsh from Llyvyr Agkyr Llandewivrevi, A.D. 1346* edited by J. Morris Jones and John Rhys (Oxford, 1894), and I.Ll. Foster, 'The Book of the Anchorite', *Proceedings of the British Academy*, XXV (London, 1950), 197-226, open up another type of source. Thomas Jones writes briefly on 'Pre-Reformation Welsh Versions of the Scriptures', in *N.L.W.J.*, IV (1946), 97-114.

The troubled years of the late fourteenth and early fifteenth centuries are the subject of three biographies of the leading Welshman of the period, Owain Glyn Dŵr: J. E. Lloyd, *Owen Glendower* (Oxford, 1931), Glanmor Williams, *Owen Glendower* (Oxford, 1966), and a bilingual study by G. A. Jones, *Owain Glyndwr, c. 1354-1416* (Cardiff, 1962). Three specialist studies are to be found in E. J. Jones, 'Bishop John Trevor (II) of St. Asaph', and C. T. Allmand, 'A Bishop of Bangor during the Glyn Dŵr revolts: Richard Young', both in *J.H.S.C.W.*, XVIII (1968), 36-46, 47-55. J. R. Gabriel, 'Wales and the Avignon Papacy', *Arch. Camb.*, VII iii (1923), 70-86, and A. O. H. Jarman, 'Wales and the Council of Constance', *B.B.C.S.*, XIV (1952), 220-222, deal with problems of international relationships as they affected Wales.

The monastic settlement in Wales has been the subject of many books and articles. J. F. O'Sullivan, *Cistercian Settlements in Wales and Monmouthshire 1140-1540* (New York, 1947), and D. H. Williams, *The Welsh Cistercians* (Pontypool, 1969) are useful surveys of their field; F. R. Lewis deals with 'Racial sympathies of Welsh Cistercians', *Trans. Cymm.* (1938), 103-118. Of studies of individual houses these may stand as examples: W. de G. Birch, *A History of Margam Abbey* (London, 1897), A. Leslie Evans, *Margam Abbey* (Port Talbot, 1958); W. de G. Birch, *A History of Neath Abbey* (London, 1902), Glanmor Williams, 'Neath Abbey', in *Neath and District: a Symposium* edited by Elis Jenkins (Neath, 1974), 73-91; David Walker, 'Brecon Priory in the Middle Ages', *Links with the Past*, 37-66; G. V. Price, *Valle Crucis Abbey* (Liverpool, 1952); R. W. Hays, *A History of the Abbey of Aberconway 1186-1537* (Cardiff, 1963).

THE REFORMATION

A number of abstracts of record sources available for the history of Wales in the sixteenth century have been published which are particularly valuable where the *Calendars* published by the Public Record Office are not easily accessible: *A Catalogue of Star Chamber Proceedings relating to Wales* edited by Ifan ab Owen Edwards (Cardiff, 1929), *Exchequer Proceedings concerning Wales, Henry VIII-Elizabeth* edited by E. G. Jones (Cardiff, 1939), with a continuation for the reign of James I edited by T. I. Jeffreys Jones (Cardiff, 1955), and *Records of the Court of Augmentations relating to Wales and Monmouthshire* edited by E. A. Lewis and J. Conway Davies (Cardiff, 1954). There is much to be gleaned from George Owen's *Description of Pembrokeshire* which can be used in the 3 volumes issued in the Cymmrodorion Record Series (1906), or in the extracts compiled and modernised in *Elizabethan Pembrokeshire: The evidence of George Owen* edited by Brian Howells, Pembrokeshire Record Society, Record Series, vol. 2 (1973). B. G. Charles has written a *Life of George Owen of Henllys* (Aberystwyth, 1974). Glanmor Williams has analysed 'The Second Volume of St. David's Registers, 1554-64', *B.B.C.S.*, XIV (1950-52), 45-54, 125-139.

A. H. Dodd published a perceptive lecture on 'The Church in Wales in the Age of the Reformation', *Welsh Church Congress Handbook* (1953), and made good use of Welsh material in his *Elizabethan England* (London, 1961, reissued, 1973). Thomas Lawrence, *The Reformation in the Old Diocese of Llandaff* (Cardiff, 1930) retains its value. Glanmor Williams published a collection of his papers on the history of the Welsh Church in this period in *Welsh Reformation Essays* (Cardiff, 1967). He has written at length on the religious history of Glamorgan in *Glamorgan County History*, IV (Cardiff, 1974), 203-256, 468-499 and on 'Carmarthen and the Reformation' in *Carmarthenshire Studies presented to Francis Jones* edited by T. Barnes and W. Yates (Carmarthen, 1974), 136-157. His contribution to volume IV of *The Agrarian History of Wales* edited by Joan Thirsk (Cambridge, 1967), 381-395, 'Landlords in Wales—The Church', explores the economic changes which affected the Welsh Church in the sixteenth and seventeenth centuries. He has examined problems arising from the study of the old diocese of St. David's and surveyed recent work in 'The Diocese of St. David's from the end of the Middle Ages to the Methodist Revival', *J.H.S.C.W.*, XXV (1976), 11-31. Civic and ecclesiastical business are both included in the *Calendar of the records of the borough of Haverfordwest, 1539-1660* (ed. B. G. Charles, Cardiff, 1967). Margaret Walker has used the records of a single parish in her 'Church life in Sixteenth-century Swansea' in *Links with the Past*, 89-116 and in 'Welsh Books in St. Mary's, Swansea, 1559-1626', *B.B.C.S.*, XXIII (1970), 397-402. A. L. Pryce produced an informative volume in *The Diocese of Bangor in the Sixteenth Century* (Bangor, 1923). For the catholic reaction in Wales two books by T. P. Ellis are still of value, *The Catholic Martyrs of Wales* (London, 1933) and *The Welsh Benedictines of the Terror* (Newtown, 1936). So is D. A. Thomas, *The Welsh Elizabethan Catholic Martyrs* (Cardiff, 1971). John Bossy's *The English Catholic Community, 1570-1850* (London, 1976) appeared after this volume was in the press, but it is a major study of English Catholicism; Dr.Bossy deliberately excluded Wales from his area of study. For John Penry and his influence see D. J. McGinn, *John Penry and the Marprelate Controversy* (Rutgers, 1966) and Glanmor Williams, 'John Penry: Marprelate and Patriot', *W.H.R.*, 3 (1966-67), 361-80. David Williams edited *Three Treatises concerning Wales* by John Penry (Cardiff, 1960).

THE SEVENTEENTH AND EIGHTEENTH CENTURIES

The literature devoted to the history of dissent in Wales lies beyond the range of this list of suggested reading. For a general conspectus see the classic study by Thomas Rees, *History of Protestant Nonconformity in Wales* (London, 2nd ed. 1883), and the many contributions made by Thomas Richards, for example, *The Puritan Movement in Wales, 1639-53* (London, 1920), and *Religious Development in Wales, 1654-62* (London, 1923). Geoffrey Nuttall concentrated on three leading figures, Walter Cradock, Vavasor Powell and Morgan Llwyd in *The Welsh Saints, 1640-1660* (Cardiff, 1957).

The problems of the seventeenth century can be gauged from J. G. Jones, 'Bishop Lewis Bayly and the Wynns of Gwydir, 1616-27', *W.H.R.*, 6 (1972-3), 404-423, Bickham Sweet-Escott, 'William Beaw: a Cavalier Bishop', *W.H.R.*, 1 (1960-3), 397-412, and J. Gwynfor Jones, 'Richard Parry, Bishop of St. Asaph: some aspects of his career,' *B.B.C.S.*, *XXVI* (1975), 175-190, E. T. Davies, 'The "Popish Plot" in Monmouthshire', *J.H.S.C.W.*, XXV (1976), 32-45, and from two major essays on more general themes, A. M. Johnson, 'Politics and Religion in Glamorgan during the Interregnum', *Glamorgan County History*, IV, edited by Glanmor Williams (Cardiff, 1974) and R. Tudur Jones, 'Religion in post-Restoration Breconshire, 1660-88,' *Brycheiniog*, VIII (1962), 11-65. Christopher Hill opened up new lines of thought in 'Puritans and 'the Dark Corners of the Land' ', *Trans. R. Hist. S.*, fifth series, 13 (1963), 77-102, reprinted in his *Change and*

Continuation in Seventeenth-century England (London, 1974). There is much which is relevant to the Welsh situation in his *Economic Problems of the Church from Whitgift to the Long Parliament* (Oxford, 1956). For John Wesley see A. H. Williams, *John Wesley in Wales* (Cardiff, 1971) and 'John Wesley and the Archdeaconry of Brecon' in *Links with the Past*, 143-164. Geoffrey Nuttall's *Howel Harris* (Cardiff, 1965) is a useful introduction to the life and work of the Welsh evangelist. Mary Clement has two important studies, *Correspondence and Minutes of the S.P.C.K. relating to Wales, 1699-1740* (Cardiff, 1952) and *The S.P.C.K. and Wales, 1699-1740* (London, 1954). Of the voluminous literature on Griffith Jones see especially R. T. Jenkins's bilingual essay, *Gruffydd Jones, Llanddowror* (Cardiff, 1930), and the essay by Glanmor Williams, 'Griffith Jones (1683-1761)', in *Pioneers of Welsh Education* (Swansea, 1964).

The Diocese of Bangor through three centuries edited by A. L. Pryce (Cardiff, 1929) continues the record of the northern diocese from the sixteenth to the nineteenth century. The *Surveys* of Bangor, St. Asaph, St. David's, and Llandaff by Browne Willis may be supplemented by D. R. Buttress, 'Llandaff Cathedral in the Eighteenth and Nineteenth Centuries', *J.H.S.C.W.*, XVI (1966), 61-76, and F. J. North, *The Stones of Llandaff Cathedral* (Cardiff, 1957).

THE NINETEENTH CENTURY

Many aspects of ecclesiastical history in the nineteenth century have been examined and reappraised in recent years. There are, for example, E. T. Davies's study of *Monmouthshire Schools and Education to 1870* (Newport, 1957), and Owain W. Jones's 'The Mountain Clergyman: his Education and Training', in *Links with the Past*, 165-184. Owain Jones has also examined 'Prince and the Lampeter Brethren', *Trivium*, 5 (1970), 10-20, and 'Mid-Victorian Introspection in Wales', *J.H.S.C.W.*, XV (1965), 47-53. His *Isaac Williams and his Circle* (London, 1971) is an extended study of the impact of tractarianism on Wales. *The Life and the Letters of Rowland Williams* by his wife (1874) has much of interest for the history of St. David's College, Lampeter. W. J. Copleston, *Memoirs of Edward Copleston, D.D.* (London, 1851) and *The Remains, literary and theological, of Connop Thirlwall, bishop of St. David's. Episcopal Charges*, edited by J. J. Stewart Perowne (2 vols. London, 1877) bring two important bishops into due prominence. There are modern assessments of Thirlwall in J. C. Thirlwall, *Connop Thirlwall* (London, 1936), and O. G. Rees, 'Connop

Thirlwall: Liberal Anglican', *J.H.S.C.W.*, XIV (1964), 66-76. Francis Jones has contributed an extensive essay on Richard Lewis in 'A Victorian Bishop of Llandaff', *N.L.W.J.*, XIX (1975), 14-56. Wilton D. Wills has looked at 'The Established Church in the Diocese of Llandaff, 1850-70: a study of the Evangelical Movement in the South Wales Coalfield', *W.H.R.*, 4 (1968-9), 235-72, and 'The Clergy in Society in Mid-Victorian South Wales', *J.H.S.C.W.*, XXIV (1974), 27-43. A closely related essay is his paper, 'The Rev. John Griffith and the Revival of the Established Church in Nineteenth-century Glamorgan', *Morgannwg*, XIII (1969), 75-102.

Ieuan Gwynedd Jones has analysed the Religious Census of 1851 in a series of articles: 'Denominationalism in Swansea and District: A Study of the Ecclesiastical Census of 1851', *Morgannwg*, XII (1968), 67-96, 'The Religious Condition of the Counties of Brecon and Radnor as revealed in the Census of Religious Worship of 1851', *Links with the Past*, 185-214, 'Denominationalism in Caernarvonshire in the mid-nineteenth century as shown in the Religious Census of 1851', *Trans. Caernarvonshire Hist. Soc.*, 31 (1970), 78-114.

E. T. Davies, *Religion in the Industrial Revolution in South Wales* (Cardiff, 1969) is a fundamental book; J. Jenkins has written briefly on 'The Church in Industrial Rhymney, 1800-1855', *J.H.S.C.W.*, XVI (1966), 77-87.

MODERN TIMES

There is much on the problems of the Welsh Church in G. K. A. Bell, *Randall Davidson, Archbishop of Canterbury* (3rd. ed. Oxford, 1952). For modern Welsh bishops see A. G. Edwards, *Memories* (London, 1927), G. Lerry, 'A. G. Cambrensis, 1848-1948', *J.H.S.C.W.*, I (1947), 72-80, Eluned E. Owen, *The Early Life of Bishop Owen* and *The Later Life of Bishop Owen* (Llandyssul, 1958, 1961), A. J. Edwards, 'Bishop Green of Monmouth', *J.H.S.C.W.*, XXI (1971), 50-65, E. Lewis, *John Bangor, the People's Bishop* (London, 1962).

For the problems raised by Disestablishment see K. O. Morgan, *Wales in British Politics, 1868-1922* (Cardiff, 1963) and *Freedom or Sacrilege? A History of the Campaign for Welsh Disestablishment* (Penarth, 1966), P. M. H. Bell, *Disestablishment in Ireland and Wales* (London, 1969), Ieuan Gwynedd Jones, 'The Liberation Society and Welsh Politics', *W.H.R.*, I (1960-61), 193-200, R. Tudur Jones, 'Origins of the Non-conformist Disestablishment Campaign', *J.H.S.C.W.*, XX (1970), 39-76, David Walker, 'The Welsh Church and Disestablishment', *The Modern*

Churchman, XIV (1971), 139-154. Two studies of the contemporary scene are especially useful, *The Church in a Mobile Society* edited by V. Jones (Llandybie, 1969), and *Rhondda Past and Future* edited by K. S. Hopkins (Rhondda, 1975). The autobiography of Daniel Richards, *Honest to Self* (Llandybie, 1971) presents an attractive picture of one clergyman's life in the Welsh Church in the twentieth century; so, also, do the books written by D. Parry Jones, *A Welsh Country Upbringing* (London, 1949) and *A Welsh Country Parson* (London, 1975).

INDEX

Aaron, the martyr, 2
Abberley, Heref and Worcs, 5
Aber, Lewis, bishop-elect of Bangor,
    44, 48
Abbot, George, archbishop of
    Canterbury, 73
Aberaeron, Dyfed, 118
Aberafan, Aberavon, West Glam, 115
Aberconway, Aberconwy, Gwynedd,
    Cistercian abbey, 34
Aberdâr, Aberdare, Mid Glam,
    123, 124, 128, 134, 136, 139, 140,
    143, n.14, 151, 155, 174, 181, 185
    vicar of, see Green, C. A. H.;
        Griffith, John
Aberdare, Lord, see Bruce, H. A.
Aberddawan, see Aberthaw
Aberfan, Mid Glam, 184, 185
Aberffraw, Aberffro, Anglesey, 13
    prince of, 40
Abergavenny, Y Fenni, Gwent, 99,
    122, 130, 134, 139, 142, n.6,
    143, n.14, 171
    Benedictine priory, 26, 50, 171
    grammar school, 105, 145
    rural deanery, 54, 143, n.14
Abergavenny, Henry of, bishop of
    Llandaff, 34, 35
Abergwili, Dyfed, collegiate church,
    58, 148
Aberhonddu, see Brecon
Aberriw, see Berriew
Abersychan, Gwent, 128, 129
Abertawe, see Swansea
Aberteifi, see Cardigan
Aberthaw, East, Aberddawan, South
    Glam, 128
Aberystruth, Gwent, 128, 136, 155
Aberystwyth, Dyfed, 118, 150, 172
Abingdon, Oxon, Benedictine abbey, 28
ab Ithel, see Williams, John
Abstracts of Dr. Woodward's Book,
    110
Academy, dissenting, 96, 97, 105
*Account of the Religious Societies in the
    City of London etc*, 110
Act for the Better Propagation and
    Preaching of the Gospel in Wales,
    75, 83, 84
Act for the translation of the Bible
    into Welsh, 66

Act in Restraint of Appeals, 57
Act of Conditional Restraint of
    Annates, 57
Act of Supremacy (1534), 57
Act of Toleration, 79, 94, 96, 99, 100
Act of Uniformity (1559), 67
    (1662), 76
Act of Union (1536), 56, 65
Addams-Williams, William, of
    Llangybi, 132
*Address to Young Persons after
    Confirmation*, 122
Afon Lwyd, 124
Alan, bishop of Bangor, 34
Albert, prince-consort, 133
Alexander, apocryphal pope, 22
Alexander III, pope, 27, 38
Alleine, Joseph, 86
Allen, William, 70
*An Afflicted Man's Testimony
    concerning his Troubles*, 84, 85, 87
Anabaptists, 76
Ancr, Y Llyfr, 46, 53, n.21
*Angenrhaid a Mawrlles Mynych
    Gymuno*, 102
Anglesey, Môn, 16, 24, 99, 109, 159
    archdeacon of, see Roberts,
        Gruffydd
Anglican-Nonconformist ratios,
    134–136, 145
Anglicans and Dissenters, 79–102
Anian (I), bishop of Bangor, 41, 42
Anian, bishop of St. Asaph, 41
Annales Cambriae, 7, 11, 12, 21, 22
Anne, queen, 97, 98, 160
Anselm, archbishop of Canterbury, 31
anti-clericalism, 56
Aragon, Catherine of, wife of
    Henry VIII, 56, 57, 59
Archenfield, see Erging
architecture, 114–116, 155–157
Ariconium, 2, 3
Arles, Council of, 1
Armagh, archbishop of, see Richard
    fitz Ralph; Ussher, James
Armorica, 4
Arthur, prince of Wales, 56
Arwystli, cantref, 24
Asquith, H., 165, 166
Asser, bishop of St. David's, *Life
    of Alfred*, 12

Lees, Harrington, vicar of Swansea, archbishop of Melbourne, 179
Leia, Peter de, bishop of St. David's, 33, 34
Leicester, earl of, 64
Leo III, pope, 22
Lerins, abbey, 3
Letter to a Friend Concerning the Great Sin of Taking God's Name in Vain, 101
Lewis, David, 150
Lewis, Evan, dean of Bangor, 150, 151
Lewis, Huw, 67
Lewis, Owen, 70
Lewis, Richard, archdeacon of St. David's, bishop of Llandaff, 138, 140–142, 181
Lewis, Stephen, of Meifod, 76
Leyshon family, 139
Leyshon, Thomas, vicar of Bassaleg, 130
Liber Pontificalis, 8
Lichfield, Staffs, 21, 22
Life and Letters of Rowland Williams, 154
Limerick, bishop of, *see* Webbe, George
Lincolnshire, 55
Lisle family, 139
Litany, Welsh, 67
Liverpool Standard, 132
Llanasa, Clwyd, 87
Llanbadarn Fawr, Dyfed, 13, 17, 26, 73, 76, 143, *n.* 8
Llanbadarn Odwyn, Dyfed, 115
Llanbeblig, Gwynedd, 175
Llanbedr Pont Steffan, *see* Lampeter
Llancarfan, South Glam, 10, 11, 13, 15–17, 19, 26, 30
Llandâf, Llandaff, South Glam, 8, 12, 13, 16, 17
bishop of, 9, 12, 13
see Abergavenny, Henry of; Athequa, George de; Barrington, Shute; Beaw, William; Bleddyn, William; Burgh, William de; Burghill, John de; Copleston, Edward; Davies, Francis; Eaglescliffe, John of; Goldcliff, William of; Gwgan; Herewald; Holgate, Robert; Hughes, Joshua; Hunden, John; Kitchen, Anthony; Lewis, Richard; Lloyd, Hugh; Lloyd, William; Marsh, Herbert; Marshall, John; Monmouth, John of; Morgan, John; Murray, William; Nicholas ap Gwrgan; Ollivant, Alfred; Peverell, Thomas; Poole-Hughes, John; Radnor,

Elias of; Radnor, William of; Rees, Timothy; Simon, William Glyn Hughes; Sumner, Charles Richard; Uchtred; Urban; Van Mildert, William; Ware, John de; Watson, Richard
bishop's palace, 50
Llandaff, Book of, 8, 11, 13, 21, 29, 30, 52, *n.* 4
Llandaff, cathedral, 26, 28–30, 36, 50, 115, 122, 137, 140, 156
chapter, 35, 36, 45, 46, 122
archdeacon of, *see* Davies, Francis; Edmondes, Frederick William; James, Gwynno; Knight, William Bruce; Williams, Thomas
chancellor of, *see* Knight, William Bruce; Simon, William Glyn Hughes
dean of, *see* Griffith, C.E.T.; Knight, William Bruce; Simon, William Glyn Hughes; Williams, Thomas
Matthew chantry, 61
residentiary canons, 128
Llandaff, diocese of, 34, 42, 43, 45, 51, 59, 63, 64, 66, 69, 70, 103, 121–142, 145, 155, 169, 171, 175, 179
origins of, 23, *n.*2, 29, 52, *n.*4
archdeaconries of Llandaff and Monmouth, 128, 129, 143, *n.* 14
reorganisation of, 125–129, 136–142, 155
Llandaff Diocesan Board of Finance, 138
Llandaff Diocesan Church Extension Society, 137, 140
Llandaff Diocesan Committee for Education, 127
Llandaff Diocesan Conference, 138, 141, 143, *n.* 19
Llandaff Diocesan Council for Education, 138
Llandaff, manor, 63, 64
Llandaff, rural deanery, 143, *n.*14
Llandaff, St. Michael's Theological College, 151, 177, 180
Llandaff Court, 122
Llanddew, Powys, 37
Llanddewibrefi, Dyfed, 20, 46, 64, 115
Idnert stone, 20
synod of, 10
Llanddewi Nant Hodni, *see* Llanthony
Llanddingad, *see* Dingestow
Llanddowror, Powys, 102, 107, 116
Llandeilo, Dyfed, 16
Llandeilo Gresynni, *see* Llantilio Crossenny
Llandogo, *see* Whitebrook
Llandough, Llandochau, South Glam, 13

Monmouth Beacon, 132
Monmouth, Geoffrey of, bishop of
    St. Asaph, 28, 34
Monmouth, John of, bishop of Llan-
    daff, 35, 46
Monmouth, Wihenoc of, 25
Monmouthshire, 70, 122, 124, 125,
    127, 129, 130, 132, 134, 135, 155,
    172
Monnow, river, Afon Mynwy, 2
Montgomery, Trefaldwyn, Roger of,
    earl of Shrewsbury, 24, 25
Mor Meirion, *see* Morgan, R. W.
Morgan, Sir Charles, of Tredegar,
    130
Morgan, Frank, 167, 168
Morgan, John, 100
Morgan, John, bishop of Swansea and
    Brecon, bishop of Llandaff,
    archbishop of Wales, 175, 176
Morgan, R. W., of Tregynon, Mor
    Meirion, 150
Morgan, William, translator, 66, 67
Morgannwg, 10, 12, 13, 15, 24, 28
    king of, *see* Meurig ap Tewdwr
Morgeneu, 18
Morley, John, 164
Morris, Alfred, bishop of Monmouth,
    archbishop of Wales, 176, 177, 182,
    183
Morris, Ebenezer, vicar of Llannon,
    158, 159
Morris, Lewis, 102, 109
Morris, Richard, of Anglesey, 109
Morris, William, of Anglesey, 109
Mortimer, Edmund, 42
Mosheim's *Ecclesiastical History*, 118
Murray, William, bishop of Llandaff,
    73
Myfi yw'r Adgyfodiad Mawr, 109
Mynyddislwyn, Gwent, 64, 128

Nantgarw, Mid Glam, 142, *n*.4
Nantyglo, Gwent, 124, 129, 142, *n*.4
Nash, Yr As Fach, South Glam, 61
National Liberation Society, 159, 164
National Society, 146
Neath, Castell Nedd, West Glam, 95,
    115, 142, *n*.6, 174
    Cistercian abbey, 60
Nennius, 8, 12, 21
neology, 152
nepotism, 35, 36, 58, 64
Netherwent, Gwent, 143, *n*.14
Neufmarché, Bernard of, 24, 28
Newcastle, Mid Glam, 174
Newcastle programme, 165
Newman, John Henry, 149, 150

Newport, Casnewydd-ar-Wysg, Gwent,
    124, 134, 137, 139, 142, *nn*.6 & 8,
    143, *n*.14, 155, 167, 171, 185
    St. Paul's, 128, 129
    St. Woolos, cathedral, 140, 171
Nicander, *see* Williams, Maurice
Nicholas ap Gwrgan, bishop of Llan-
    daff, 34
Nicholl, John, 137
Nicholls, Benedict, bishop of Bangor,
    50
Nonconformist, The, 135
Norman incursions into Wales, 24–26,
    28
Northumbria, 21, 22
Norwich, bishop of, *see* Lloyd, William
Now or Never, 88

Occasional Conformity, 95
    Act, 97
Oculus Sacerdotis, 46, 53, *n*.21
Offa's Dyke, 14, 144
Ogmore, Ogwr, valley, 137
Olchon, Heref and Worcs, Baptist
    Church, 74
Ollivant, Alfred, bishop of Llandaff,
    122, 132–138, 140–142, 143, *n*.12,
    145, 151, 153–155, 160
Origen, 1
Oswald, king of Northumbria, 7
Oswestry, Salop, 85, 91, 93
Oudoceus, *see* St. Euddogwy
Owain Gwynedd, king of Gwynedd, 27,
    28
Owen family of Plas Du, 61
Owen, Charles, 93
Owen, Goronwy, 109
Owen, James, 91–96
Owen, Jeremy, 100
Owen, John, warden of Llandovery,
    dean of St. Asaph, principal of
    Lampeter, bishop of St. David's,
    143, *n*.13, 166–168, 170, 171, 173–
    176, 185, 186
Owen, W. H., of Rhyllon, 132
Oxford, bishop of, *see* Wilberforce,
    Samuel
    diocese of, 63
Oxford University, 71, 73, 116, 148–
    150, 177, 179
    chancellor of, 46
    Christ Church, 59
    Jesus College, 71, 82, 85, 113
    Oriel College, 127
    Worcester College, 149
Oxford movement, *see* tractarian
    movement
Oxwich, West Glam, 75

Thomas, J. J. A., vicar of Swansea,
bishop of Swansea and Brecon,
179, 183
Thomas, Joshua, curate of Llanllywen-
fel, 109
Thomas, R. S., 180
Thomas, William, canon of St. David's,
75
Thomas, William, dean of Worcester,
bishop of St. David's, bishop of
Worcester, 83, 84, 100, 101
Thoresby, John, bishop of St. David's,
bishop of Worcester, archbishop of
York, 43, 47,
his catechism, 47
Tillotson, John, dean of Canterbury,
archbishop of Canterbury, 87–89,
94
Time and the End of Time, 109
Times, The, 132
Tintagel, Cornwall, 2, 4
Tintern, Tyndyrn, Gwent, Cistercian
abbey, 61
Tithe Act, 161
Tithe commutation, 129
Tithe Commutation Act, 161
Ton Pentre, Rhondda, Mid Glam, 184
Tours, archbishop of, 32
tractarian movement, 140, 149–154,
156, 157, 159, 181
Tracts for the Times, 149, 150, 159
Traethodydd, 154
Traherne, John Montgomery, 127
Trawsfynydd, Gwynedd, 74
Treatise Concerning the Lord's Supper,
102
*Treatise containing the Aeqvity of a
Humble Supplication, A*, 71
Trecastell, Trecastle, Powys, 132
Tredegar, Tredegyr, Gwent, 124, 128–
130, 156
Tredegar, Lord, 171
Tredwstan, Powys, 81
Trefddyn, Trefethin, Gwent, 128
Trefeca, Powys, 111–113
Lady Huntingdon's College, 113
Trefor, John (I), bishop of St. Asaph,
43
Trefor, John (II), bishop of St. Asaph,
43, 44
Trefyclo, *see* Knighton
Trefynwy, *see* Monmouth
Tregaron, Dyfed, 115
Trellech, Tryleg, Gwent, 142, *n.*6
Tully, Robert, bishop of St. David's,
51
Twistleton, George, 75
Tyddewi, *see* St. David's
Ty Gwyn, 3
Tyndryn, *see* Tintern

Uchtred, bishop of Llandaff, 34
Uganda, 180
Ultra Aeron, Dyfed, rural dean of, 115
United Reform Church, 184
Urban, bishop of Llandaff, 28–31, 34
Usk, Brynburga, Gwent, 72, 128, 142,
*n.*6, 143, *n.*14, 171
grammar school, 145
Ussher, James, archbishop of Armagh,
152

Vale of Glamorgan Railway, 138
Valor Ecclesiasticus, 54, 64
Van Mildert, William, bishop of
Llandaff, 122, 125
Vaughan, B. N. Y., bishop of British
Honduras, dean of Bangor, bishop
of Swansea and Brecon, 187, *n.*9
Vaughan, David, 170
Vaughan, John, 61
Vaughan, John, of Derllys, 96, 100
Vaughan (Fychan), Rowland, 67, 87
Vienne, archbishop of, 32
Villiers, George, duke of Buckingham,
73
visitation, episcopal, 32, 44, 45, 69, 73,
90, 125, 151
royal, 67
Vortigern, 21

Walbeuf, James, 61
Walden, George, 143, *n.* 17
Wales, archbishop of, *see* Edwards,
A. G.; Green, C. A. H.; Morgan,
John; Morris, Alfred; Prosser,
David; Simon, William Glyn
Hughes; Williams, Gwilym Owen
Wales, Celtic Church in,
architecture, 18
bishop, 3, 5, 10
status of, 10, 12, 13
bishopric, kingdom-, 10–15
bishopric, territorial, 27, 29
synods, 15
role of abbot, 10
Wales, Church in,
case for an independent province,
32, 33, 48, 49
creation of independent province,
166, 167
Electoral College, 177
financial policies, 170, 171, 177
Governing Body of, 169–172, 176,
178, 182, 183, 186
Representative Body of, 167, 169,
170
Standing Liturgical Commission,
180

p. 112, *for* Cefnamlwch *read* Cefnamwlch

p. 188, *for* Aberriew *read* Aberriw